FREEDOM DREAMS

by

Dasarath

The Book Tree
San Diego, CA

ISBN 1-58509-130-8

Cover layout & design: Marc Rubin

Text layout and design: Lee Berube

Printed on Acid-Free Paper

.

Published by
The Book Tree
P O Box 16476
San Diego, CA 92176
www.thebooktree.com
We provide fascinating and educational products to help awaken the public to new ideas and information that would not be available otherwise.
Call 1 (800) 700-8733 for our *FREE BOOK TREE CATALOG*.

To Papaji
Beloved Master
Sri H.W.L. Poonja, 1910-1997

Acknowledgments

I want to thank Brooke Halpin for his perseverance in finding this book a home, and my publisher Paul Tice for his meticulous editing and bringing it all together so graciously. I'm grateful to many friends for their advice and support: David Mulveny provided constant encouragement and ongoing dialogue that helped clarify critical questions in the text. Mitch Bobrow and Avery Solomon read parts of the manuscript and offered valuable suggestions. Vidya Frazier gave an early draft of the whole book a thorough, insightful editing that saved me much embarrassment. Marc Rubin designed a cover that beautifully expresses the essence of the message. Sue Williamson transcribed the satsang dialogues and provided unwavering love and advice throughout the crucial period of writing. Timothy Smith wisely counseled me over the years on my trips to India and the master. A deep bow to Pamela Wilson for generously offering her loving, clear wisdom in the final stages of editing. And finally, the steadfast friendship of Lal and Komalama—who led me to Papaji and shared the entire journey with me—truly allowed this book to be.

Publisher's note: Within the text the words "bodymind" and "mindbody" are often used. In traditional grammar these words would require hyphens, however, the author wishes to suggest that an holisitc unity is at work rather than mind and body being separate and connected. The word "nondual" also remains unhyphenated, as many in the field of consciousness research have begun to employ it in this way.

CONTENTS

Foreward

What Is Freedom?

by John White
Author of *The Meeting of Science and Spirit* and *Enlightenment 101*

Dasarath has written an excellent introduction to the theory and practice of enlightenment as it is described in the spiritual tradition known as Advaita, or nondual awareness. Advaita is an ancient and universal spiritual tradition which declares that freedom is the true nature of everyone, our native condition. That is so, Advaita declares, because the universe is a uni-verse—i.e., unified, whole, without division, seamless—and the multiplicity of things in all their variety are nothing more than waves on the surface of the Ocean of Being which are temporary expressions of that Ocean, that Source.

However, it adds, the process of growing up imposes psychological and cultural conditioning and blinders upon us so that we lose sight of ourselves—our true self which is the Self of all. Thereby we become lost in a maze of physical, mental and social activities that divert our attention from our real identity and generate a false sense of who we are.

That false sense of separate, autonomous self has a name: ego. The result of the ego-formation process is unhappiness, fear, worry and all the secondary forms of identity confusion which they generate, such as arrogance, hatred, addiction, greed and their social manifestations, notably conflict, oppression and war. In fact, as Dasarath points out, the entire spectrum of human suffering and evil can be understood as being due to our false I-dentity, our egoic delusion that we are anything less than the Infinite and Eternal Source of Creation, the Undivided Being, the One-in-all-and-all-in-One, temporarily operating through an individual form who carries our own name—and the names of all other beings. For at rock-bottom reality, we are all one. I am you are he is they are us is me, Amen.

Awakening to that great truth is the point of spiritual practice. However, Dasarath says, as long as one continues to believe in an individual practitioner who is crossing the great gulf that is assumed to exist between you and your goal of spiritual awakening, then practice can actually reinforce the delusion of separation from the Whole. This subtly strengthens the sense of being alienated, lost, alone.

The perspective of Advaita, which Dasarath shares with his students and audiences, asks instead, "What is happening in your consciousness at this very moment which generates the false notion that you are apart from the cosmos, apart from God, apart from the fullness and harmony that is the condition in which everything, including you, exist all the time? Who is separate from that? And if you think it is you, who is the one who holds that idea in mind? Who is the one who asks that question? Who is the one who fails to see the universal field of consciousness in which the thought of 'I' arises?"

By pointing out the delusion of separate self, Advaita shows that the "problem" is nonexistent and thereby it "cures" the disease. It is as if the individual person makes a fist, squeezes the fist so tightly that it hurts like hell, and then identifies himself with it (or perhaps even with just one finger!). Advaita says, "Look, the fist didn't make itself and you are not the fist. You are the one making the fist. Recognize that. Then relax your hand. You'll feel better. And if for some utilitarian purpose you should need to make a fist again, you can. You can use the fist but without mistaking yourself for it."

With that insight and wake-up call comes healing which is actually wholing—that is, restoration of awareness of the cosmic wholeness which is your true state. From that proceeds a radical change of stance for your being-in-the-world. It is a stance characterized by ease, by happiness and a clear understanding that your role in the grand scheme of creation is to enjoy life while possibly also helping others to awaken from their own self-centered dream into reality.

Advaita has been exemplified by many sages, ancient and modern, of various religions ranging from Hinduism, Buddhism and Taoism to Christianity, Islam and Judaism. Among the best known of the ancients are Shankara, Gaudapada and Kabir. More recent ones include Ramakrishna, Ramana Maharshi, Swami Sivananda, Sri Nisargadatta, Ramesh Baleskar and Dasarath's own teacher-mentor, H. W. L. Poonja, better known as Papaji.

The "heart" of the book is Part One, in which Dasarath discusses how and why we, in our essential freedom, create a dream of unfreedom and how we wake up. Part Two consists of transcripts from dialogues he's had while being a friend and teacher to people who come to him so we can see how the student-become-teacher actually applies the theory, actually practices what he knows. In Part Three Dasarath speaks with honesty and humility about his life and the journey to awareness which he made, including his particular version of the mistakes and false turns which are inevitable for us all on the spiritual path. Dasarath has not only offered a very useful text, he has also written it in a beautifully clear and engaging style that is a pleasure to read. I'm happy to recommend freedom's dream to you.

John White

INTRODUCTION

All wisdom and holiness are but streaks of lightning. —Huang Po

You are invited to share the most intimate of human experiences—the direct knowing of your true nature. In my last book *Wisdom at Work*,* I discussed the awakening of consciousness in the workplace and how we could be free, fulfilled and effective in our work. While I framed it within the nondual perspective—that there is one essence showing up as everyone and everything—there was still considerable attention given to the development of the individual. Here the invitation is to see through the separate "I" and its story—rather than improving it—to the presence that is free, here and now.

This wisdom resides within all hearts. My intention is to point directly to the knowing within you. Anything I could say you already know, so deeply and intimately, as it is your own nature. In this sense there is nothing new to be learned. There is simply the direct recognition of what is already here prior to all thought and effort. Awakening is literally a disillusionment, a dropping of all expectations and fantasies of what it might be, to come face to face with what is. In this uncompromising awareness there is no separation. All beings are its forms, all life its dance and expression.

This book is based on daily journals I began keeping in 1991-92 to describe the awakening that occurred over the course of five years of visits with my teacher Sri H.W.L. Poonja (Papaji) in India. The master's passing in 1997 inspired further insights into freedom that had to be expressed through writing, and the idea for this book was born.

I explore the mystery of freedom from three approaches—exposition, dialogue and narrative. Each describes a traditional way of knowing and expressing the Self. We each have our own unique combination of these elements. You may find some more fitting or appealing than others. The three together embody my particular way of sharing this awareness.

Part One is a thematic portrayal of nondual awareness. It explores the mysterious play of the Self which seems to dream itself into manifestation, then appears to lose itself in its imagined individuality, and finally, awakens to the realization that it—the essence of you, I, all beings—has always been free.

The second part includes transcripts of my satsang talks, dialogues, and correspondence with lovers of freedom that provide a close-up of the process of inquiry by which the Self is revealed. It has been a great joy to participate in such an intimate, one-on-one communion in which consciousness can recognize itself.

I love the mystery of it all. I love the ancient Chinese Zen Master Huang Po's declaration that all our spiritual insights are at best momentary lightning flashes in the vast mystery beyond all understanding. I am delighted that thought can never grasp its source and that there is no way to explain it. "Those who know, do not speak. Those who speak, do not know," Lao-Tzu cautioned enigmatically. So why speak at all about That which cannot be described? How to convey the pristine reality beyond all concept and language?

While mystery is often seen as a problem to be solved or a code to be cracked, for me it is an irreducible reality to be enjoyed, sufficient unto itself. Truth is so simple, the mind addicted to complexity and analysis cannot get it. Paradoxically, knowing is present in the silence of no-thought itself. The unspeakable wisdom arises from the total acceptance of mystery.

Knowing that there is no way to speak the truth lets us play with explanations without holding them as absolute positions. In this light, explanation is just metaphor. Understanding is the game of consciousness for its own enjoyment—a bone the dog of mind gnaws on for the pure activity of it. One of its most delightful tools is paradox, a way the intellect tries to grasp the elusive. Paradox holds apparent contradictions in an embrace that cradles the truth hidden within the opposition. In Lao Tzu's conundrum above, that one cannot speak the truth, the subtle wisdom is revealed in the paradox that he *said* it.

Though language can never grasp it, mystics speak of it anyway—through paradox, poetry, riddle, parable and song, through indirection and allusion, full of nuance and apparent contradictions—for the same reason that I must describe the indescribable here. What must be said, must be said. This reality is my truth and joy. It cannot contain itself and literally bursts to express itself. So while no concept captures it, all creation is its expression. Every sound is an echo of the silent source; every word, a declaration of the unutterable. And while it is continuously saying the same thing, each new iteration is a unique expression of the joy of awakening.

The narrative in Part Three views the phenomenon of the guru through the lens of my awakening with Papaji. While my experience was not unusual—many people had realizations in the master's presence—the story shows how the awareness presented in the book emerged from my encounters with Papaji, and expresses my gratitude for what he revealed to me. I want to celebrate and share his wisdom, and provide an inkling of the play of grace and how the guru worked.

The story also details the subtle nuances in the play of consciousness. For while the awakening is to a timeless, unchanging reality, paradoxically, I also find it to be a dynamic, ever-deepening realization. The narrative conveys the ups and downs, pitfalls and breakthroughs, I went through with Papaji. It includes a dramatic roller coaster in which the most sublime clarity and bliss alternated with fear, doubt, arrogance and the whole range of human emotions and mental tendencies.

During a quarter-century of spiritual study and practice I had built up an ideal picture of a pure state of consciousness where such fluctuations would no longer exist. Yet only by going through all the ups and downs, and through exposing my most embarrassing foibles and self-delusions, did it become clear that I am not limited to the ever-changing stream of experience with which I had been identifying.

The full acceptance of my ordinary human experience revealed the spacious awareness that is free of all experience—free *from* it as well as *within* its fluctuations. It includes the realization of being nobody, while it also embraces the full humanity of this unique bodymind process called Dasarath playing out the mystery of life. Within this presence ordinary thoughts and feelings continue to come and go. The human flows on, rising and falling like a wave on the ocean of being. There are times of identification, of emptiness and fullness, of expansion and contraction. The awakening is reborn and refreshed each day as quiet releases, small epiphanies, gratitude and wonder. *And each time it is the same awakening*—the realization of being the silent presence, the enduring ground of wholeness and peace that is always here beneath the surface activity. All the variations in experience—including identification and the sense of separation—are seen to be expressions of this ever-present reality underlying and sourcing it all.

Freedom dreams. . . . The Self that is always free dreams the story of its own sleep and awakening. Like a fever dream, it seems so real you could swear it is happening. Ironically, while I began to journal my experiences as a way to assure myself that it was not some fantasy I was making up, it soon became clear that consciousness truly is imagining the author and all the characters. While the narrative is written from the perspective of an individual, it sees through the dream of the "I" to the truth that there is no one who is unenlightened, no one to get enlightened. In this sense it is hard to say whether it is fiction or non-fiction. It begins as "my story" and ends up revealing That which is untouched by all stories, all identities. The dream story itself—all of life—is the invitation to this freedom.

An individual account such as this is at best a mixed bag. It can provide inspiration, as well as pointers to the elusive deceptions in consciousness. If it leads you to measure your experience against another's, however, you may not recognize the truth of who you are here and now. Comparing one's way against another's sustains the belief that there is "someone" and "others" moving along a progressive path toward some attainment. While the Self is one, it is realized in as many ways as there are individuals. Each awakening has a different flavor or expression that arises through the particular life stream of the bodymind organism, and no two streams are the same.

May all these words remind you that you already are what you seek, that you need only turn to your own being, the presence that is available here and now. Here you discover that you *are* the fulfillment, freedom and peace you have been looking for, that there is no path or progress to what you already are.

As there is plenty of paradox and apparent contradiction in the account that follows, I find relief in Emerson's reminder that "consistency is the hobgoblin of small minds." In light of the indescribable absolute, what we can say is shifting and relative, appropriate to the specific context and the mind of the listener. When taken all together, perhaps the deeper whole will be intuited. There is also quite a bit of repetition here, since there are so many ways of saying essentially the same thing. Consciousness is incessantly referring back to itself, until it is obvious that you really are here, that there is no leaving or returning to what you always/already are.

∞ ∞ ∞ ∞ ∞

* *Wisdom at Work. The Awakening of Consciousness in the Workplace.* Larson Publications,1998. Published under the name Let Davidson.

PART ONE

MYSTERY PLAY

All is a dream and is known to be a dream only when you are awake. —
Papaji

I. ORIGINAL NATURE

Mystery

What does it mean to say it is all a dream? What does it mean to be
awake? How do we approach this mystery, knowing that it lies beyond the
grasp of mind to understand and words to express? "The Tao that can be
named is not the eternal Tao," advised the ironic Lao-Tzu. And yet we speak,
for it is the very nature of mystery to express itself. Existence mirrors the
unseen, continually reflecting a reality self-evident to those with eyes to see.
The nondual tradition has its story, and while none of it is literally true, it still
echoes the wisdom of silence and invites us to awaken. If we remember, as
in the ancient analogy, that words are only fingers pointing to the moon, then
the unspeakable can be revealed. Here then, is a metaphor for what can never
be told.

Nothing

Prior to everything, original nature is beginningless and endless, neither
existing nor not-existing. It is without qualities or attributes, thus limitless,
boundless, measureless, locationless, timeless. We use words like "void" or
"nothingness" or "infinity" to hint at this intangible, unthinkable mystery. Yet
it is beyond even that, the origin of emptiness and nowhere, the source of
both absence and presence. To call it infinite is not enough. What is more
than everything? To call it emptiness is to say too much. What is less than
nothing? What is there when even emptiness is removed?

Vast silence, absolute stillness—this is sunyata, the void of the Buddha.
Jewish mystics and Kabbalists called it the En-Sof, the infinite nothing, root
of all roots, indifferent reality. The ancients and the Christian mystics called
it the abyss, which derived from the Greek word for depthless or bottomless.
Or they referred to the godhead, that original Self which is prior even to God,
which corresponds to the quantum vacuum that some physicists theorize pre-
ceded the big bang.

All these words point to the reality that is your own original nature. It is
the unchanging context in which all life, form, experience, universes arise—

13

always present within and behind everything. It is the silent space in which the planets are hanging, the same emptiness within the atoms of the material world. I sense it as pure spaciousness, the weightlessness within my physicality. There is a diaphanous quality, the transparency of all form. Absolute rest, perfect peace, you are That here and now.

Something

Yet simultaneously this inconceivable nothing is also something. Absence is also presence, as if non-being projects itself as being. The intangible transcendent brims with its own immanence. It is said that nature abhors a vacuum—as if emptiness cannot bear its own imagelessness and thus must manifest. And so the void by its very nature fills itself. This is pure a-void-dance. The self-negation of the void is the birth of presence which shimmers within itself, a reflection of the unseen, an appearance within the nothing.

We are not speaking in terms of time or sequence, as if there were first nothing, and then there was something. They co-exist simultaneously, implicit in one another. Everything and nothing are the inseparable faces of mystery. The presence is immanent *in* and *as* the absence, as the self-expression of nothing. And nothing remains the implicate essence of something, the insubstantiality that underlies the world of form and materiality.

Original Taste

While the Self-as-nothing is attributeless, within the Self-as-something, there are certain qualities or functions that describe the subtle, original taste of oneself. The ancient Hindus called it *satchitananda*, which I find a succinct description of being myself. *Sat* is truth or being, *chit* is knowledge or consciousness, *ananda* is bliss or delight. The Self is, it knows that it is, and that is joyful. This is the bliss of being awake—conscious presence delighting in being itself.

These primary qualities of source are multiple, simultaneous dimensions of a single indivisible totality. In the same way that water can be described as having the characteristics of wetness, liquidity, and transparency, they are in fact inseparable and interdependent aspects that always include one another. They form the fundamental ground in which all existence and experience arise. Everything shimmers and vibrates within it.

Being

Put simply, you just are. Being is. It is fullness, wholeness, sufficient unto itself. It needs nothing and everything is contained within it. Being is the ancient, familiar presence that is and always has been. "Before Abraham was, I am" is a declaration of timeless presence without beginning or end. The advaitic "I am That" or the biblical "I am that I am" is the subliminal intuition of being itself. The untranslatable absolute presence, prior to all name and form, refers to itself as being. Out of this single ground of "I am" is projected the multiplicity of all beings. Here is the original subject, the essence of all subjectivity which is always present beneath the surface of all relative identity. If "human" is our given name, then "being" is our last name—the ultimate, nameless identity of all beings.

This "I am" is the constant, unchanging thread of continuity of our existence. In truth we are already familiar with the existence of our own Self. The intuition that you are is always with you. Everyone has the experience "I am." You say it and think it constantly: I am happy, I am sad, I am young, I am old, I am hungry, I am full. Yet when you identify with your constantly changing experiences and roles, you ignore the presence that you have always been. If we turn attention to the source of all our identifications, the unchanging "I am" within changing phenomena reveals itself—not an identity but the source of all identity, not a person but the source of all personhood. When we cease to identify with everything else, then the pre-existing reality shines by itself. It is self-evident. "The Self proclaims itself at all times as 'I, I'," Ramana said. "It is self-luminous. It is here."

Awareness

"I am" implies consciousness. The luminosity of the absolute is the light of knowledge radiating in primordial darkness. I am knowingness awake to myself, an awareness of being aware. This is pure nondual awareness—*jnana* or gnosis—in which there is no knower or known, no subject that knows or objects to be known, just awareness itself without form or content. You are this being-consciousness which mysteriously knows nothing and can never be known by anything other than itself.

In order to know itself, consciousness has the capacity to imagine form and content, to perceive and experience its imagined forms, and to identify with its experience. This capacity activates the movement we call thought within the unmoving awareness. The ocean of consciousness gives birth to waves and currents of thought arising and disappearing within it. These are the seed-forms of all mind and experience. By focusing on these thought-forms, awareness imagines itself as all existence—a mirror in which to see itself. In this mirror of existence the formless is reflected as form. When awareness faces outward toward form, it sees itself as the world. When it faces back to itself, there is no reflection, no world, just the reality of the unmanifest Seer.

Bliss

Ananda is the bliss of being awake. This quiet joy and wellbeing is the original and most subtle way the Self experiences itself. It is revealing that "Eden" means delight or bliss in Hebrew. The Garden of Eden story mythically depicts the original domain of innocent delight inherent in consciousness before the "fall" into experience. The garden is not a place in the ancient Near East, nor an experience that existed before in time, but a reality within you here and now.

Bliss is the fundamental feeling tone at the heart of all specific experiences and emotions. All experience flows from this. All feelings, emotions and sensations are transformations of this basic underlying essence. Just as the multiple gradations of color of the rainbow are refractions of the underlying reality of light, so all emotions and feelings are modifications of the underlying ananda. We might say that when the original, unmediated delight is poured through the prism of thought, it is experienced as the spectrum of physical and emotional sensations, pleasure and pain, desire and fear, attraction and repulsion. While we ordinarily consider these to be departures from our inherent underlying happiness, in truth they are all expressions or refractions of the one original taste. To the Self all experience is nothing more than its own bliss in form. The sense of wellbeing is present regardless of the specific emotion seeming to arise.

In the play of duality, when there is attachment to the specific forms of experience, there is an immediate forgetting of the prior happiness and fulfillment of the Self. Yet no experience, no matter how sublime, can equal the original taste. Hence there is the nagging, underlying sense of unfulfillment and our life becomes the quest to regain that happiness. Sooner or later we may be fortunate enough to realize that it cannot be found in the spectrum of experience, that we are looking in the wrong place. When we give up that search and surrender to the source of all experience within us, we rediscover the bliss of our own self-nature.

Energy

The vibrancy of bliss, the luminosity of consciousness, the movements in imagination are all expressions of a vital force that pulsates in the empty stillness. This energy is the fundamental dynamism that permeates the Self, the power that vibrates, oscillates, throbs, moves, generates, pervades and animates existence. It is the breath of life, the *chi, ki,* the force that makes your heart beat and blood flow, that drives your thoughts, feelings, behaviors, your body functions, that moves everything.

The ancient Hindus called this power *Shakti,* the divine mother, the creative matrix of all existence, the voluptuous goddess who gives birth to—that is—becomes the universe. Shakti is pure formless potentiality, a fertile womb of all possibility. Nisargadatta Maharaj pointed us directly to this awesome creative power to become. "You are the infinite potentiality, the inexhaustible possibility. Because you are, all can be. The universe is but a partial manifestation of your limitless capacity to become." Inexhaustible, yes, a shimmering pulsational field in which anything and everything can occur. Here is the womb of plenitude, brimming, seething, pulsing, endlessly giving birth to creation.

II. THE APPEARANCE OF SELF AND WORLD

Big Bang Here & Now

The equivalent of the mother womb in quantum mechanics has been called the "quantum vacuum, a void that seethes with possibilities that arise and vanish like bubbles on boiling water, bubbles so ephemeral as to be essentially nothing, possibility without actuality." Some physicists believe that all of existence can arise from one of these bubbles of possibility erupting or exploding. Such an explosion—or big bang—they speculate, could be the origin of the universe.

What I like about the big bang idea is its sense of an explosion of energy in void by which potential/nothing becomes actual/something. It is the presence of energy within being-consciousness-bliss that gives birth to everything. Energy pulsing through being generates existence. Energy moving consciousness takes the form of thought. Energy inherent in bliss radiates as all experience. Within the immaculate void the absolute as being-consciousness-bliss-energy takes shape as existence, not as some objective creation separate from itself, but as a transparent projection, immanent within itself.

This is taking place within you here and now. While scientists may view the big bang as some discrete event in the distant past, I experience it as a manifestation showing up all at once in this timeless moment. Everything is arising presently as an expression of the underlying energy. The explosion is now. It is the ongoing intensity that animates life itself, the pulsational energy within our experience, present as the vibration in every cell of the universe, in every cell of the bodymind.

The Dance of Love

A magnificent, voluptuous version of this ongoing big bang is the Indian tantric vision of the sexual embrace of Shiva-Shakti. Shiva, the male, unmoving consciousness is joined in ecstatic union with Shakti, the feminine, dynamic moving energy. Mystery divides into two to generate itself in form, and all life is born from this interpenetration of the two-in-one, the loving embrace of consciousness and energy.

The interplay of these polarities is an expression of the force we call love. We might say that the Self manifests as both lover and beloved for the exquisite experience of loving itself. The One imagines the arising of subject-object to play out the dance of love. Paradoxically, it creates the appearance of separation, yet it is always in union with itself. In the appearance of duality, love is the force that both separates and joins, the way it seems to divide and then embrace itself. It is fascinating that the act of separation is also the act of joining within the undivided totality—literally, the way the Self cleaves to itself. Alan Watts pointed out that the word "cleave" has two opposite meanings—both to separate and to join. Here is the mystery of creation in the nondual vision.

In this sense the big bang is the original formless Self bursting into form and giving birth to creation as an expression of love. Here we see all manifestation as the dance of love loving itself. Multiplicity is its loving communion with itself. Within this appearance, love is the cohesive force that holds everything together. Like the gravitational pull that keeps the planets and heavenly bodies together, love holds all beings in relationship to one another. All forms of relationship—be they personal, social, political, ecological, be they intimate and caring or violent and hateful—are all modifications of this underlying love. Love is the submerged feeling-tone inherent in all the feelings beings have for one another—be it anger, fear, like or dislike. No matter what the experience, all relationship is the Self loving itself.

In the world of appearance, where we have forgotten our true nature, this subliminal love remains unknown, hidden beneath the surface. Momentary glimmers may show through from time to time as we go through the ups and downs of relationship. When we become aware of our reality, love shows up naturally as the recognition of the unity underlying all multiplicity. It is the experience of seeing your own Self as all beings and realizing that they are all included within you. Love is the Self recognizing itself in the "other." It is the way the One relates to itself.

The Play of Consciousness

While all of this seems to come into existence, it is just an appearance in consciousness. Here we enter the heart of the great mystery of how something seems to arise in nothing—the exquisite ability of consciousness to imagine manifestation as a multi-dimensional, holographic, fully sensory experiential projection arising within itself. Within its unchanging invisible essence, in the timeless, locationless void, the Self projects all existence, all form, all experience as its own imagination. The Hindus call this *lila*—the divine play or dance. Here the birthless appears to be born, the ever-tranquil seems to move, the undivided One refracts as the many, and the intangible emptiness simulates the felt experience of life, all of it dancing like a mirage in consciousness. "Those who are experts in the Upanishadic wisdom," wrote the ancient sage Gaudapada in his commentary on the *Mandukya Upanishad*, "look upon this world as if it were a cloud-city seen in a dream."

Metaphorically, we can say that the appearance of manifestation is the way formless consciousness can know and experience itself. "The wave arises to know its own unknowability in the mind of the unknown," Papaji explained enigmatically. Sheer mystery, which in its unmoving, undivided nature cannot know itself, imagines the mirror of manifestation that reflects itself as the diversity of form. The visible is a reflection of the invisible. In this sense all creation is the University of Self-Knowledge which the absolute attends for the sheer joy of self-recognition.

The capacity to imagine form and then to become caught in it is what the Hindus call *maya*. Maya refers to the power of consciousness to lose itself in its own imagination, as well as to the appearances it projects. It is the capacity to dream as well as the dream itself. Maya is the seemingness that makes it look like something is happening in the midst of nothing. Often associated with the feminine Shakti, it is the voluptuous attractiveness of the dream that sucks awareness into its own projections.

Maya is sometimes translated as illusion, in the sense that what we ordinarily take for real—the manifest world of physicality and materiality and our experience of it—is realized to be just imagination. Since all of creation is only an apparition of thought, it can be considered unreal. Yet at the same time, when you see that it is all the formless absolute projecting itself, then we know it is all real. The eye of wisdom sees only the Self in all appearance. There is only reality showing up as all. Real and unreal, here is the mystery of maya.

Consciousness is like a mirror that reflects images within itself. The image is a three-dimensional projection within the mirror, just as life is a three-dimensonal projection within the ground of consciousness. The image is here and not here at the same time. It is an appearance that never touches the mirror. Images leave no stain on the mirror, which remains always pure, always empty. Like the mirror, the Self is never affected by the images and experiences that arise within it. While experience is felt by the mindbody organism, the consciousness that imagines all experience *does not experience any of it*. All experience is known to be an empty, insubstantial projection within this spacious awareness. It all just happens and you—the Self—is untouched by it all. Nothing ever happens to you.

In the same way, no matter how much activity takes place in the appearance, the Self is unmoving. Within you the projection of form arises and moves. The entire manifest world is constantly changing, coming and going. That's why I call it the movie. Yet while it moves, you never come and go. If you travel to India or in the States, if you are in your bedroom or your car, you do not go anywhere. The movie is moving within you and you are the unchanging presence within which it is all happening. You are the stationary witness of all the moving, which is never separate from you.

To the absolute, the entire process of imagination goes on unconsciously—as digestion occurs unconsciously within the individual. In this sense, imagination is the unconscious of the conscious Self. The entire world process is just the unconscious dreaming of formless consciousness. And paradoxically, no matter what the dream, the Self only seems to sleep, only appears to be deluded. It is always free of its own projections, free of the bodymind drama. It abides awake, empty, still, unchanging.

In this sense there is no "coming down" from the formless source into something separate we call "creation." The very concept of coming down is a judgment on manifestation which is often seen dualistically as less than source. It is a prejudice born of attachment to the "purity" of the formless unmanifest, which is held to be "higher" than life. To the nondual sage all form is an expression of the Self. "Form is emptiness, emptiness is form" is the mysterious truth of the *Heart Sutra*. Wisdom favors neither formlessness nor form, in truth, makes no distinction between them. Everything is the Self.

Consciousness imagines existence through the instrument of thought, which is the technology of the dream. In the empty stillness, unmoving awareness seems to move. I say, "seems to move" because the essential nature of awareness is always unchanging repose, always at rest. Yet somehow movement seems to occur within the stillness, the inherent energy/potentiality pulses and generates currents of thought-forms in the ocean of awareness. All these movements in consciousness—thoughts, ideas, images, archetypes, seed tendencies, perceptions, beliefs, desires, fears, emotions, that collectively we can call "mind"—are merely modifications of its own self-nature, the way the real vibrates into existence as form. Like ripples on a pond, they reflect the light of the one moon of consciousness as many moons, and give the appearance of a world of multiplicity.

When the pond is still, it is clear that there is only one moon, one light, one reality. It is only the movement of thought-waves that creates the appearance of multiplicity. Hence the silence of no-thought reveals the underlying undivided reality, the unmoving depths of the ocean which is here beneath the surface activity. The stillness of awareness is always present as the space within everything, even as the movement of imagination takes place within it. Imagination does not disturb the stillness. Thought is not an obstruction to no-thought. Thought occurs within no-thought, just as everything appears within awareness.

The magnificent power of maya projects a full-blown, three-dimensional multi-sensory world of experience within the boundless immensity. In the midst of timeless nowhere, it projects dimensionality—time and space—as the location and duration within which creation can take place. Time and space are fundamental tools of consciousness that define the imaginary boundaries in which life appears to happen. What we perceive as physical space—the seemingly endless universe around us—is a function of depth perception that creates the impression of distance, as in a 3-D movie. It projects a "here" in the midst of nowhere, a location for existence to exist. Simultaneously, consciousness projects the time sense as the experience of duration. The time sense allows for a continuum in which manifestation can endure as a process of transformation and change. Without time and space nothing happens. In truth, in the here now of wakeful awareness, none of it is happening. The spatio-temporal realm is known to be an elusive transparency within which the lila seems to take place.

Self as selves

Dimensionality is the theater in which the Self plays out the magnificent movie of embodiment. Imagined existence becomes the playground of the "I am," the absolute subject, which incarnates as the multiplicity of all beings and plays all the characters in its own movie. The One shows up as a world of someones, the Self a world of selves, each individuated form a microcosmic, holographic image which both reflects and hides the formless absolute within it.

This is maya's greatest trick and crowning glory, as described succinctly by Shankara: "The mind oscillates as subject and object to produce an appearance of duality through illusion." By this vibration, undivided consciousness seems to bifurcate into a perceiving subject and a perceived object. Subject and object arise simultaneously, mutually co-dependent upon one another. They require one another and exist only in relationship to one another—two poles on the continuum of consciousness which oscillates between them without ever losing its inherently undivided nature. By arising as subjective knower and experiencer in a world of knowable, experiential objects, the Self lives the dream of knowing and experiencing itself.

The play of the absolute knowing itself is expressed in a magnificent, cosmic game of hide and seek. Life is the adventure of hiding and then finding itself, of forgetting and remembering its own eternal nature. By imagining itself into existence as all beings, it seems to forget itself and become hidden in its own individualized consciousness. It then seeks through that same impersonation to rediscover itself, all for the sheer joy of awakening, by its own grace, to what it has always-already been. The forgetting and remembering, the sleep and the awakening, are all the play of the supreme consciousness, like the peek-a-boo games an infant or young child plays, always knowing it is a game, done for the sheer delight of play.

For the human being, Ramana taught, the key to the whole play is the I-thought. The I-thought is the original thought, the way the formless "I am" refracts and localizes into individual self-consciousness. The "I" resides at the core of each individual, the eye by which it sees itself, the center from which it experiences itself, and the basis for its illusory sense of separate identity. The very process of giving itself subjective identity is the way the Self pretends to forget itself. Identification with the I-thought creates the fundamental ignorance that I am not the Self, that I am an independent subject separate from the totality. When consciousness identifies with its own thought-forms and thinks: "I am the mind," "I am the body," "I am my experiences," it seems to forget itself and goes to sleep as ego-consciousness.

While colloquially used in the west as arrogance or selfishness, here "ego" simply means the belief that I am a separate subjective self, rooted in identification with the bodymind and its survival programming—the mechanisms and strategies that sustain the organism in which the Self has taken form. Ego is how it imagines itself as separate and maneuvers through the world of its own embodiment. Self-forgetting is the dreaming of the human drama. Seen in this light, ego is a divine instrument of creation so the play can go on. If there were no identification there would be no play, no world. To see this is to realize that there is no dilemma in ego, that the individual "I" has no existence independent of the source consciousness that is dreaming it. The Self-in-hiding plays its parts so well, it becomes so fascinated with its own projection that it is only natural that "I" get totally sucked into the mind-movie of individual existence and live out the drama of being someone in a world of others.

Once there is the belief in a separate "I," one sees through the filter of that identification. The sense of a separate self projects a world of objects in its own image as the domain in which it can exist. The technology of projection is the attachment to the stream of mental activity that creates the dream of individual existence in a world of multiplicity

Thought creates the appearance of separation and multiplicity by defining "things." To "de-fine" literally means to create an "end" (*fin*) or limit around something. It draws a boundary line (which is what "de-scribe" means also)

which delineates a limited thing, that is, which factors something out of the undifferentiated whole. Within the reality of "no-thing-ness," mind creates things by defining them. This understanding is consistent with the uncertainty principle in physics which suggests that the act of observation itself defines a specific, locatable "thing" within the undifferentiated quantum potentiality, in which specificity and location are purely possibilities.

It is telling that maya also means "measure" in the Sanskrit. Measurement is an instrument of definition, another way the mind creates things. In our materialistic, scientific culture, what can be measured is considered to be real. The English word "real" comes from from the Latin *res*, which literally meant "thing." And so we live in the assumption that separate things are real, and the underlying undivided reality is ignored.

Naming also creates separation. In the biblical account God (supreme consciousness) gives Adam (individual mind) the power to name things. In the Sanskrit it is called *nama-rupa*, which refers to the superimposition of name-and-form which generates the appearance of division and separation. This is also expressed in the analytical quality of mind, the ability to divide into bits for the purpose of understanding. To understand or give meaning to something is to give it separate existence.

Here thought performs a control function for the separate "I" which is always seeking a sense of solidity and security in the midst of flux. Its illusory existence continually threatened, ego is resistance to dissolving into Self. Without bounded objects around it, ego loses its imaginary boundaries of separate identity and dissolves. The power to conceptualize freezes the undifferentiated flow into things, which then become manageable, or so we delude ourselves. By naming and defining, ego-mind attempts to exert dominion over the vast unknown. Adam's power to name the animals is expressive of humanity's drive to survive by dominating nature, and each spoken name is a declaration of our hoped-for power and security in a fluid world fundamentally beyond our control.

While thought creates the appearance of division, there are no boundaries in reality. The seams in the fabric only seem to exist. If attachment to thought creates the perception of separation, then the silence of no-thought reveals the seamless unity. While it seems to multiply into a world of forms, it is all an appearance within the One that never loses its undivided nature. There is differentiation, but no separation. All forms and distinctions are known to be Self. Even language like "one with the whole" or "interconnected" fails to grasp that there are no "things" to be connected, that separation is a misperception to begin with, a divisive thought within unitive consciousness.

The Movie of Experience

Creation means both *appearance* and *experience*. Consciousness literally fleshes out the picture it imagines by generating sensate experience in the mindbody organism. Here we have the incarnation of consciousness—literally, the word becomes flesh—as vibrating energy densifies into physical-emotional experience. When awareness fixes attention on its own thought-forms, it feeds the sensory solidity of that form. Attention is the way consciousness focuses energy with laser-like power to create experience. Attachment to thought sustains the experience of solidity for the illusory "I."

The mind and its extensions, the senses, simultaneously project and receive the movie of experience. This is the creative power built into the mindbody organism that becomes a projecting/receiving node of the dream. Through seeing, hearing, feeling, touching, tasting, sensing and interpreting, consciousness imagines and experiences its own manifestation. Projection and reception are two aspects of the same creative process occurring simultaneously.

The senses are the instruments that give us a fully tangible experience of the movie. They project out the world of experience. You see *in and with* your eyes. There is nothing out there to see. Your eyes both project and receive vision. You hear *in and with* your eardrums. There is no sound separate from the vibration in the instrument that receives it. The senses both generate and experience the movie. No wonder we get totally sucked into it. The mind-senses create a closed system.

You walk into a movie theater and take a seat. You know that up front is a polyester screen, and in the back is a projector that shines light through a film upon that screen. Basically all you will be seeing is light and color on a screen, moving images accompanied by sound. But as soon as the movie rolls—if it is a good movie—you forget that you are sitting in a theater watching a movie and get sucked into the story. You identify with the characters and vicariously go through their experience. When they are happy, you are happy. When they are in danger, you are tense or scared. When they are making love, you are aroused. When they are sad, you cry. We are literally played by the movie. In this sense all experience is vicarious. It is not really *yours*, that is, the true Self has no experience of its own. It is all identification. Identification with the mind-movie, that is, attachment to thought-forms and images on the screen of consciousness, causes experience. Our life unfolds as the fleshing out of our thoughts, an incarnation of consciousness. "We are what we think," taught the Buddha. "All that we are arises with our thoughts. With our thoughts we make the world."

The mindbody organism generates neurophysiologic experience in response to the images we see on the screen of consciousness. The sciences of holistic health and psychoneuroimmunology show how the flow of energy-consciousness in the mindbody generates experience at the cellular level. Thought stimulates neuronal activity in the brain which generates protein-based chains of amino acids that flow as neurotransmitters carrying chemical messages to the cells of the body. Cells have receptors which receive and decode the message injected by the neurotransmitter. The cellular reaction then becomes the basis for our physical and emotional experience. In the same way, in reverse, the nervous system carries sensory messages to the brain which translate the perceptions of the senses. While the physical brain is in the head, intelligence literally flows throughout the body carried by the biochemical substrate and the nervous system. Consciousness courses through, and is resident in, every cell of the body and is in continual communication with itself through its self-regulating network. The drama of energy-consciousness is enacted within the neurophysiology of the mind-body organism which is projecting and receiving simultaneously.

The mind-senses create our sense of ordinary "reality." We think that because we can see it, smell it, taste it, touch it and feel it, it must be real, that I and the world must exist. This is the great success of maya, to convince its own projection of its existence. Attention is captured by the forms of consciousness and thus ignores source-reality, the formless ground of all forms. In a materialist culture, reality is defined by what can be perceived, experienced and measured through the senses, founded on the belief in the validity of the senses as the avenue to truth. Yet they are just the instruments of consciousness that give the appearance of substantiality to what is actually an empty mirage in consciousness. There is really nothing here. The senses are an aspect of the transparent hologram, just as in a dream you can feel sensory experience (sexual arousal, fear, anger, etc) and it is all still a dream. Sensory experience is fully valid within the world of form, yet it is not a measure of what is deeper than the mind and senses. You cannot taste, touch, see, feel or hear the formless source and essence of all experience.

We can appreciate how the movie has such holding power if we see that it is simultaneously the entertainment of the Self and the distraction of the individual "I." The Self a-voids itself by imagining. You fill your own voidness with the mind-movie, and enjoy your own a-void-dance. This is world-class distraction. "My Maya," Krishna told Arjuna in the *Bhagavad Gita*, "is difficult to get over." It makes sense that maya has to be captivating. It has to be so voluptuous to entice consciousness into forgetting itself. Otherwise, the play could not go on. This is the artistry of the absolute, to create such alluring splendor and beauty, to make the dream so irresistibly attractive, that it produces enchantment. Maya is so compelling that it "entertains" the individual "I." That is, it "holds" it, which is the root meaning of "enter-tain" from the Latin. To entertain thought means to hold it, explore it, get engaged with it, and probably, get lost in it.

So the cosmic entertainment of the Self *is* the distraction of the individual "I." Our fascination with the movie pulls awareness off the void and puts it on form. This serves the ignoring of the formless, a turning away from source which sustains the projection and the sense of individuality. If attention goes to the formless, the "I" and the movie disappear, the entertainment is over. So the "I" feeds on the manifestation, nursing continually on the teat of Mother Maya. The perceiving subject becomes addicted to the experience of the movie which gives it a sense of solid existence.

The entire process of thought we call the individual mind is a diversion that sustains the sense of the "I." Diversion—as in both enjoyment and detour—is the way we divert ourself from reality. We go to the movies to be distracted from our Self. Which, of course, is exactly what is needed to sustain the play of manifestation. If there were no "I" caught in thought, there would be no existence at all. Papaji said that the only reason everyone is not realized now is that they are so fascinated with their own dramas.

As we can see by the wide range of movies and videos showing today, people are entertained by just about anything. They enjoy comedies and tragedies, romances and dramas. They are fascinated by heroism and violence, love and horror, brutality, torture and pain. People go to be titillated and amused, challenged and inspired. They get scared, terrorized. They purposefully subject themselves to being disgusted, violated, outraged. How can we be entertained by all of this? It is important to remember that entertainment does not mean "amusement." We may be turned off and repulsed by the images we are captivated by. The point is to be engaged.

Of course, in the movie theater, there is some awareness that no one is really dying on the screen. While we may be momentarily disturbed by the show, we know it is just a movie. In the same way, freedom knows that ego-mind, that all of life, is the play of light and sound on the screen of consciousness. You are the light that projects, you are the screen upon which all is projected. You are never touched, never affected by the drama being played within you, just as the screen in the movie theater is not affected by the images on it. When there is fire in the movie, the screen does not burn. While suffering occurs in life, no one is suffering. Awareness is free of experience at all times even as it is occurring and being felt by the mindbody organism.

No-One Suffering

This is the great paradox: No one is living, no one is dying, no one is suffering. The sense of self we call ego lives out the dream that it exists and continually seeks to insure its survival. The "I" takes on a life of its own, yet this life is no more separate from source than the wave is separate from the ocean. A separate self is only an appearance in consciousness created by attachment to thought. The challenge in speaking about the imagined "I" is that we run the risk of reinforcing its non-existent existence.

Be that as it may, to review what we have said so far: Ego is the refraction of the absolute into the individual I-thought, which is the way the Self knows itself, the way it shows up and plays the game of selving into form. For the perceived world to exist, the perceiving subject must arise. The appearance of the world is sustained by the sense of separate identity. In this way ego is a divine instrument of creation. At the same time, it is pure ignorance, the misperception that you are not the Self and that you are limited to the mindbody organism. It is rooted in attachment to the I-thought and identification with the conditioning and survival programming that run the organism and keeps it alive.

Once this identification "takes," the "I" ignores its inherent, already-existing wholeness and gets caught in two fundamental operating principles that shape our experience as individuals—separation and incompletion. The "I" subliminally suspects that it has separated from source and is plagued by the sense that something is missing. Because we have severed ourself from the rest of our Self, we feel incomplete. This is similar to what the Biblical tradition calls original sin—the sense that one is "off the mark," that this is not it. These beliefs generate dissatisfaction and suffering while they also impel us to reclaim the fullness of our original nature. One lives driven by the nagging, unconscious suspicion that I am not whole and must fulfill myself. Life becomes a process of seeking what I think will complete and perfect me.

Ken Wilber has pointed out that as the fundamental unity differentiates itself into selves, each organism is moved by two apparently opposing drives simultaneously. One thrust is to pursue its survival and success as a separate entity through the quest for self-actualization—the development of the full potential of that organism. At the same time the organism is driven by the equal and opposite drive toward self-transcendence. It yearns to go beyond its sense of separate existence and merge with the whole, to rest in its original nature. These two drives embody the dance of the Self, which is simultaneously coming into form and returning home through its egoic manifestation.

Taken together, the drives toward self-actualization and self-transcendence seem to be in conflict and may give some clue why suffering is inherent in the "I". It is both hiding and seeking at the same time. One is simultaneously running away from Self and toward Self, trying to be separate and trying to dissolve. The "I" yearns to be and it yearns not to be. If it is held as either/or, as in Hamlet's question, it generates the anguish of being torn in two.

So the "I" is actually doomed to failure and can never reach its goal. In reality, we can neither get away from Self nor can we reach it. All such beliefs and drives together reflect the false assumption that I am not home now, and in that denial all striving is futile. This rebellion against source— the "I's" arrogant claim of independence—is the molten core of all human suffering.

What makes it even stronger is the narcissism inherent in ego. The hypnotic trance of Narcissus, fascinated with his own reflection, keeps the "I" locked into its drama of separation. We are obsessed with the story of our own individuality and uniqueness, our own experience and emotions, our own pain and suffering. We romanticize our predicament. We worship it through our egocentric culture dedicated to the pursuit of individual self-interest. This devotion to the separate "I" is systematically sustained by cultural conditioning, especially in the west, and most of all in American culture, which is infused with the most extreme version of individualism on the planet.

While the imagined individual self experiences the emotional ups and downs of this process, from the perspective of the absolute, of course, there is no dilemma, just the play of consciousness. The whole movie of the egoic self struggling to survive or trying to be free is the heroic dream of the Self.

"I" Can't Get No Satisfaction

The belief in a separate "I" is continually reinforced by attachment to the bodymind's survival programming. Encoded there are the key strategies of desire and fear to ensure that the organism gets what it needs to survive and avoids what threatens its existence. While they may be valid and useful functions for our daily needs, attachment to desire and fear sustains egoic suffering unless we see clearly what they are and how they operate.

We can best appreciate desire if we see that it is actually the driving force behind all creation. Desire is a highly focused form of the supreme power that moves all things. It shows up originally as "the wanting to be" which impels the womb of emptiness to give birth to manifestation. Nisargadatta Maharaj pointed out how this process takes place in microcosm every morning you wake up from sleep. "The absolute is Paramatman. From this total Reality comes the chidakasha—the wanting to be. From there the physical space, the entire manifestation, comes into being, in a fraction of a second. In deep sleep there is nothing, then there is the slightest feeling that I want to be awake, then the entire manifestation takes place within a split second." Referring to this same wanting, Shankara pointed out that the Self's "fondness for the unreal is alone the cause of birth." This fondness for its own form is the motor force behind manifestation.

In this sense, all desire is the Self's own yearning for itself. Deep within us is the inherent, subliminal knowing of our own divinity and the longing to return to source. Intuiting its own incompletion, the "I" yearns for itself-as-wholeness. The very sense of impoverishment is the way the Self calls itself home. The divine power that generates form is also the engine that drives the self-forgetting individual back to its formless nature. So desire is a divine capacity. It is the supreme energy itself, at the service of the play of forgetting and remembering. And because it plays both functions simultaneously, desire drives both separation and return to source.

The one holy desire gets diffused through the separate "I" as the vast array of secondary desires for whatever it thinks will give it fulfillment. All specific desires—whether for love, fame, fortune, success, approval, security, material possessions, sex, food—are subsets of the one great desire for fulfillment and union. We want the Self above all things, yet as long as we seek it in the specific objects of desire, we cannot find it. Focused outward on objects, desire sustains ego and suffering. Turned inward on the Self, it frees. When desire is focused on waking up, it comes full circle back to the Self it never really left.

Gaudapada saw a lack of symmetry in the power of desire. It is easier to get caught in it, he implied, than to be free of it. "Because of this passion for any object, whatever it be, the [absolute] becomes ever covered up easily, and it is at all times uncovered with difficulty." The difficulty makes sense when we remember that desire creates and sustains the dance of creation. If it were too easy to let go, there might be no manifestation. Desire is an aspect of maya's ability to draw consciousness into the movie and forget itself. Not only does she create an alluring movie, she imbeds in us a yearning for and tenacious clinging to it. Shankara's commentary on Gaudapada's word "passion" is "eagerness to grasp," which seems to be about the same as Buddha's concept of clinging or attachment which he declared, in the second noble truth, to be the cause of suffering.

This passion-clinging-grasping reveals how ego *needs* the movie to exist. Because subject and object are not really separate, desire actually expresses their mutual interdependence within the underlying undivided Self. As soon as the split into subject and object appears in consciousness, the seeming subject needs the world of objects to survive. It draws its illusory lifeblood from them. Without objects, there would be no subject, only the totality. Desire is one way ego tries to hold onto the movie and shore up its sense of existence. The subject's fundamental dependency on the world of objects proliferates into a wide spectrum of intensity ranging from mild interest-attraction-like-preference to attachment-need-dependency-craving-addiction. We seek whatever we think will give us the experience of fulfillment and communion. And, as we know so well, we can get addicted to just about anything.

The process of desire follows an endless loop, which reinforces the sense of separation and incompletion. The interplay of desire and the "I" is a kind of circular chicken-and-the-egg conundrum. Desire arises as a natural consequence of identification with the "I." If I think I am separate and incomplete, then I desire something to fulfill me. And, in reverse, attachment to desire elicits an "I" out of formless consciousness. Wanting projects a wanter and a wanted. The wanting introduces or reinforces the belief that I am a needy, separate subject in a world of objects.

If we look more closely at the process of desire, we see it arises out of a shift in awareness. Awareness shifts its focus from its formless emptiness and looks out at its own projected thought-forms. If attraction to form arises, if attention is focused more intently on the object of desire, if we want it and get attached to it, the prior desireless peace of the Self is ignored, and the original, fulfilled nature of ananda is forgotten. Attachment to desire creates the experience of being incomplete and generates the belief that an unfulfilled "I" needs the object or experience. As thought or desire channels energy into that experience, the pure undifferentiated bliss of the Self takes on the form of that experience. All experience is a transformation of the underlying bliss-energy, yet no experience, no matter how intense, can equal the blissful wellbeing of our true nature. Hence the lingering dissatisfaction that sustains the cycle of desire.

This cycle is exercised to the max by the current high-tech global consumer economy, especially in the United States which may be the most egoic, materialistic culture the world has ever seen. The economic system and advertising industry promote a consumerism designed to feed ongoing need and addiction by dangling before our eyes the never-ending promises of more, better and different. We are told that you can have anything you want, and that it will give you satisfaction and happiness. Yet the ego-based economy can never deliver the real goods as long as it continues to reinforce the belief in a separate, incomplete subject in a world of objects. This too, of course, is just the play of consciousness, which sustains the movie of creation. Maya has never been more successful in creating a closed system in which you can't quite get enough to satisfy desire.

The Rolling Stones' classic rock refrain "*I can't get no satisfaction*" expresses the bare truth about the unfulfilling nature of ego and desire. There is no real satisfaction in the egoic domain, only clever counterfeits and momentary gratifications within its ongoing impoverishment. Sooner or later we learn that yearning for, or clinging to, pleasure produces pain. The play of polarity is ruthlessly efficient. As the Zen saying goes, there is but a hair's breadth difference between heaven and hell, and to know one is to know the other.

We won't be satisfied until we understand the bottom line about desire—that desire itself is never satisfied. We feed off experience yet we are no more nourished than a dog gnawing on a bare bone. Buddhism calls this pattern the "hungry ghost," a big-bellied desire cruelly frustrated by a tiny mouth and neck.

You might sometimes experience a temporary gratification when you obtain a desired object or experience. We think that if we gratify our desires we will have peace and satisfaction. We assume that fulfillment is the result of some action—like scratching an itch, eating when hungry, or having an orgasm—that by getting what we want, we will be satisfied.

But momentary gratifications do not satisfy the *process* of desire, which goes on and on. When you gratify a desire, another one comes. This is the way the survival programming works to keep the organism functioning. One desire follows another. No matter how delicious and filling the meal, we are soon hungry again. No matter how ecstatic the sex—or perhaps because of it—we want it again.

If you look more closely, you see that it is actually the *absence* of desire—the state of desirelessness—that reveals the inherent satisfaction of the Self. You see that desirelessness exists in the space between two desires, when one is no longer here and the next one has not arisen yet. When desire is not here, the original fullness is revealed. The yearning, the neediness, the straining and sense of incompletion that disrupted our original underlying sense of peace is gone. You do not *create* satisfaction by fulfilling a desire. Rather, it is *revealed* in the empty space between desires. This desirelessness *is* satisfaction. It is freedom, freedom from the "I" which cannot exist in desirelessness. Since the key function of desire is to sustain the survival of this transparent ghost, in the absence of desire there is no desirer.

What we have been seeking is already here and now. It was merely hidden by the grasping, by the sense of being the needy "I." Freedom from the endless cycle of desire and gratification comes in the realization that happiness, fulfillment and satisfaction are already within you. This awareness itself is liberating.

When you know the always-abiding peace of your original nature—that you need nothing, that you are nothing—then you can see the automatic mechanism of desire for what it is and relate to it appropriately. Through this witnessing certain needs, demands, and attachments may become more light-ly-held preferences. You can experience the whole process freely without either denying it or clinging to it. And, ultimately, if you boldly face desire as your own power, you see there is nothing wrong with it, there is no point in judging it or feeling bad about it. As we shall see later, one can ride that desire home and enjoy it as ripples of bliss-energy of the Self.

Know Fear

The other side of desire is fear. Like desire, fear is a function of the ignorance of our true Self. It too is a form that the underlying power takes when it is filtered through an ego-mind organized around its own survival.

As a survival strategy, fear is generated by the perception that something may threaten my survival. There is nothing objective about this. Fear of mice, heights, rejection, failure, loss, criticism—whatever the object—are all based on the fundamental misinterpretation that I am at risk. From the egoic point of view, these may in fact seem like real threats, since the "I" has forgotten its eternal nature and sees itself as a physical entity seeking to make it in a material world filled with a myriad of dangers.

In the play of duality, desire and fear are polarities that arise interdependently, co-generate and reinforce one another. We often fear the opposite of what we desire or are attached to. If you desire love and approval, you fear rejection; if you must have success, you fear failure or risk; if you hold on to power, you will avoid being controlled; if you desire winning, you are threatened by losing; if you are attached to life, you fear death.

In daily life fear takes shape along a continuum of extremes—at one end mild worry, doubt or anxiety, on the other end, panic, dread, terror and paranoia. The ultimate fear, of course, is the fear of death, of dissolving back into emptiness, of erasing the boundaries of one's separateness. Fear is the contraction the energy takes, an implosion that protects against dissolution and reinforces one's imagined existence. It is the strongest way we resist our immersion in source. The resistance is so strong precisely because, at the core, fear is based on ego's subliminally correct intuition that it is not really separate—that it doesn't really exist—and that it must continually shore up an imagined sense of solidity.

Fear, like desire, gives a jolt of energy to the "I" which revitalizes its sense of being a solid, real entity. Actually, we get off on fear. It is ironic that while we seemingly don't like fear because it is so uncomfortable and scary, its very intensity, uncomfortable or not, is what the separate self sense feeds on to reaffirm its existence. All those horror movies that "scare us to death" actually give us a shock of electricity, like the EMT applying the defibrillators, that brings the "I" back from the dead. So fear is basically an energy jolt that the ghost feeds on for its sense of aliveness. Ma Shakti so loves her imagined forms that she seeks to revive them with a taste of her power.

While fear serves the survival of ego, it is also the opportunity for freedom. Because fear is energy itself, the more intense the fear, the more we feel the power of our own Self. The intense fear of intimacy, commitment and love that arise in romantic relationships is a signal one is close to the union that love can reveal. In spiritual life, intense fear may arise as a shrinking back from the fire of devotion and surrender that could usher in realization.

In these moments when fear is so intense, if you face it head on, allow it to arise, accept it and feel it thoroughly, it can flow unobstructedly through the body. By being completely present with it without resistance, and without clinging to any concept or story associated with it, it is experienced for what it truly is—pure energy, intense aliveness itself. At the heart of fear is the ecstasy of the original taste. It is your own power, a burning, transformative fire that consumes all sense of separateness and limitation, and reveals one's own nature. The feelings pass and the underlying peace, the spacious awareness remains. What a relief to discover that no matter how intense the shocks of fear may be, the intensity has no effect on the intangible presence that underlies it at all times. When you look even more deeply into that and trace it back to its source, fear is seen to be just the play of consciousness in space. It is pure imagination without substance, actually nothing at all. If you know fear, there is no fear.

This experiential knowing allows you to see clearly through the fundamental mindstates that generate fear to begin with. Beyond the I-thought, beyond the beliefs in separation and incompletion, beyond the denial of the Self, there is no ground for the core existential fear to grow in. Once you know that your true nature is birthless and deathless, once you know that survival is no longer an issue, then fear has no hold on you and can play its appropriate cautionary role in protecting the bodymind organism. After all, we still prefer not to step on poisonous snakes or drive off cliffs.

The Time is Now

While attachment to the I-thought makes it seem that the "I" is a continuous presence, in truth it is discontinuous. The I-thought comes and goes, like all thought, all experience. It seems to be here, then it is not here. There are many gaps when the I-thought is not here—in sleep, whenever we are fully engaged in experience—and in those gaps there is nobody home. If we gave attention to the silent gaps between the thoughts, we would realize that identification is really a strobe-like, on-off process that creates the appearance of a permanent entity. Ignoring the gaps and connecting the dots creates a purely mental picture of something that has no enduring existence.

Since mind is geared up for the survival of the separate "I," it focuses on the *presence* of the I-thought and ignores its *absence*. This seems to be a basic tendency of ordinary attention to focus on form rather than on the formless, on thoughts and objects rather than on the spaces between them. By jumping over the gaps we imagine that the "I" is always here.

The time sense strings these familiar I-thoughts along to create the appearance of an ongoing entity. The memory of previous I-thoughts and the anticipation of future ones gives the semblance of continuity to what in truth is just an oscillation of consciousness.

Time is one of maya's most effective tools for ensuring the duration of its illusory individual self. It has already been noted that the time sense arises in the now as the continuum in which the imagined manifestation can endure as a process of change. Time provides duration and direction for the "I." The self-sense, we could say, buys time for its existence, for without time, it would not exist. The sense of movement and evolution is a distraction from the unmoving timelessness in which no form or identity can exist. It expresses and serves a kind of restless momentum which must keep striving, running from the vague intuition that to stop means extinction. The felt movement of time, then, is another form of resistance to dissolving into source, which, in the exquisite wisdom of consciousness, allows the imaginary movie to continue. Time is a divine instrument that serves the egoic illusion and the unfolding of creation.

The conventional linear time sense divides into past, present and future to elongate the sense of individual identity. The mind is like a movie projector facing in opposite directions at the same time. It projects backward and forward simultaneously through the twin functions of memory and anticipation. Memory is the mind-function that projects the impression of a past. Anticipation is the mind-function that projects the chimera of the future. Past and future do not exist. There is only now, and in the now memory and anticipation are technologies that create the appearance of a continuum of time on the screen of consciousness. Past and future are short film clips in which the "I" can see itself: this is who I was, this is who I am going to be. They assure the "I" that it is coming from somewhere and going to somewhere. And as long as it is coming and going, it feels like it exists. Remembering a past behind me and anticipating a future ahead of me, the "I" lives out its drama in the theater of imagination.

What we call the "past" is just memory, a mental image, taking place now. This record or recall of experience projects a movie backward that creates the appearance of a past. The sense of having come from somewhere is one basis for identity. We think we are what we've been, what we've done, our credentials, our resume, the accumulation of our experiences and learnings. Our preoccupation with past experience, be it accomplishments or failures, joys or disappointments, even hurts and traumas as painful as they may be, define and give "I" a sense of solidity. We drive through life with one eye on the rear view mirror, not only to maintain identity, but also for a sense of ongoing direction. Imagine waking up one morning without memory, without a past. It pulls the rug out from under the sense of purposeful movement. Without the past the egoic momentum will wind down. At its core, focus on the past is a denial of the reality of the timeless now, an avoidance of living in the moment where the Self abides.

Like the past, the future is an idea occurring now. It is a projection of anticipation, the capacity to look forward and envision a goal and a trajectory toward it. The "I" also defines itself by its future, by what it wants to become, do and have, by something to look forward to, or for that matter, to fear and avoid. Whether it is a bright, promising future, or some dreaded one, the specific content is less important than the fact that imagination is engaged looking forward. The egoic sense feeds off the anticipatory image. To have no goal or sense of future is literally disorienting to the sense of self. Imagine living without goals, without knowing what you will do or where you are going. The future-idea actually energizes the sense of a separate self, giving it motivation, incentive, a carrot on the stick, something to live for. Seeing images of a positive future charges the organism and empowers it to move forward, thus enhancing its sense of substantiality.

Beneath this is a fear of stopping, which suggests, especially to the restless, achievement-oriented, forward-looking western ego, an aimless lethargy or boredom, a kind of bogging down or ego-death. Which of course, is not far off the mark. Like the past, the future functions as a refusal to be in the moment, ultimately, a resistance to dissolving into timeless presence. Anticipation is the energy running away from source, even as it thinks it is heading toward it.

The survival functions of memory and anticipation, like desire and fear, reinforce one another. The momentum of where I've been points me in the direction I'm going. And our changing concept of the future continually revises the past, as we rewrite our resumes for the new jobs we anticipate.

Ironically, the time-sense conspires to avoid the present by conceiving it as the division between past and future. While theoretically we speak of time as the triptych of past-present-future, in truth, there is no room in mind for the present as an experiential reality, only as a concept. Because mind defines itself through memory or anticipation, to hang out in the timeless moment literally reveals its non-existence. So the closest it can get to the now without dissolving is to create the concept of "the present," an infinitesimally narrow line, drawn between past and future. No wonder we conventionally refer to it as the "fleeting moment" which doesn't last. Thought can never grasp that which is always here.

Only when there is no concept does the time-illusion cease. Time is just thought, and when you are free of thought, you are free of time. In the silence of no-thought the always-abiding timelessness is revealed naturally. You see that time doesn't exist; that it never existed. The classic spiritual cliché "be here now" really means: *see that you already are here now*, that you are the timeless awareness that abides untouched by all of it. Freedom is now, reality is now, you are now.

Paradoxically, when you abide as timeless awareness, memory and anticipation continue to serve the effectiveness of the mindbody organism in a purely functional way. Appointments are made and kept, plans are set and revised, schedules are followed. Each situation arises and dissolves, everything happens as it does. The clock keeps moving, yet it is still always now.

An historical aside: As a former historian, I've observed how deeply embedded the linear time sense is in western culture. The west's pronounced historical sense provides the scenario for our egoic materialistic culture to live out its romantic agony of suffering. The Biblical fall, let us remember, is the fall into time. The Garden of Eden mythically depicts the place of timeless eternal consciousness, that which is always now. The "original transgression" literally projected consciousness out of timelessness and into the drama of linear time, human mortality and suffering. History is both a consequence of biting the apple and a record of the pain that followed.

The suffering is sustained as the linear historical sense operates as a denial and running away from the garden of now. A major trend in western historical thinking has posited a continuum in which we are heading from some remembered past golden age and progressing toward some anticipated future state of wholeness, salvation, revolution, perfection, utopia, New Age. Actually, both the intimation of a past "paradise lost" and the hope for an ideal future are deep, subliminal intuitions of what is here now, metaphorical images of this true knowing. Yet as long as they are projected into past and future they prevent us from realizing the underlying reality of the now-garden and keep us locked into the anguished historical momentum moving headlong into nowhere. History becomes the busy make-work of an anxious culture that doesn't know how to rest, existing both as an expression of suffering and the context that sustains it.

The end of history-as-suffering is not some historical endpoint, but rather the awakening from the dream of time. Freedom is in knowing yourself as the timeless wholeness in which the dance of history and individuality takes place.

Vision of Impermanence

Since the time-sense is the way we measure change, seeing through time means seeing through the ever-changing manifestation to the underlying changeless reality. If we look deeply at the appearance of change, if our human perception were fine-tuned enough to see what actually is, we would see that everything in the world of phenomena is impermanent—all of it evolving, expanding, contracting, vibrating, arising and passing away, infinite variations of the dynamic pulsing energy which is projecting creation. Life is a continual flowing stream of becoming—being born, growing, maturing, decaying, dying.

From the perspective of ongoing transformation there are no things, only processes. No thing stands still long enough to be anything. Hence the truth of "no-thing-ness." The "thingness" of things is created by the analytic mind craving fixity and control, hoodwinked by the inherent limitation of perception itself, which imagines the dynamic movement of flow as fixed entities.

And hence the truth of selflessness. From the moment sperm meets egg until we become ashes and dust, the human being is a constant process of change. The individual "self" is nothing more than an idea that conceptually freezes the moving stream of tendencies into an appearance of a solid object, held together by memory and anticipation. Acknowledging this underlying selflessness reveals our apparent individuality as just a wave in constant motion, rising and falling as an inseparable expression of the totality.

What we call solid objects only exist at the most superficial levels of perception. Beneath the surface of the apparent physicality of objects is the process of continuous molecular composition and decomposition. Within that is the ongoing subatomic activity of particles and waves, which are themselves interchangeable forms (wavicles) of the underlying energy. Only a tiny part of the atom is mass. 99% of the atom is space, an emptiness filled with pure potentiality. Taken deeply enough, science itself shows that all manifestation arises as the play of intangible energy in space, the fundamental source generating this three-dimensional, sensory mirage of existence.

When you see that our world is constantly changing and insubstantial, it becomes obvious that you cannot hold on to what cannot be grasped. Suffering comes from clinging to the elusive, ephemeral flow of impermanence, and to the belief that you can find happiness, peace or freedom in the transient. But if you turn to what is permanent in the midst of change, if you truly face the emptiness within all matter, including your supposed "self," you relax into the peace of your unchanging home.

III. THE PATHLESS PATH

The Romance of the Path

If one is fortunate, at a certain point in the dream there are the stirrings of awakening to reality. The forgetting begins to become remembering, and the game of hiding from Self shifts to seeking. Of course, the yearning for the peace, happiness and freedom of our original nature has been going on unconsciously beneath the surface of the "I" all along. But the submerged drive to self-realization is not satisfied as long as it is focused outward on the world and the passing experiences of the supposed individual.

We may become conscious of that drive for what it is. Perhaps the suffering has become too great. Perhaps you have gratified your worldly desires and found that the promises of materialistic culture were false, that you are still lacking real satisfaction. Perhaps you begin to realize that there is more to life than you thought, that you have intimations of a deeper reality. Or a teacher or lover or new circumstance gives you a sudden insight, a taste of the bliss or peace of who you really are. You sense that there is something more and must get to it.

Grace is a word we give to the ineffable force pulling oneself home. It is the inherent magnetic attraction, like gravity, recalling the individual mind-stream to the ocean of consciousness. This force is literally the intuition of our original being, our remembering, through the fog of identification with the individual personality. We intuit this pull in nature. It arises in the intimacy of romantic love, and when we lose ourselves in our creative passions. It flashes momentarily in the psychedelic experience. It speaks to us clearly from the enlightened ones of all ages and cultures whose wisdom stirs and awakens us.

Whatever the external catalyst, they are the ways consciousness calls attention back to itself and launches the "I" toward "transformation," or "self-realization" or "enlightenment." Within the dream the spiritual path arises as the way out of suffering and toward freedom. This is the crucial turning point in spiritual life, when you become aware of that pull, when you feel the opening of the heart or the stirrings of a vaguely familiar knowing. If you are willing to follow and give it your full attention, the individual consciousness may fix itself into a homing orbit, impelled by desire and drawn by grace. And if you are so blessed, you may see that the push and pull are one and the same force, and in that realization individual effort dissolves into the effortless flow of the totality.

So we get "on the path." It is thrilling, comforting, exhilarating. You are on the heroic journey home. You have sighted the goal and are moving toward it. It is a righteous feeling. The "I" is now a seeker, a spiritual person. We are no longer wandering around lost in the wilderness. We begin to live on purpose with intention and direction. We clarify and simplify our lives. We discover the rich, fascinating treasure house of world philosophies, spiritual traditions, methods and practices that promise us clarity, bliss, freedom. We are turned on by teachers, preachers and sages, led and misled by charlatans and fools. You study, you learn the practices and techniques, become fluent in the languages of spirit, acquire the ritual paraphernalia, the clothes and emblems of the ever burgeoning tribe of seekers. You meditate, pray, breathe, practice yoga, raise the kundalini, balance the energy, heal, dance, drum, study your chart and cast the hexagram, stare deeply into each other's eyes. And indeed it does bring comforts, glimpses of illumination, tastes of peace and happiness. Inspired by these successes we push on, dogged, steady, believing in progress; or, lacking such signposts along the way we may flail in despair, sensing it is endless or fruitless, or just not for me.

The radical nondual vision sees that all this striving and seeking is still more identification, albeit in a spiritual mode. The "I" has now taken on the identity of a spiritual seeker. "I" am purifying myself, "I" am making myself better, "I" am getting closer to God. The concept of a spiritual path itself is a more subtle instrument in maya's bag of tricks to project duration so that the separate self-sense can sustain its illusory existence. It buys it even more time and allows it to remain in business. As long as there is a path, the "I" can continue to delude itself that it exists as something separate from source, at the same time reassuring itself that it is getting "closer." The struggle along the path, the heroic journey crossing the vast distance to reach some goal, reinforces the experience of solidity.

For all its dignity and romance—indeed, *because* the dramatic interpretations of this journey sustain our subtle self-deception—the path is more postponement. It is another way to avoid the Self in the very process of seeming to move toward it. It is still the busy make-work of the imagined "I" which continues to shore up separation and incompletion even as it seeks their solution. As the Tibetan Buddhist Master Chögyam Trungpa Rinpoche pointed out thirty years ago to idealistic Americans flocking to eastern spirituality, it is the supreme opportunity for the spiritual materialism by which we feed our fascination with ourself. One more book to read, one more teacher to find, one more secret practice, one more out-of-body experience, then I'll get it.

Sooner or later—if you are fortunate—you realize that the very concept of "someone on a path" itself is the impediment. Perhaps you have the grace of meeting a true guru who reflects your immaculate reality back to you. You see that you are holding to the belief that there is an "I" that is separate from the Self, and that by practice it can somehow diminish or purify itself. You see that "diminishing" or "purifying" is simply more striving. There is nothing to diminish or purify. The concept that "I am not already That" is pure ignorance. It imagines the condition we call "unenlightenment" and posits a goal called "enlightenment." It then creates a spiritual path that will take this "unenlightened" me from my imagined "bondage" to some imagined "freedom." Yet the non-existent "I" can never bring about its own demise. The ultimate freedom comes in seeing that there really is no separate "I," that there is no path and no need for any one to walk it, that there is no bondage to escape nor freedom to attain.

No Way

Here we come face to face with the fundamental paradox of the nondual realization. The big joke is that you already are what you seek. You already are peace, you already are happiness, you are the love, the knowing, the consciousness that pervades everything and that manifests as the universe. You are That. The absolute is all there is. Since you already are what you seek, there is no way to get here. There is nothing to do—no effort or practice is necessary—to become what you already are. All you can do is be. This is the true art of being. In the pathless path, the means and the end are one and the same.

I love how the great Chinese Zen Master Huang Po roared to his disciples:

" . . . All dharmas such as those purporting to lead to the attainment of Bodhi [enlightenment] possess no reality. The words of Gautama Buddha were intended merely as efficacious expedients for leading men out of the darkness of worse ignorance. It was as though one pretended yellow leaves were gold to stop the flow of a child's tears. . . . It must by no means be regarded as though it were ultimate truth. If you take it for truth, you are no member of our sect; and what bearing can it have on your original substance?"

Here the true teacher boldly declares that all the noble teachings and practices are simply pretending—compassionate stopgap gestures intended to soothe our suffering until we can face the reality of what is. If you cling to them they become distractions from the already existing truth of your buddha nature. Continuing, Huang Po cautioned his students:

"As to performing the six paramitas [virtues] and vast numbers of similar practices, or gaining merits as countless as the sands of the Ganges, since you are fundamentally complete in every respect, you should not try to supplement that perfection by such meaningless practices. When there is occasion for them, perform them; and when the occasion is passed, remain quiescent.

. . . Only awake to the One Mind, and there is nothing whatsoever to be attained. This is the *real* Buddha. The Buddha and all sentient beings are the One Mind and nothing else."

And finally Huang Po shows them the truth of Buddhism that is beyond even Buddha:

"So the sutra says, 'What is called supreme perfect wisdom implies that there is really nothing whatsoever to be attained.' If you are also able to understand this, you will realize that the Way of the Buddhas and the Way of devils are equally wide of the mark."

There is no way to what already is.

When asked to sum up his teachings, Papaji often said: "No teaching, no teacher, no student." "No teaching" cuts through all concepts, approaches, methods, and practices to the discovery and celebration of truth here and now. Papaji was uncompromising in his rejection of any evolutionary way. He would not allow us to indulge the belief that you are not That and that you had to develop toward it. For him there was no movement toward a goal, no need for practice to perfect yourself. No transformation or purification was required. His advice was always the same: Just be quiet. In the silence all is revealed. What you are in truth is already here and has always been so. "No teacher, no student" sees through the veil of duality that imagines the separation of your undivided nature into subject-object, self-other, into an enlightened teacher and an ignorant student. In fact there is no separation, there is no duality, there is no enlightenment and no ignorance. There is only the undivided nature of reality. Knowing this is the essence of freedom. There is only the absolute, and it understands it all.

Understanding It All

The pathless path of *Advaita* (literally, "not-two" or "undivided" in Sanskrit) is the way of understanding—also called *jnana* in India—the penetrating wisdom that sees no separation. The nondual knowledge *is* the Self. While this wisdom cannot be grasped in concept, we can directly taste our true nature by understanding what the word "understand" really means.

First, I am not referring to the rational, logical method by which we attempt to divide and analyze existence. While this approach is useful in describing and manipulating the world of phenomena, it cannot grasp source consciousness itself, the origin of all mind and phenomena. It can neither limit the limitless nor divide the undivided. Like a stick that burns away in the very attempt to stir the fire, dualistic analysis cannot enter mystery.

If we examine the driving force behind analysis itself we discover the why-thought. "Why?" is the questioning quality of mind. Like an itch the "why?" arises and calls to be scratched—to be pondered, to be answered, based on the assumption and hope that if this "why?" is answered, everything will fall into place and the itch will go away. Questioning is an intellectual form of desire, a seeking of the understanding that the mind thinks will bring peace, security and control. Like the process of desire, which is never quite satisfied by its temporary gratifications, intellectual answers come and go, yet the mechanism of questioning continues seeking ever new content.

The question—this wanting to know—is a crucial piece of technology in the self-perpetuation of mind, one of the ways it sustains its functioning and reinforces the appearance of the "I". The why-thought is a servant of the I-thought. Deathly afraid of unemployment, it ongoingly seeks busy work to stay in action and sustain its imagined existence. It ennobles understanding as its heroic adventure of explaining reality and coming to ultimate truth.

Yet this hope is the sucker bait on the fishhook of the question. If you turn the question mark—"?"—upside down—"¿"—it looks like a hook. Questions have a barb on the end that hooks attention into continued thought activity, which in its pursuit of truth continues to mask it. It generates ever-more refined questions and answers and the whole body of profound philosophical and spiritual discourse arises. It seems like such a heresy to the acquisitive, knowledge-seeking mind to suggest that there is really nothing to know and no point in thinking about it.

No matter how sublime the expression, all explanation is just a metaphor for the unutterable mystery. In the silent knowing beyond words, mystery is sufficient unto itself and needs no explanation. Ultimately, "why?" has no answer. Or, we could say, the real answer to "why?" is "because." That is, "be-cause" in the sense of an injunction to be-the-cause itself, to abide as source. When you realize that you are the cause of all, the source of all questions and answers, then the true meaning of understanding becomes clear.

Reverse the two concepts within *understand* and you get *stand under*. To stand under something might be to place yourself below it or lower than it, which suggests that one approaches mystery by humbling yourself before it, bowing to it. Thought must give up all attempts to define the infinite and comprehend the unknowable. It must kneel, indeed, prostrate itself fully upon the ground of silence and release all its conceptual positions, no matter how lofty. In the surrender to no-thought, the real knowing is revealed. Wisdom arises in the total acceptance of mystery.

The meaning of *understand* gets even clearer if we see the word's Latin origins: *sub* (under) *stance* (stand). The *sub-stance* or essence of something is that which *stands under* it, that is, it underlies it. To understand reality is to realize that it stands under everything and everyone. It is the unchanging substrate within everything, the Self within everybody. You are that truth.

Thus, understanding means *being the substance* that stands under everything. In this sense truth understands it all. In this mysterious self-knowledge where knowing is being, there is no individual knowing subject and known object. "Substance is what remains," wrote Eli Siegel, the Jewish mystical poet, "when everything you can think of has gone."

The Paradox of Practice

The nondual vision may seem severe and uncompromising in its refusal to entertain any notion that there is someone seeking or something to do or somewhere to get. It is exactly this unhedging directness that I most love about it. There is only the Self here and now, and absolutely nothing to be done about it.

Yet because the absolute stand permits of no self-indulgence whatsoever, it is clear that it is not for everybody. Sri Ramana Maharshi, a magnificent embodiment of the nondual realization, would often divide spiritual aspirants into three categories. There are those who are so ready that simply upon hearing the truth they realize their nature. The second group needs to focus on self-awareness for a while before their reality is fully apparent. Other seekers must undergo years of spiritual practice until they realize what is already so. While for Ramana there is only the Self now, he also understood that within the dream it may be appropriate for an illusory doer to engage in illusory practice. So even though you are home now, even though you are already the Self and there is nothing you can do to attain what you already are, the nondual sages still offer injunctions to those attached to the belief that you are not already That.

The paradox of practice is enriched if we recall that whatever happens within the dream is all the play of consciousness. There is no choice in the matter precisely because there is no chooser. There is no separate agent bringing about its own realization, just the self-knowing of the whole. How and when one awakens is not up to the imagined "I" but to the supreme power that moves everything. No matter what the "I" seems to be doing—whether you practice or not—realization happens inexorably at the appropriate time as a function of the totality. Whether the wave rises or falls is not up to the wave, but is simply the activity of the ocean. If you are moved to practice, you will. If not, you won't. Awakening occurs—or not—when consciousness so moves it. There are many examples of awakening without practice. There are even more examples of years of practice without awakening. This is not said to encourage passivity—after all, whether you are passive or active is also perfectly moved by the Self—but to challenge the persistent identification with a willful doer and its addiction to doing. There really is nothing to do and no one to do it.

People have a hard time getting what "nothing to do" means because we are so conditioned to doing as a means to an end. In western culture, especially in the US, this is embedded in what was originally called the "Protestant ethic," which believes that salvation—be it spiritual or secular—would come through accomplishment and hard work. If you work hard enough, it justifies you, purifies you, makes you worthy of grace, brings you closer to God. This conviction is extended by the science and technology-based, positivist belief in progress and perfectibility. We are moving "toward a better future." Somewhere, down the road, it will all come together if we keep working on it. To the spiritualized ego, work—whether we call it "working on yourself," "transformation," "sadhana," or "practice"—is the doing that will get us to that perfection.

These fundamental operating principles of a workaholic, achievement-oriented culture are supported and expressed in the western sense of linear history as the continuum in which we collectively work out our freedom and salvation. The progressive historical sense is the cultural, macro version of the "I"s micro sense of time as the continuum in which it can prolong its existence. The history-based culture and the individual mind conspire to support the obsession with working on oneself over time, which blinds us to the perfection of our being now. Doing just reinforces doership and more doing. It cannot lead to being, which already is.

Perhaps practice does have some usefulness. While it may seem that it enables you to *attain* unitive wisdom, I would say—at best—practice exists to *exhaust* you, to lead you to surrender your striving, to give up. In the giving up, the truth of your being is revealed.

Yet this does not necessarily mean giving up practice. Ultimately, we must inquire: *Who is practicing?* As long as we believe there is someone practicing, then practice reinforces the "I" and its belief in separation. It perpetuates the search and postpones the realization of what you already are. When you see through the "I" that is practicing, then if you continue sadhana, you see it for what it is—the play of consciousness. You see that no one is going anywhere or attaining anything, that the entire process of someone going somewhere through practice *is* the dream. No one is meditating, no one is visualizing, no one is chanting, all of it is the play of consciousness.

The great Chinese Zen Master Dogen made it very clear: *practice is enlightenment.* In the nondual vision, when you sit on the meditation cushion you are not *attaining* your buddha nature, you are *expressing* it. When you sit quietly, chant, sing devotional songs, pray, whirl, follow the breath, visualize, it is all the Self contemplating itself, celebrating itself, loving itself, worshipping itself, declaring itself, playing out its exquisite dance of freedom.

Here one can enjoy all the rich and glorious ways of self-experience that we call practice—not as a means to some distant goal or to become someone else, but to be what you already are.

The Mother of All Desire

Within the dream-paradox of following injunctions, Papaji repeatedly said that the single most important condition for awakening is to *want freedom above all things*. Since desire, as we noted above, is a specific form of the divine motor force behind all manifestation, it is also the engine that drives awakening. The supreme desire that generates creation, ignorance and suffering is the same will that turns back to its own self-recognition. Desire is liberating if we see that it is the Self's own yearning for itself, the subliminal knowing deep within consciousness of our own divinity and the longing to return to source. If one channels this holy longing fully toward freedom, laser-like in one direction only—rather than diffusing it though the endless diversity of desired objects that usually capture our attention—it has extraordinary liberating power. Focused outward on objects, desire sustains the experience of separation. Focused inward on the Self, it frees. You ride the divine creative force full circle back to the Self you never really left.

Papaji also explained that if there are unfulfilled desires, or desires that are higher on your list than freedom, the energy will be organized toward the pursuit and satisfaction of those desires sooner or later. (Hindus and Buddhists tend to think long-term in terms of lifetimes). If one thinks one wants freedom, but actually has other priorities, one will experience the conflict of this self-deception. So get clear about what you want and go for it.

Freedom is a choice you make, a total focus on the Self. "Have this burning desire," advised Papaji: "'I want to be free. That is the only thing I want. Nothing else interests me. I have been enjoying myself for thirty-five million years, fulfilling every possible desire. I have experienced all possible enjoyments, but now I don't want any more. I want freedom and freedom alone.'. . . If you want freedom, you must want it to the exclusion of everything else. You cannot keep your other desires pending while you try to win freedom. You just reject them completely. When the desire for freedom is strong enough, nothing will prevent you from walking into the Heart and claiming your kingdom."

Papaji loved to tell the story about the man who is on fire, running to the river to douse his flames, and a friend stops him and asks if he'd like to go out to dinner. If you are on fire and running to the river, what are you going to do? Will you let any other desire get in the way of this relief? You must want it that much. Who is truly burning for freedom above all?

Nisargadatta Maharaj was equally insistent on channeling desire toward the Self: "Increase and widen your desires till nothing but reality can fulfill them. It is not desire that is wrong, but its narrowness and smallness. Desire is devotion. By all means be devoted to the Real, the Infinite, the eternal Heart of Being. Transform desire into love. All you want is to be happy . . . . To imagine that some little things—food, sex, power, fame—will make you happy is to deceive yourself. Only something as vast and deep as your Real Self can make you truly and lastingly happy."

So turn your face totally to the source. Choose it, make a total commitment to freedom, and live in this absolute dedication. "Earnestness," insisted the Maharaj, "is the only condition of success." "Thinking of that alone, speaking of that, conversing of that with one another, utter dedication to that alone—this is called *abhyasa* or practice by the wise," spoke the wisdom of the *Yoga Vasistha*. Jesus taught: "Seek ye first the kingdom of God, and his righteousness; and all those things shall be added unto you." Which is the essential meaning of the ancient Hebrew injunction: "Have no other gods before me." Give your full attention, your full love, devotion, worship, only to God, to freedom, to the Self. Give in to the longing for your own Self, face it entirely and let it consume you. If you give in to this fiery passion, it will burn you up. When you want the Self above all things, the process of desire dissolves into a single yearning. When freedom is your only desire, there is only freedom.

This burning desire is a driving force in many spiritual traditions. The exquisite love poetry of Rumi and the great Sufi mystics lyrically expresses the passionate longing of the Lover for the Beloved. The Indian bhakta sings in heartfelt devotion to God. The fervent prayers of the Jewish Hasidim and Kabbalists, and the Zen student's burning concentration on the koan, also channel this ardent intensity toward liberation. The practitioners of Hindu and Buddhist tantra skillfully use sexual desire in opening up blissful nondual consciousness. In all these ways the deepest desire and longing is sacralized and channeled toward the Self.

From the dualistic perspective, this desire is the yearning of the separate self for freedom. In the nondual vision, however, the adept sees through the appearance of duality to the play of the one supreme energy itself. Here the bhakta is both the lover and the beloved dancing in sweet harmony with oneself. The tantrika is both god and goddess, the two faces of the absolute eternally joined in ecstatic, sexual embrace within you. The Jewish mystic knows that prayer is really Self-talk, the single monologue of the unspeakable, unaddressable One. There is only the undivided reality in union with itself, and this passion—the intensity of desire—is its own energy and love, the very cohesion of That which has never been sundered.

If you have not tasted the sweetness of your own true nature, then wanting nothing but the Self may seem like a forced ascetic sacrifice of what you think you want. However, when one has known its pure satisfaction, one wants to return to it again and again. And the more we savor the peace of the Self, the more acutely do we feel the pain of our unfulfilled desires and attachments to experience. Here suffering itself is its own blessing, for it drives one back to the peace. Our pain is the grace that leads us to return repeatedly to the Self until we have had enough suffering and are unwilling to get stung again. We realize that no experience in the movie can come close to the magnificent wholeness of our own being.

So want freedom above all things. Turn to it incessantly, over and over again with one-pointed devotion. As the great Sufi poet-saint Rumi beckoned: "Come, come, whoever you are, this caravan has no despair." Though you may wander away a thousand times, you only need turn your face Selfward once again to be welcomed home. As you turn to it, it pulls you. You see that your very yearning is the gravitational force of grace itself, pulling from—and to—the center of pure silence and fullness. It is the irresistible attraction of absolute being calling its own reflection home—a black hole in which nothing and no one can exist. To desire only the Self means to yield to that dissolution into source—to surrender to one's own truth as the moth abandons itself to the flame. In this way total desire is surrender.

Surrender's Just Another Word for Nothin' Left to Do

Surrender lies at the very heart of the paradoxical pathless path. In dualistic spiritual language, the word "surrender" implies some kind of action by a doer. It suggests that there is a letting go, some giving up that must be done to realize oneself. Yet in the mystery of the no-way, surrender is not so much a letting go as it is a *seeing through* the I-thought itself and the belief that there is something "I" must do, somewhere to get, more effort to make to realize myself. Even the concept "letting go," as passive and mellow as it sounds, suggests an unnecessary action. While conventionally we might say that one relinquishes the I-thought, it seems more precise to say one merely abides as what you are before thought and action arise and after they pass away—the being-awareness that recognizes no doer, no duality. So, rather than an action or effort, surrender is the seeing that no action or effort is necessary, and that no separate agent exists to perform it. It is the awareness that you are and always have been home free. To be That involves no doing.

Papaji said over and over again: "Don't try. Make no effort, have no intention." It may seem as if it takes a great intention to have no intention. It may seem like a tremendous effort to give up all effort. But this is just because the mind—addicted to doing—cannot grasp the simplicity of being and so reverts back to its habitual trying. Deathly afraid of unemployment, it continually generates the make-work of giving itself a sense of solid existence. Surrender is a huge challenge to the addiction to busyness, which seeks more, better, different.

Responding to a student who said letting go is difficult, Papaji explained: "That's because you have the idea that letting go is something you have to do. To move from one place to another may be difficult if the journey is long and hard. But if you don't have to move at all, how can you say that it is difficult? Just give up the idea that you have to do something or reach somewhere. That's all you have to do."

In this sense surrender is a full relaxation of effort and striving. It is ultimate stress relief, a release of the contraction, of the holding-on muscle. It is the end of identifying with the survival functions—the desire-grabbing-controlling impulses and the fear-avoiding-resisting tendencies that lock in the separate self-sense. Surrender is simply letting yourself be as you are. It is like going to sleep: In order to sleep you must surrender the world, give up your relationships, let go of your body, your thoughts. You can only sleep if you give all of that up. You surrender into non-existence. Each night as you die into source, you are refreshed by this surrender.

In this refreshment we come to know the immense richness of the Self, and relinquish the impoverishment of the separate self-sense. The master told us repeatedly: You are an emperor, not a beggar. You possess the untold wealth of the universe, unimaginable riches. Don't beg for enlightenment, don't plead for it. You are the Self, don't assume that you are impoverished. Give up that yearning and be quiet, and the treasure will be self-evident as your very nature.

Because the I-thought is the lynchpin that holds the separate self sense and its suffering together, the essence of surrender is seeing through identification with the "I" and its story. It is the end of belief in the doer. Are we willing to cease being the star of our own movie and give up the heroic romance of the arduous path? Are we willing to see how much we hold on to the hopeful quest—that hope is still suffering. Can we see how addicted we are to longing and struggle, and see through the whole drama? Who has had enough?

To not entertain the I-thought exposes the illusory nature of separateness and reveals the always-already presence that underlies all sense of self. If you plunge into the depths of yourself it is seen that the individual "I" is just a refraction of the one "I am," your real being and the sole subject from which all being arise.

I love Emerson's simple account of his awakening: "Standing on the bare ground,—my head bathed by the blithe air, and uplifted into infinite space,—

all mean egotism vanishes. I become a transparent eyeball. I am nothing. I see all. The currents of the Universal Being circulate through me; I am part or particle of God."

From the egoic perspective, surrender looms as failure and defeat. It may seem an admission of weakness, that you couldn't handle it or do it by yourself. It triggers the illusory doer's fear of not being able to control its destiny or pursue its agenda. Surrender faces this fear head on, staring directly into the eyes of an individualistic culture that worships free will as its most precious quality—a worship that sustains the rebellion against source. In relaxing that resistance, surrender claims the ultimate victory of resting as one's own Self.

A Generous Acceptance

Surrender comes as well through the unconditional acceptance of all our experience, whatever it may be. Remember that the sense of separation is sustained by attachment to experience—to our desires and fears, likes and dislikes, to the pursuit of pleasure and the avoidance of pain. The "I" continually seeks to feed off experience—grasping what it wants and rejecting what it doesn't—to give it a sense of solidity, To fully embrace whatever comes, to accept our experience as it is without trying to control it, undermines the sense of "I". Its imagined boundaries and strategic, manipulating tendency cannot endure this receptivity. "Enlightenment," Zen Master Joshu Sasaki Roshi defined succinctly, "is the unconditional embrace of your karma." It is in our full acceptance of all our experience that we find liberation in the midst of life as it is.

Nisargadatta Maharaj cautioned those who came to him seeking some idealized state by saying, "Realization comes through a conscious and deliberate plunging into life, not in retreat from it," "through a generous acceptance of finite experience, not in blotting it out of mind; through utter willingness to be what one is, not in trying to lift oneself to Heaven by one's own bootstraps. The Self realizes freedom from the finite world by deliberate self-abandonment to its limitations." Again, the paradox of the pathless path—just be yourself, allow yourself to have ordinary experience, accept your limitations.

Self-abandonment to our limitations is a challenging, scary concept to the ardent spiritual student filled with perfectionist notions of some ideal "enlightened state." We hear that there is a place of unblemished peace and love and bliss and kindness. One of the biggest traps in spiritual life is this expectation of permanent purity, absent of everyday experience, a perfectionism that subtly rejects our humanness. We then measure ourselves and our experience against that ideal. We somehow believe that we "get there" by always being peaceful, always being loving, always kind or equanimous, and that if we are experiencing something else, we are not there, nor will that ordinary kind of experience help us to get there. We scrutinize all our experience and judge whatever doesn't seem to approximate the ideal. So naturally we don't want to accept the ups and downs of our experience as it is. We want to manipulate it and purify it, we want to get rid of some experiences and cultivate others. We want to elevate ourselves to the ideal.

We thus hold up an ideal that, in the very process, means there is "someone" who is never quite living up to it. This perfectionism sustains the impression of a self "less than" its own true nature. Recall that maya projects the appearance of division through measurement. Measuring, which in this sense means judging our experience against an image of perfection, literally traces the boundaries of a non-existent separate self. In so doing you forget that you are without qualifiers of any kind, what Buddha called "suchness," that which is prior to all judgment.

If we read the Biblical story of the Garden of Eden as a myth of consciousness, our original unconditioned nature is evident. Adam and Eve were free to live eternally in innocence. God had presented Adam with only one commandment: "You must not eat from the tree of the knowledge of good or evil, for when you eat of it you will surely die." (Genesis 2:17). The commandment was very clear: Do not bite into the distinction between good and evil. Do not judge. If you remain in innocent consciousness, free of judging, you abide as your original nature, which is eternal. If you distinguish good and evil, you no longer know your perfection. This was the simple, straightforward promise; this was the unambiguous warning.

Eating the apple—the judging quality of mind—divides the inherent perfection of reality into right and wrong, good and bad. The myth describes the origin of dualism, the separative mentality that projects upon the primordial unity the multiplicity of existence. It cleaves our whole being into subject and object, separates the individual from the totality, creates the distance between the human being and God, and projects the endless path of return to that original state.

This dualistic mentality literally casts us out of the garden of innocent consciousness into the forgetting of one's own Self. No wonder they felt "shame," the feeling tone of separation from one's pure nature. The divided mentality ejects us from paradise and into the world of suffering—as the myth says, into the pain of childbirth and the "painful toil" of work and subsistence. It casts us out of the eternal now and into mortality, into time, old age and death. It is the fall into mind and its dream of struggling to survive outside the garden of source consciousness.

There was just one commandment at first. When they didn't follow that one, then we got ten! And now the seemingly endless stream of do's and don'ts which no one can ever live up to. Hence the vicious cycle of perfectionism—the process of continually falling short of oneself—spins the wheel of suffering.

All this is the consequence of judgment. The "fall" did not take place in some mythic or historical time, somewhere in the past in the Near East. It occurs now. Every moment that one judges one's experience or oneself, one is cast out of the garden of one's own unconditional Self.

As the old saying goes: "What you resist persists." Paradoxically, your very judgment and resistance holds you captive to the experience you are trying to avoid. Resistance is the way we hold on and stay stuck. Like the old Brer Rabbit story of the tar baby, the more you try to push it away and get out of it, the more you get stuck in it. The experience persists, and the experiencer persists, caught in some "attainment-mode" trying to let go of the attachment and reach the ideal, pure state. We get stuck in the thought that this isn't it, that all our human experience isn't it, that attachment and reactivity aren't it, and that we have to attain some other state.

Yet if one is fortunate to be close to the great sages, we see that the masters have their ordinary human experience, their moods, their emotional outbursts and ups and downs, their personal idiosyncrasies. Papaji got angry and cranky. It just happened in a totally different context than most people. When asked if he got angry, Papaji subtly replied. "Yes, but 'I' don't get angry, anger gets angry." That is, experience comes and goes, moods and reactions come and go. It is all a perfectly natural flow of experience, yet it doesn't happen to anyone. There is no experiencer there judging the experiencing, or pushing it away, or clinging to it.

So you don't have to change your experience. Just allow it to happen, receive it all with equanimity. The essential key is to *feel it fully*, without holding it or pushing it away. You take what comes, the pleasure and pain, what you like and dislike. Be with it when it's here, let it go when it is gone. That is all you can do—allow it to come up fully into consciousness. Feeling is the crucible of transformation, the fire that burns the experience away. When we feel fully, we give the experience the opportunity to complete itself and dissipate. Emotions follow a simple basic law: if you feel them they will pass. That is, if you feel them as pure sensation without clinging to the story we tell about them, then they come and go naturally. They live out their life span and disappear. If you resist them, deny them, judge or repress them, they have a tendency to stick around. They get stored in the mindbody as some form of stress or may show up eventually as illness.

The willingness to feel is the litmus test of true courage. I am not speaking of the popular concept of courage as "no fear." While fearlessness is, indeed, a quality of our true being, we do not realize it by denying fear or making an end run around it. In fact, courage is the willingness to feel fear, to be fully open to it. "In order to experience fearlessness," Chögyam Trungpa Rinpoche advised, "it is necessary to experience fear. The essence of cowardice is not acknowledging the reality of fear." Courage, then, is the willingness to face our fear. We no longer hide or shrink back from certain experiences, but welcome them, as uncomfortable or scary as they may be. Hell can come and go, lifetimes can come and go, in what is a second on the clock. When one is truly open and courageous in the face of all experience, there is no impulse to run from any of it. On the contrary, one embraces the mystery itself.

When you are willing to feel the entire spectrum of human experience as it is, you come to know its true nature—transitory, ever-changing, modifications of the underlying source. Sensations are not felt any less than before. In fact, they might be felt *even more* intensely when there's a greater openness and receptivity to the energy in its raw state. When powerful feelings arise we are given the opportunity to taste an unimagined poignancy of existence. The intense grief and sadness many of us experienced during the September 11 attacks threw us into the fire of overwhelming feeling. It felt like molten lava flowing through me, burning everything in its path and leaving an indescribable awe and mystery. Such utter intensity went beyond pleasure and pain, beyond all the categories and interpretations we place upon feeling. Even the most painful experiences became exquisitely beautiful and sacred. It was clear these feelings were not personal, but rather arising from source itself, manifesting through the medium of my bodymind programming and conditioning. By not placing upon it any judgment or identification or story, all experience, all suffering, is felt as the sensate forms of the intangible formless. While the sensation is felt, it is also known to be insubstantial and spacious.

As you fully accept the flow of mindbody experience as it is, a shift in identification takes place. Instead of identifying with the *changing content* of your experience and believing yourself to be the experiencer, you realize that you are the *unchanging context* within which it is all occurring. Experience comes and goes and you are always here, allowing the flow of thoughts, feelings, and actions to occur without attachment or judgment. You are the simple loving space that witnesses the mindbody process, including the personality, living out its programming.

It is an odd paradox—to fully accept the individual persona is to be free of it even as it flows on. This is what Maharaj meant by the "utter willingness to be what one is, not in trying to lift oneself to Heaven by one's own bootstraps. The Self realizes freedom from the finite world by deliberate self-abandonment to its limitations." We lovingly accept our humanness, our programming, conditioning, tendencies, preferences, our individual quirks, moods and so-called foibles. The American nondual sage Robert Adams jokingly told his students how amused he was at the way his personality turned out. By compassionately observing the whole person with gentle acceptance, you are freed from identification with it. As long as you are trying to make yourself perfect, you are stuck identifying with an imagined imperfect self. It is a tremendous challenge to see through the attempt to change, improve, fix the personality. Any change that may occur is simply the destiny of the organism. It is a great relief to see that there is no "perfecting" the individual, that there is no one working on oneself or purifying character or cultivating virtue or shaping one's development. To truly give this up is liberation. Ultimately, then, self-acceptance is self-transcendence.

The unconditional allowing of experience reveals your true nature. On the one hand you know yourself as the awareness that is untouched by the mind-body process. The Self is always free of experience and never limited to it. It is so difficult to describe: all experience occurs, recorded and felt by the senses—vividly, tangibly—yet the being-awareness experiences nothing, just as the images in the mirror never really touch or stain the mirror. All states come and go, and you just are, free of it all, even as it is all happening within you. The inherent happiness and peace of your original nature are independent of what happens in the movie of experience.

Ultimately, however, in the mystery of nonduality, to be free of experience does not mean you are separate from it, as if you are some independent subject witnessing the flow of sensory objects. This is just another trap in dualistic consciousness, an attachment to emptiness that sustains a subtle sense of separation by pushing away the world of experience. The fully open embrace of experience actually reveals the undivided reality, that all experiences are forms of your own formless reality. It is a welcoming celebration that it's all just you experiencing yourself as the endless variations of the one taste. This is the "return" to the garden of innocent consciousness, which you discover has always been here, awaiting your acceptance. Neither a place in time nor a state of mind, this unconditioned perfection is your very nature here and now.

Don't Even Think About It

Ramana Maharshi pointed out that the essence of the Advaita approach is summarized in two Biblical sayings: The first is, *Be still and know that I am*

God. (Psalms 46:10). In silence the wisdom of your original nature is revealed. "The experience of silence alone is the real and perfect knowledge," Ramana taught.

"Silence is a raft across the miserable ocean," Papaji reassured us. It is the place of refuge, the source and abode of peace. If thought is maya's tool in projecting the appearance of multiplicity and the separate "I," if attachment to thought creates the experience of suffering, then no-thought cuts through the root cause of all ignorance and bondage. "It is only the cessation in the mind of all notions," Shankara emphasized, "that can lead to true knowledge of the Self." Silence is the unspoken communion of the undivided. In the stillness beyond mind it is seen that there is no separation—it was only a thought in consciousness.

Based on this logic, one of the most common injunctions in the paradoxical no-way is simply "Don't think." "Be quiet," Papaji told his students over and over again. Depending on the situation, this command might be interpreted in various ways. It might mean to have no thought, to not give rise to a thought. If, however, thought arises, then make no effort to stop it. If it persists, do not indulge it or follow it, neither cling to it nor push it away. Basically, have no relationship to thought. As the Maharaj suggested, just don't read your mail.

The dictate to be still boggles the mind. Because the sense of a separate doer exists only in mental activity, to not-think is the equivalent of suicide. Our fascination with thought reinforces the experience of a separate self and its suffering. We are dealing here with a fundamental, unconscious addiction to thought. The "I" sense works over thought the way a cow chews its cud. The activity feeds our narcissism and keeps us glued to the fascinating movie of our own imagination, which by entertaining the "I" holds it captive to its own projections. No matter whether we are addicted to the most attractive, voluptuous fantasies or to the most horrifying, repulsive fears and worries, they are all the ways we cling to the personal drama and distract ourselves from the silent peace of our original nature.

So we earnestly pursue the simple injunction to be still and know. Typically, initially, we may think of silence as the opposite of sound or thought. We seek quiet, peaceful relief as a clear contrast to the noise of our life and the chatter of everyday mind. We go on retreat, preferably to some idyllic setting, where the absence of intrusive sounds invites us to discover the quietness within. We learn the rich menu of meditation techniques to quiet the mind. Through such focused efforts we may discover momentary relief from our compulsive chatter. The blessed oases of peace and bliss seem obvious proof that we are on the right track to the ultimate silence that awaits our diligent commitment to meditation.

Yet no matter how often or wonderful those moments of peace may be, sooner or later the inherent momentum of mental activity reasserts itself and those pesky, familiar thoughts begin swirling once again. Then we think we're not doing it well and our peace is continually interrupted by thoughts we obviously cannot control.

At this point we may realize that one cannot—in fact, need not—make oneself quiet. *The quiet is already here.* Rather than quiet the mind or restrain thinking, simply be aware of the silence that is already present. This is the most subtle shift of focus. Ordinarily, just as our eyes tend to focus on objects, our attention habitually looks at thoughts rather than the space between them. When you focus on the silent gaps between the thoughts, your experience of that space expands and deepens. The silence between the thoughts pulls with the force of a black hole. It has a magnetic attraction that generates a willingness, a yearning, to listen more deeply, to yield to it, to be immersed in it. It's like making love with silence, both a full embrace of it and a surrender to it. This listening is consciousness turning to itself, sensing the gravitational pull it has on itself, calling itself home.

Home is the immense silent space that is everywhere. What we call inner space and outer space are the same all-pervasive context—the emptiness in which everything exists. The space in which the planets and galaxies hang, the very space within matter itself, is the same silence in which all mental activity comes and goes. Everything occurs within this great peace which is the context for all movement and manifestation. It is the source from which everything arises, in which it abides, and to which it returns. The magnificence of this silence allows for everything—sound, thought, and action—to occur within it. Thoughts come and go and the silence is always here, just as the sky is always here no matter what the weather. Sky is the unchanging context for the ever-changing, ephemeral weather. Silence is the permanent space in which the weather of thought, sound, action take place. All mental movements are only apparent modifications of the peace that is always here, undetected by the active mind.

In the silent depths of no-thought, the wisdom of the Self abides. Here not-knowing and knowing are one and the same—an unfathomable intelligence without form or content that simply knows that it is. There is no one who is silent, no knowing subject, just silence itself which is your original nature. So the injunction to "be quiet" is not a call to more effort or doing, but literally the invitation to be what you already are, to see that you abide as the silent emptiness.

It is a calming paradox that silence is not some passive antithesis to action and thought, but the ever-present spacious background and inner dimension of active life. In realizing that silence is everywhere, we don't have to seek idyllic, quiet physical settings. Wherever you are the silence is here. Abiding as this stillness, you are always on retreat regardless of the surrounding physical noise and activity. Of course pleasant physical surroundinds do soothe us, and it is wise to follow the call to retreat when it beckons.

Once you discover the underlying reality of silence, there need not be a problem with thought or mental activity. The waves of thought arise naturally and do not disturb the ocean of silence. Why should the ocean mind if it has waves, if it is turbulent or smooth? Their movement is just its play, and the depths are unaffected by the surface activity. Ocean and wave are one. Silence, thought and activity are one. From the ground of silence we see that intellect and thought form the technology of consciousness and the code that runs the bodymind organism. Without a thinker to claim them, thoughts come and go freely as natural, functional expressions of the being-awareness that sources all life.

Being Awareness

Ultimately, then, freedom is not about not-thinking, but simply *being the awareness* that sees and allows all thought and experience to come and go. In the paradox of the pathless path, awareness is the way and awareness is home. To abide as consciousness, one turns awareness back to itself to discover that consciousness is already abiding. "Face the Self incessantly," Papaji urged. "You are That. You must look to your Self right now. Don't postpone." "Attention to one's own Self," claimed Ramana Maharshi, "which is ever shining, the one undivided and pure reality, is the direct, infallible means to realise the unconditioned, absolute being that you really are."

The process by which awareness turns back upon itself Ramana called *vichara* or self-inquiry. It asks you to face the "I" that thinks it is seeking, that thinks it is meditating, that thinks it is the doer. Ask the ultimate question "Who am I?" Focus attention on this "I" and trace it back to its source. Where does this "I" come from? The point is not to come up with some intellectual answer but rather to turn your face directly to yourself. In so doing you become aware of being aware. It is as if the eyes are rolled backward 180° to the awareness behind it all. Rather than focusing on thoughts, I am aware as the knower of the thoughts. Rather than focusing on the perceived objects, I am aware as the conscious subject. Rather than focusing on the seen, I am the seeing, the seer behind it all. Just as the eye cannot see itself, for it is the seer, so consciousness cannot know itself because it is itself the knower. To face the Self is to realize you are that consciousness. When awareness looks upon itself, the split between an observing subject and an observed object disappears. *There is just awareness aware of itself.* The knower, the known and the knowing are one and the same. The Self reveals itself as being-awareness, a burning fire that burns away any sense of a separate "I". When you face the sun, Papaji would say, the shadows are behind you. Instantly there arises the joy of self-recognition. The eternally abiding presence is what you have always been. Awareness doesn't bring you "there," it reveals that you are always here.

Within this pure, unmediated knowing reverberates the second Biblical phrase that Ramana considered to complete the Advaita vision: "*I am that I am*" (Exodus 3:14) is the lion's roar, the radical self-intuition of being-awareness awake to itself. It is not a "creative affirmation" that brings something new into existence, but rather a subliminal knowing of what is already so, the self-revelation of consciousness present to itself. Deeper than the I-thought, the presence of the true "I am" is sensed, the intuition of one's being, prior to and within all identity.

Because the Self reveals itself in all forms and experiences, every event, every situation, every thought is an opportunity to realize this conscious presence. Every experience invites you to realize that you are the awareness within which everything comes and goes. When I am sad, I am the awareness that sees the sadness. When I am lost, I am the awareness that knows I am lost. When I am found, I am the awareness that knows I am found. The particular objects of awareness come and go endlessly. Awareness remains. It is neither lost nor found. It neither appears nor disappears. The different states of consciousness change continually. Awareness is the unchanging context in which all states come and go.

In awareness there is no need to stop any activity or attain any particular state. Awareness allows—it doesn't cling, it doesn't reject, it makes no demands, it doesn't identify with the experience that is occurring. It is simply relaxed alertness that involves no effort or striving, no tension or concentration. It is aware of striving, aware of making an effort, aware of trying to concentrate. In this seeing there is only awareness awake to itself.

To rest as this presence is to see that everything occurs within awareness without ever touching it. In the same way that clouds pass through the sky without affecting or obstructing space, nothing disturbs your empty original nature. Like space it allows for everything to exist within it while remaining untouched by it all. When sadness is here, the awareness is not sad. When anger is here, the awareness is not angry. The ever-changing forms of imagination play out the movie while the underlying screen of consciousness remains free of the experiential drama occurring within it. The mystery of freedom reveals that nothing obstructs freedom.

While everything exists within awareness, paradoxically at the same time, nothing can exist within it. No matter what experience is arising, when awareness turns back to itself, the experience dissolves into the seeing. You realize that awareness is all there is, that all apparent forms are nothing but the play of consciousness without boundary, everywhere reflecting itself as all dimensions, forms, beings, worlds.

IV. LIVING FREEDOM

Realization Revealed

Spiritual seekers have romanticized the concepts of "realization" or "enlightenment" to mean some wondrous event or experience you have, or some accomplishment you attain. Actually, realization is the ultimate non-event or non-experience—not a happening at all but the revelation that nothing is happening to anybody. It is a true disillusionment in which all illusions of being someone on the path to enlightenment fall away. There is the clear seeing that there is no individual "you" to be realized, simply the presence that is always here.

"The state of Self-realization, as we call it," Ramana compassionately admonished the yearning souls who came before him seeking enlightenment, "is not attaining something new or reaching some goal which is far away, but simply being that which you always are and which you always have been. " And again: "You are the Self. You exist always. Nothing more can be predicated of the Self than that it exists. Seeing God or the Self is only being the Self or yourself. Seeing is being."

On the one hand we can say that in realization nothing new is added, only the ignorance has ceased. Yet, paradoxically, we can also say that realization doesn't destroy ignorance, it reveals that it never existed. There is no ignorance in the Self and there never was any. Ignorance is just its dream. The whole cycle of ignorance and realization, bondage and liberation, occurs solely in the imagination. Neither bondage nor liberation are real. They are simply appearances in consciousness that are dreaming the whole process, while in reality nothing happens. The absolute undergoes no change from bondage to liberation. No one is ignorant, no one forgets, no one wakes up, no one is free.

Because there is no attainment and no one to claim it, all claims are false. If I say I am *not* enlightened, it is a denial of my true nature—the absolute, which is always and already free. If I say I *am* enlightened, it is just more identification, which ignores the truth that there is no one to claim anything. Both statements are claims by the illusory separate self-sense that arrogantly demands recognition of its doubted existence. The "I" creates and claims both bondage and freedom. It personalizes unenlightenment and enlightenment as the domains in which it can exist. Yet freedom can never be possessed, precisely because it is free of a possessor. It is absolutely impersonal, revealing that which is free of the personal. It is nothing in itself. It has no voice and makes no claims. All this endless discoursing about it has no bearing on one's pristine state, which is beyond description. What remains is the natural state of our unconditioned being.

Papaji made a distinction between *enlightenment* and the natural state called *sahaja*. Enlightenment, he defined, is a state someone gains through effort over time, and whatever can be gained can be lost. Sooner or later it will disappear. Anything that comes and goes is not the real thing. If you think you have attained it, then it is not the ultimate.

On the other hand, sahaja is here all the time, and is known naturally and effortlessly. "Everyone is in the natural state whether one is aware of it or not," Papaji pointed out. "The *sahaja stithi* can never come through effort or practice. It cannot be attained because it is there all the time. It neither comes nor does it go. If you simply keep quiet and let things happen by themselves, you will find that it is that which is present all the time. You are never away from it or apart from it." That which is always here is pure presence without quality or limit. So subtle, so simple. It is you.

Tyranny of the Glimpse

One of the mixed blessings of spiritual life is the "glimpse." We have all had such moments—the falling away of the mirage of appearance, a burst of revelation, a wave of bliss, a taste of stillness, in which the clouds of thought dissipate and the "I" disappears. It confirms the teachings and reveals our true nature. In this sense, the glimpse is a touch of grace.

Yet it becomes a hindrance to resting as presence here and now if the thought arises that "I had a glimpse of truth." When a sense of separateness returns, the glimpse is held in memory as a distinct experience in time rather than the reality of now. I then struggle to regain that glimpse, to do what I did before to experience it again. I measure it carefully and describe it lovingly: it lasted an instant, minutes, hours, days, months, intermittently in varying strength. I refer back to it for solace and reassurance. The glimpse I had in '92, the great awakening of '93, these memories become part of my spiritual credentials and identity as a seeker. In the attempt to hold on, we draw a thought-boundary around the infinite. The very act of grasping loses it. What is here now cannot be known when it becomes a "then."

So as soon as it is held in memory, the glimpse becomes part of the content of ignorance. It is now a "spiritual experience" in the past that the "I" uses to support its agenda of independent existence and inspire it to greater spiritual work. It becomes an experience that demonstrates one's "progress along the path to realization." The memory of the glimpse becomes a tyranny, a rope binding us to time from which we can never be free as long as we hold to this memory and anticipation of its return. Since presence does not exist in time and is beyond all experience, to place the glimpse in time and label it an "experience" denies the reality of our being here and now.

The attachment to "high" experience is one of the great traps in spiritual life. Bliss, kundalini experiences, visions, psychic incidents, rushes of ecstasy, all the usual spiritual phenomena that people mistakenly associate with freedom, arise and pass away as temporary adornments of the being-awareness that underlies and sources all experience. Attachment to any of it blinds us to our formless nature.

Our clinging to these precious moments is the other face of doubt, the belief that I am not it, that I am not free or realized. Seeking to recreate the highs continues to feed doubt. As long as I held on to doubt, I made even stronger efforts to confirm my freedom. Yet the whole process of doubt and seeking affirmation creates the impression that freedom is somehow vulnerable, a changeable state that comes and goes. The I-thought projects its own transcience on its source. It clouds the awareness that freedom is no "state" at all, but rather the context in which all states come and go, be they high or low. What goes up must come down. What comes and goes, Ramana told Papaji, is not real. Freedom is always here and now, deeper than all experience.

The invitation is to give up the idea that "I" had a "glimpse" in the "past," to give up clinging to any state or experience. The surrender of the "I" and its temporal framework, its attachment to experience, its credentials and progress, its doubts and need for affirmation, reveals the natural stateless state now. When you don't try to hold on to it, it holds you. Right here is the peace and wholeness that we seek.

The presence that is here cannot be lost. Even such thoughts as "I am lost" or "It has disappeared" or "I am not it" are just projections of consciousness within the always-existing reality. There is nothing outside of it, and nothing within it that can disturb it. "Getting it" and "losing it" arise within it. "Trying to hold on to it" takes place within it. You are the being-awareness in which all these notions take place, in which all these claims and doubts, the pursuing and rejecting of experience, take place. Presence embraces both getting it and losing it, remembering and forgetting, wakefulness and distraction. All of these are the perfect expressions of consciousness. If you hold to one and reject the other that is still duality. To have no preference for any of these states is home.

The "I" holds on to "stabilizing" in the Self as part of its belief in an illusory progress toward the goal. There is a quite logical assumption that there is some gradual, incremental movement of consciousness in the direction of stabilization. We think: If I could just build upon these glimpses, they will expand and deepen and eventually culminate in the unbroken state. On the one hand it certainly looks like a process of stabilization takes place—a kind of progressive embodiment of realization in everyday life, in which nondual wisdom permeates, and is integrated in, the bodymind. Embodiment, then, shows up as the simple living of what is true. Yet, while embodiment does occur, the concern for stabilization still arises from doubt and hope, which feeds the belief in a doer that is not quite there yet. It measures its progress based on thoughts, feelings and sensations, and the persistence or disappearance of conditioning. Paradoxically, however, all of this is consciousness, and consciousness—which is all there is—has no need to stabilize.

Papaji refused to entertain any notion of progress or development toward some final stabilization. In response to a student who asked, "How can I stabilize in the moment of truth that I once lived?" He replied: "The idea of stabilization is a disturbance within awareness. Why do you want to fix the awareness? Only because you have accepted that you are unaware. For the awareness itself, what difference does it make whether you are aware or unaware? Is awareness not everywhere, both in attention and in inattention? . . . Why should you want to remember or stabilize That when it is That itself which is the power that enables you to remember or stabilize?" And he always came back to the ultimate question: "The idea of stabilization comes from your mind, from a thought you have stored in your memory. But tell me, where is your mind now?"

In the blessed silence of no-mind all questions of realization and stabilization fall away. Here the Self is already realized. Here shines the brilliant clarity of Gaudapada's radical vision: "All the souls are, by their very nature, illumined from the very beginning . . . . No soul ever came under any veil. They are by nature pure as well as illumined and free from the very beginning." This was the Buddha's simple realization: the nature of all beings has always been realized.

Egoji

The pesky enigma in the play of consciousness is the appearance of ego. On the one hand, we can define ego as the belief in being an individual doer, rooted in attachment to the I-thought and identification with the bodymind process. While the unconscious survival programming of the organism automatically sustains the bodymind, it is the attachment to and identification with those functions that generates the experience of separation and suffering. In this sense ego is both the technology of ignorance as well as its repository, and thus is the target of a rich array of spiritual theories and disciplines designed to dissolve or transcend it.

On the other hand, we come to realize that ego is nothing other than the individuated refraction of the one consciousness, a microcosmic, holographic image which both reflects and hides the formless absolute within it. It has no real independent existence, merely an appearance in consciousness created by thought. There is differentiation, but no separation. While the "I" seems to take on a life of its own, it is just a wave on the ocean of Self. In truth, there is only the ocean, and the wave or "I" is simply its movement. Functionally, we could say, it is the way the formless absolute knows or experiences itself. Seen from this perspective ego is a divine instrument of creation so the play can go on. It is always at the service of Self despite all appearances.

Thus, in the ocean of realization the wave of individual consciousness continues to rise and fall as an appropriate activity of the tides of freedom. The awareness-ocean simply witnesses its ebb and flow. Papaji and other masters referred to themselves interchangeably as the body and the totality. To the absolute there is no conflict between wave and ocean. The wave is just the natural form or movement of the source-reality.

More specifically, we could say that a functional ego continues as the survival programming of the organism, yet without anyone identifying with it. On this matter Papaji took a clear stand that was liberating to hear: When asked if he had ego, the master enthusiastically affirmed: "Yes, I have! I have ego. She likes to serve me as a maidservant. Without a maidservant the house cannot run. I have no complaint against ego. Let her live in my house. I have no problem with her. I don't find any emnity between her and me. She is quite happy." On another occasion he said: "Ego is the servant that runs my household so I don't have to worry about it. So I can remain on vacation."

Freedom from the separate "I" doesn't means the programming stops or disappears. It means there is no longer anyone identified with it. The delusion is not the survival function, but in thinking you *are* those functions. Identification with fear and desire, memory and anticipation, and other typical survival activities, locks you into the belief that you are limited to the bodymind, rather than being the presence within which all of this is taking place and which includes all of it.

Thus egoic programming is a natural and inherent part of the life process. To see through it doesn't invalidate its functionality, it just places it in the proper perspective as the natural intelligence that runs the organism and makes sure it operates well in the movie. It keeps you from driving in the wrong lane, gets you to the plane on time, and makes sure you eat when hungry. When you know who you are, the programming continues as the servant of the Self rather than as the master.

Shunyata, the eccentric Danish mystic, brilliantly referred to this functioning as "egoji." "Why harass or kill egoji, when one can be free in its play as a needed, useful tool—free in the divine Swa Lila's graceful Self-interplay." In India the reverential suffix "*ji*" is reserved for gurus, respected elders, beloved family and friends. Appending it here suggests the divinity of ego as well as its intimate role in the playing out of our lives.

So it is absurd to think about getting rid of ego. Alan Watts put it in his typical tongue-in-cheek way: "Getting rid of one's ego is the last resort of invincible egoism." It simply cannot get rid of itself. Besides, in the radical nondual vision, what is there to get rid of? Who is getting rid of it? Once you see the illusory nature of the "I," then residual I-consciousness is no obstacle to freedom. It *is* the Self. Dwelling as impersonal consciousness allows for the continuity of individuality in the ongoing play of the totality.

Moreover, it is also possible that the realization of one's impersonal nature can free up the individual bodymind process to experience its most fulfilled expression. That is, self-transcendence can generate self-actualization—the fruition of inherent individual potentialities. In the knowing of your true Self the particular abilities, traits, qualities, talents you were born with are freed up to flower naturally and spontaneously. As impersonal formless consciousness manifests through you, it allows this individual form to take on its ultimate uniqueness and even to thrive as a transparent instrument of the Self, which shines through it. Egoji is but an expression of the light.

Emerson eloquently depicted the transparent individual fully illumined and actualized by the divine: "From within or behind, a light shines through us upon things and makes us aware that we are nothing, but the light is all. A man is the façade of a temple wherein all wisdom and good abide. What we commonly call man, the eating, drinking, planting, counting man, does not, as we know him, represent himself, but misrepresents himself. Him we do not respect, but the soul, whose organ he is, would he let it appear through his action, would make our knees bend. When it breathes through his intellect, it is genius; when it breathes through his will, it is virtue; when it flows through his affection, it is love. And the blindness of the intellect begins when it would be something of itself. The weakness of the will begins when the individual would be something of himself. All reform aims in some one particular to let the soul have its way through us."

The nondual awareness arises within a unique bodymind process with its own inherent tendencies, preferences and personality. Radical change may or may not occur within it. Some individual characteristics may disappear or get

ironed out, others may be accentuated. The process may highlight the uniqueness of the individual rather than reduce it to some bland homogenized state.
Many sages live on with distinct, often highly idiosyncratic personalities.
They get moody, angry, sad, silly, nervous, melodramatic. They simply have
no identification with the tendencies that arise. The organism lives out its
programming and undergoes change according to its conditioning.
Personality is the expressive face of the impersonal.

One lives the joyful mystery of being the invisible essence and the immanent manifestation simultaneously. This exquisite dance of full participation
is the *Heart Sutra* in action—the absolute abides as emptiness and form
simultaneously without dilemma. Living consciously as the individual and
the whole, one engages in life while seeing through it to its fundamental
insubstantiality.

This selflessness is the ground of all relative, situational identity. Each situation evokes an appropriate response. An identity arises to function in that
situation and dissolves when it is not required. With clients I show up as a
consultant or coach; with my daughters I arise as their father. Name, form,
role come and go, while the formless presence remains—pure potentiality
full of seed possibilities of what one could be. The situational "I" arises functionally and disappears when not needed. The pull of relationship defines a
"me." Without the external object, no individual subject exists. There is a
playing out of roles while presence is unaffected by the activity going on.
The bodymind lives out its programming, conditioning, karma—call it what
you will—which is the script of the movie, the lines it is following.

Beneath the surface there is only the Self playing out its dance of multiplicity, showing up as everyone. All parts are played by the one Actor, the
sole Subject behind all the characters. The words "person" and "personality"
derive from the Greek *persona*, which referred to the masks worn by actors
in the ancient Greek tragedies and comedies. From *per* (through) and *sona*
(sound), it literally meant the mask through which the sound came. The person or personality is the form through which the formless essence enacts its
movie of life, the face it wears.

Joshu Sasaki Roshi used to say you could only be naked for so long each
day—you could only hang out as emptiness for so long—then you had to get
dressed, so to speak, put on your persona, go out there and act like you are
someone and play the game of life.

Early Retirement Plan

While certain ascetic or monastic traditions have prescribed the renunci-
ation of ordinary relationships and activity in the world, the radical nondual

realization requires no separation from work, family or society. For those willing to be free in the midst of the daily challenges of the workplace, I offer a special Early Retirement Plan. Rather than giving up one's employment, this unique program allows one to be on permanent vacation while the work gets done effectively and the paychecks keep coming in. All it requires is retiring the sense of individual doership—seeing through the one who works to That which is doing everything.

Ramana never encouraged spiritual seekers to leave their work or everyday life circumstances in the pursuit of self-realization. He just asked them to inquire who is working? "The feeling 'I work' is the hindrance," the Maharshi pointed out. "Ask yourself 'Who works?' Remember who you are. Then the work will not bind you, it will go on automatically. Make no effort either to work or to renounce; it is your effort that is the bondage. What is destined to happen will happen. If you are destined not to work, work cannot be had even if you hunt for it. If you are destined to work, you will not be able to avoid it, and you will be forced to engage yourself in it. So leave it to the higher power; you cannot renounce or retain as you choose. . . . Do not imagine it is you who are doing the work. Think that the underlying current is doing it. Identify yourself with the current."

Like Ramana, Papaji never counseled seekers to leave their work or family, and explicitly insisted that no such change in living conditions was required for freedom. He constantly reiterated that you only need to be quiet in whatever circumstances you find yourself. In fact, after his realization in the 1940's with Ramana, Papaji continued to work for a living to support his family, functioning effectively in business and as a mining manager. As cited above in his description of returning to work, Papaji discovered he could perform all his job tasks perfectly in silence without any thought whatsoever. "When one abides as the Self," he found, "some divine power takes charge of one's life. All actions then take place spontaneously, and are performed very efficiently, without any mental effort or activity."

One retires when one abides as silent awareness. When you are simply empty and present in each task, each meeting, each activity, the sense of individual doership dissolves into the flow of stress-free work. You witness the work happening on its own through the bodymind process. The mind and senses operate functionally as instruments of the underlying power. All thoughts, words, gestures, actions, responses seem to flow on automatic from the inner stillness. Everything gets done, and may even get done better than ever before.

The essence of freedom at work is being fully engaged and non-attached simultaneously. It allows you to be productive while sustaining your wellbeing, to be proactive, vital and alive while remaining calm and centered. It allows you to experience freedom and true security while making a useful, creative contribution to life. In the current organizational jargon, we could say that ultimate high performance arises in the absence of the performer. In this recognition, of course, it is no work at all, but truly the play of grace.

Everything Just Happens

When there is no identification with a separate doer, it is clear that everything is just happening on its own. It is all the Self doing everything, moving everything. "What is done," Papaji would often remind us, "is done by the supreme power which moves all things. Without that supreme power I could not even lift my hand. The problem starts when you think, 'I am lifting my hand.' Don't bring in this egotistic idea at all. Let this supreme power take charge of all your activities and be aware that it is the supreme power alone that is doing them. . . . Nothing can function without this power, but no one is aware of this."

To be aware of this is to see the indescribable beauty and perfection of the whole. "The things that emerge from the Self are all in the way that they have to be," Papaji affirmed. "The whole of samsara that we see around us is a manifestation of the Self. Everything that is seen, smelt or tasted is very beautiful. There are no mistakes in the Self. Everything is the way it ought to be. It is all a beautiful unfolding of perfection itself."

"Perfect" here doesn't mean perfect as opposed to imperfect, but rather the suchness of existence prior to all judgment one way or the other. It is the vision of everything just as it is without any filter of interpretation, likes or dislikes, judgments of good or bad, right or wrong. Ordinarily, if life doesn't conform to our values or desires, we can't see it as perfect. When our vision is free of that filter, the inherent beauty is self-evident.

The innocent eye sees everything happening inexorably. "What must happen will inevitably happen, without exception," the sage Ramesh Balsekar declares uncompromisingly. "There is no kind of intensity of supposed volition of any supposed individual that can in the least alter the inexorable causation of the Totality. No one can will anything but what the Totality causes him to will." Whatever happens, says Balsekar, is God's will. What we call individual will is simply the will of the totality playing itself out through the bodymind process. And, of course, "will" is merely an anthropomorphic metaphor for what is simply a causeless arising without anyone who wills, be it the individual or the totality.

True freedom within this automatic unfolding is freedom from doership. "I don't say do this or that," Nisargadatta Maharaj told his students. "Do what you like; just know that you are not the doer. It is just happening. The destiny that has come into existence on the first day of conception is unfolding itself. There is nothing that you can claim the doership of. Once you know who you are, that destiny does not bind you."

So destiny happens, but in freedom there is no one bound by it. Even "destiny" is just a concept arising in mind. The movie is playing itself out as it must, all of it the dance of the cosmic imagination. There is no individual doer, no "I" who acts, feels, thinks, desires and fears. The organism just lives out its programming or destiny, while the seer, the consciousness, allows the movie to be what it is.

No one has any control here. "Control" is just an idea, a function of the survival programming. Whatever you do is the Self. Whatever you feel or think, decide or choose, is the play of consciousness. Every time you think you are making a choice, that choice is just a thought arising in consciousness. If you get caught in doership, if you identify with the movie and believe there is a "you" that has control, you are caught in the suffering cycle of the strategic, manipulating sense of self.

Suffering ends when one realizes it is all entirely up to the supreme, and that, in any case, peace and happiness are not in how the movie turns out. They reside in That which is home free now, regardless of what is happening in the play. To make our happiness and wellbeing dependent on the changing circumstances and relationships of one's life is to live as a yo-yo, going up and down mechanically on the fickle finger of fate.

This vision of perfection goes beyond the traditional debate in western philosophy of "free will versus determinism," which resides within the either/or thinking of the dualistic framework. From the nondual point of view, it is both and neither. You choose and there is no choice. Choices are made and there is no chooser.

It is fascinating how the Advaita sages address the paradox of free will and destiny, each of them affirming the automatic flow, yet still acknowledging the illusory play of individuality. In discussing his awakening with Ramana, Papaji admitted with not a little irony: "If you read my life you will understand that it had to happen, that I was destined to meet him. I was scheduled to meet him. But at the same time I can say that I don't believe in destiny, because for most people destiny means a kind of resigned fatalism. People with weak minds blame destiny for everything that happens to them. My mind was never weak, I never accepted that my life had to follow a particular pattern. I knew what I wanted and went out to fight for it."

So he was destined, and yet he acted as if he weren't. Papaji points out that people will abuse fatalism to remain passive. Of course, Balsekar would say that if you are passive, it is your destiny to be passive, and that Papaji was programmmed to be feisty, that it was his destiny to take destiny into his own hands. "What you like to do at any particular moment according to your sense of right and wrong is exactly what the Source wants you to think at that moment," Balsekar clarified. "Otherwise 'you' have initiative, and my point is that there is no individual at all." For nondualists, the undivided Self is always the absolute reality and the individual perspective is the relative, a mere function of the absolute and not a real category in itself. The wave is only a movement of the ocean and all its activity—the entire destiny of the wave is moved by the source—ocean which is all there is.

Ramana stated clearly that there is no free will in reality, that the *concept* of free will is a function of the "I". It exists as a concept only as long as one mistakenly assumes oneself to be a separate individual. The true freedom of the individual is to see that there is no individual, only the absolute. "The only freedom man has," the Maharshi declared, "is to strive for and acquire the jnana [wisdom] which will enable him to not identify himself with the body. The body will go through the actions rendered inevitable by prarabdha [karma/destiny] and a man is free either to identify himself with the body and be attached to the fruits of its actions, or be detached from it and be a mere witness of its activities."

"Free will holds the field in association with individuality. As long as individuality lasts there is free will. All the scriptures are based on this fact and they advise directing the free will in the right channel. Find out to whom free will and destiny matters. Find out where they come from, and abide in their source. If you do this, both of them are transcended."

In the silent source neither concept applies. Here is absolute mystery. As Papaji put it: "Things just happen. There is no question of destiny or free will, things just happen, and you are one of those things." Only in the dualistic realm does the polarity of free will and destiny seem to exist. In the silent Self there is neither.

Still, in the busy realm of thought, there has been an ongoing debate among the spiritual traditions over the question of responsibility in life. The radical nondual response points out that there is no one to be responsible, that the whole is doing everything, and that if the concept of responsibility has any validity at all, it is the undivided totality that is always responsible . . . period. This response does not satisfy those who refer to it as the "Advaita shuffle," which they consider a clever ruse to avoid personal responsibility and discount the importance of being concerned about one's actions in the movie or facing the social problems of humanity.

Ramesh Balsekar has addressed the enigma of responsibility in his elegant description of living "as if." You act as if there is free will, knowing that there is no such thing. You live as if you are responsible, knowing that the totality is responsible for everything.

"You must act in life *as if* you are the doer," Ramesh suggests, "knowing that you are *not* the doer. The human being lives on fictions. For example, the human being knows that the sun is stationary and that it is the earth that is in movement, but nonetheless in his daily life he accepts the fiction that the sun rises and sets."

"So the understanding is that this is all an illusion and that you do not have any free will, but in life you must act as if you have free will. . . . You have to act. In fact, you cannot *not* act. The bodymind organism must react to an event."

"By acting as *if* you have free will you have assumed responsibility for the consequences, but deep down you know that whatever the consequences are, they are the destiny of that bodymind organism . . . . Living one's life in society you cannot ignore the sense of responsibility. Therefore what do you do? Act as responsibly as you are programmed to do."

"Over the course of time, this intellectual understanding that you are not the doer will go deeper and all actions that happen will be recognized as spontaneous actions, not 'your' actions."

This spontaneity expresses the ultimate meaning of responsibility— the *ability-to-respond* appropriately within the larger flow. When we are simply aware, when there is nobody to react, then we see action arising spontaneously out of the awareness of the moment. Here is the perfection of the selfless totality in harmonious response to itself, operating fluidly as an undivided whole system. It reveals the mystery of doing and not-doing simultaneously, what the Chinese Taoists called *wei wu wei*—active non-action. Action flows spontaneously from emptiness. The body is the vehicle through which action occurs, yet no one is doing anything. It is all just happening and the movie is what it is. Nothing we think we know about ourselves or life can capture the newness of the unfolding unknown.

To allow this to happen, to "surrender to the flow," means to be here in the moment and let life be what it is. Freedom is acceptance that this totality is doing it all, and that you are that totality. In this full acceptance you know that no matter what occurs, you are the peace that is not touched by what is happening. Life may be falling apart around me but I am not falling apart. I am That which is neither thrilled when it goes well nor sad when it doesn't. Life happens and I am the freedom in which it happens.

Acceptance sees through the doer and its survival. Even when you think there is a doer planning and controlling, *the totality is still doing it all*, but you experience the suffering generated by the illusory sense of a controlling "I". Without the "I" and its concerns, it is seen that it is all being taken care of. There is such relief, such joy and ease in allowing it to unfold. It is playing itself out perfectly through you.

One sees that living mystery has no special form or way. There is no right way to do it. There are no mistakes, no wrong turns. These are all just the projections of desires and interpretations on the suchness of what is. Life just shows up as it does. The circumstances of one's life are no indication of one's realization. Your life could fall apart or come together, your relationships might flower or whither. You could lose your job or your business could become unexpectedly successful. All of this just happens on its own.

God and the Devil in the Same Hand

People have a hard time accepting the perfection of life because it challenges conventional morality and our expectations about "spiritual" behavior. There is a widespread assumption that awakening or enlightenment should show up in traditionally defined moral or responsible behavior. Yet I see no such obvious relationship between realization and behavior. In my observation, being awake does not necessarily mean one acts according to socially accepted morality and does the "right thing." There are many examples of highly revered, apparently awakened individuals engaging in socially disapproved sexual behavior, alcoholism, financial improprieties, lying, and the whole litany of human foibles. An extreme example was debated in Buddhist circles recently about a Zen master who supported Japanese imperialism, racism and anti-Semitism during World War II, positions anathema to most freedom-loving, tolerant, non-violent people.

What are we to do with this? Measure each individual's realization according to specific moral and ethical dictates? Some spiritual traditions clearly do so. Others, as some Buddhists did in the above debate, make a distinction between the legitimate realization of buddha nature and behavior.

Ethics and morality are relative cultural and psychological definitions evolving through a complex web of historical traditions, social and family conditioning, and individual tendencies. Realization reveals That which is free of all conditioning and programming, free of all cultural and psychological identities. Though it is the source of it all, the Self has no beliefs, no values, no standards of behavior. Yet the persona in which self-realization takes place may still carry certain social and cultural conditioning, individual biases and eccentric, unconventional tendencies that continue to play out through the bodymind mechanism. One may be awake and still exhibit behaviors or attitudes considered "unenlightened."

Papaji was adamant that "Behavior is not a reliable indicator of egolessness or enlightenment." He explained: "'Should I do this, or should I do that?' are questions that arise in an unenlightened mind. When there is no mind, the question cannot even arise. The Self will make the body perform various actions and all those activities will be correct and perfect because they are promoted by the Self. Mind will not intervene to decide whether or not some course of action is correct or not, because mind will no longer be there. *Enlightenment ends all debates about behavior.* Problems of conduct and morality are problems of the decision-making mind. They do not arise in the Self at all. This is hard to understand because understanding cannot penetrate or encompass what I am talking about. This state cannot be described, cannot be imagined, and cannot be touched." [italics mine] No one can understand the behavior of the awakened one.

It is especially hard for people on the side of "good" to understand that the Self is beyond good and evil. At first it seems blasphemous. We cannot reconcile that with traditional, anthropomorphic concepts of a just and loving God. As we noted above in the discussion of the Garden of Eden, duality arises with the distinctions mind makes, in this case the knowledge of good and evil. As soon as that distinction is made, separation is projected upon undivided, innocent consciousness. Duality appears within the divine as the division into good and bad, right and wrong, God and the devil, righteousness and sin.

In dualistic thinking such polarities require each other. Opposites co-generate each other and can only exist co-dependent on one another. Yes has no meaning without no; hot requires cold; there is no good without evil. So those who identify with good *need* evil for their goodness to exist. Their attachment to goodness literally creates and sustains evil as its opposite/co-genitor. Dualistic thinking equates God with good, then creates evil or the devil as the source of the bad. Thus it divides the inherent perfection. It sees grace in the flower blooming but not in the flower wilting, in a body healing but not in a body dying, in hoped-for outcomes but not in senseless and random misfortune and failure. It sees God in a saint's realization but not in a criminal's action, and cannot fathom that all behavior arises perfectly from the same source, moved by the same play of consciousness. The absolute plays all functions—in Hindu terms—as creator, sustainer and destroyer of all life.

This vision of divine immanence threatens the very existence of good. It endangers the survival of those attached to goodness, and hence the dualistic religious mind devoted to good has fought "pantheism" as a direct threat to its unique "chosen" role. Yet, in the clarity prior to all judgment, no moral identity can be sustained.

In the awareness of your true nature, which is pure and stainless, it is clearly seen that there is no sinner. To a seeker who confessed to committing "sexual sin," Ramana Maharshi responded: "Even if you have, it doesn't matter so long as you do not think afterwards that you have done so. *The Self is not aware of any sin. . . .*" When a seeker asked for advice after admitting that he was tempted to commit adultery with an attractive neighbor woman, Ramana replied: "You are always pure. It is your senses and body which tempts you and which you confuse with your real Self. So first know who is tempted and who is there to tempt. *But even if you do commit adultery, do not think about it afterwards because you are yourself always pure. You are not the sinner.*" (Italics mine) What a radical stand, to abide beyond all judgment and doership as the purity untouched by the senses and behavior.

Sasaki Roshi used to tell his Zen students that we must hold God and the devil in the same hand. That hand is the unconditioned absolute, source of both good and evil, of values and judgment. It is the undivided awareness that sees the divine expressing itself as the dance of duality itself. The play of light and dark, yin and yang, right and wrong cycles on and on, not as if the "good" will win in the end, but rather, as if all polarities are complementary aspects of the whole whose pristine unity is never really cleaved by mind. This pre-existing wholeness is the ultimate solution to the imaginary division. Who is willing to die into that undivided consciousness which is neither good nor bad?

We may think that because everything is inherently perfect, one should then remain indifferent to suffering and passive in the face of perceived injustice, oppression, abuse, violence. There is a fatalism in which acceptance means not taking constructive action. Yet, since whatever you do is an expression of the underlying perfection, whether you are passive or proactive is the activity of the totality. So one is free to follow one's heart to address those issues if you are so moved, free to work for the betterment of the world or not, free to be socially engaged or to be a hermit.

Following one's heart puts one in touch with the deepest wellspring of authentic behavior. If you truly dive into your heart and follow it, you discover a love prior to all morality, ethics and values which is the source of appropriate action. In the undivided heart, where there is no egoic suffering or self-interest, the roots of separation, violence, conflict, oppression, greed do not exist. Here there is no distinction between individual action, love, and the flow of the totality.

A Seat in My Heart

Love abides in the heartfelt recognition of the undivided perfection of what is. It is an exquisite openness and receptivity to all life as your own Self. When you see that all beings are forms of you, how will you relate to your-

self? How will you treat yourself? Kindness, mercy, service all flow naturally from this realization. Love, which in the Judæo-Christian tradition is the
supreme commandment, is the only guide to behavior we need. It is the way
the absolute relates to itself. Ultimately, love is the fundamental energy
underlying all human experience and emotions. No matter what you are feeling, it is a form of your own love. Like the expanding universe of the physicists, the fathomless ocean of love knows no limit. It fills the emptiness,
ever-deepening into the boundless heart.

Love is death to the individual "I". In that precious moment when lovers
die into one another, there is a dissolving of individuality. In love one sees
the beauty and perfection of the other. The very otherness of the other falls
away. There is no separation in such intimacy. The word "intimacy" derives
from two Latin words meaning to know and reveal one's innermost essential
nature. This intimacy is love recognizing itself in the mirror of the beloved.
No wonder people worship romantic love, for there we are at the threshold
of self-transcendence. But usually we aren't aware that such human love is
just a taste of a vast reservoir within us, just a glimpse of our true nature. So
rather than cling to the other who you think is the source of love, if you turn
fully to the source itself, you would know that you are this love. To allow this
love free reign in your heart transforms your experience of yourself and others and the world.

As the heart looks out upon the world of suffering, love takes the specific form of compassion. "This compassion is not for the individual,"
Nisargadatta Maharaj explained, making a subtle distinction, "but [for] that
beingness which has trapped itself into identifying with a number of individuals." Compassion arises spontaneously as the One's own loving response to
the suffering inherent in its own projection. Maharaj continues: "At the same
time that the Unmanifest became manifest the reason for this compassion
arose spontaneously. . . . The entire manifest world is a very clear expression
and the spontaneous arising of this compassion. One does not realize the
instant expression of this compassion in the world. Before the baby is born
the milk is formed in the breast of the mother, and the compassion to feed the
baby arises at the same moment."

What perfect, enigmatic symmetry! Compassion and suffering arise
simultaneously at the birth of the manifestation—a kind of full feeling yin-
yang that cogenerate one another—as the way the Self experiences its own
projection. As consciousness identifies with its finite forms, compassion arises to touch, assuage and heal the suffering inherent in the play of duality.
Having seemingly divided itself in order to show up as form, the absolute
tenderly embraces itself as the suffering object of its own materialization. In
this compassionate embrace, the undivided mercifully reassures itself that, in

truth, it has never let go of itself, that it has never been separated, that it has always been One.

So compassion is Self-Love. It exists only for one's own Self, born of the recognition that there are no others, that there is only you. As Papaji makes clear, there is no compassion in ego, in the dualistic illusion of "someone" helping or serving "another": "Having known the supreme state, our own Self, from inside there arises compassion. Automatically we are compelled. It's not service. Service has to do with somebody else. When the command is compassion, there's no one doing any service to anybody else. When you are hungry, you eat. You are not in service to the stomach, nor are the hands the servant when they are putting food into the mouth. We should live in the world like this. Service is the responsibility of the Self. Otherwise, who is doing this service? When the action is coming from ego, there is hypocrisy, jealousy, crises. When the doer is not there, compassion arises."

Zen Master Taisen Deshimaru saw compassion arising in *mushotoku*, which is the "total abandonment of self, thoughts, goals, the whole mental structure that is the foundation for the development of the ego. True compassion is this abandonment; it begins with it and ends with it." In the non-dual realization there is no one helping, no one being helped, no one serving, no one being served. There is only compassion, the tender, loving expression of awakened being for itself.

The eye of compassion sees only the divine, even in the midst of suffering. I was struck by Mother Theresa's joyful admonition to her Missionaries of Charity who were dealing with the abysmal suffering and poverty in India: "Never let anything so fill you with sorrow as to make you forget the joy of Christ Risen. We all long for heaven where God is, but we have it in our power to be in heaven with him right now—to be happy with him at this very moment. But being happy with him now means: loving as he loves, helping as he helps, giving as he gives, serving as he serves, rescuing as he rescues, being with him twenty-four hours, *touching him in his most distressing disguise.*" (Italics mine)

Here is the loving, transcendental vision that sees through suffering to the truth of Christ Risen. The suffering itself is absolved by the beatific vision. No matter what it looks like out there, it is all God, albeit "in his most distressing disguise." Every leper Mother Theresa touched was Christ, her Lord. And so compassion sees the perfection in suffering itself, all of it the living expression of the divine. In the same way, from the Buddhist perspective, the current Dalai Lama has described how his compassion for the suffering of these apparent selves springs from his realization of the selflessness of reality. Emptiness itself, the ground of change and impermanence, gives compassion the possibility of relieving suffering.

Again, the mystery of the radical nondual awareness: Recognizing the insubstantial transparency of existence doesn't invalidate its suffering, nor does it prevent you from touching its pain or working for peace in the world if you are so moved. The paradox itself is so poignant, so awe-filled. It frees you to move through the dream, sensitive to its suffering and awake to its perfection, responding as the totality moves you.

The realization opens the heart and allows living beings a place within you. I was deeply touched when Papaji confided to his biographer David Godman, who asked him how he looks at the people in satsang. "First of all, I absorb them all and give them a seat in my Heart. As the lover gives a seat to the beloved in his Heart, you are always seated in my Heart."

The heart has no limits, excludes nothing. All imagined boundaries dissolve in this openness. Abiding as spacious loving awareness, everything takes place within me. Love allows all to be as it is, tenderly embracing everything as its own. The heart loves all beings because there is no other. There is only love touching itself, loving itself as all life.

Playground for the Wise

While Advaitins have often been accused of emphasizing the illusory nature of consciousness in a kind of static, world denying nihilism, the radical nondual vision also sees that, because everything is the Self, *everything is also absolutely real*. Ramana, echoing Gaudapada, captured the paradox succinctly: "The Self is real. The universe is unreal. The Self is the universe." Yes, the whole manifestation is all consciousness, all a projection of imagination in space. *And yes*, because everything is the absolute projecting itself, it is all real. The formless, invisible emptiness shows up as visible, tangible form—the movie of life. The absolute is both *transcendent*—beyond it all—and *immanent*, dwelling in and as everything. There is nothing that is not the Self, there is nothing that is not reality. So—exquisite mystery—the manifestation is real and unreal simultaneously. True wisdom favors neither formlessness nor form, neither transcendence nor immanence, neither reality nor unreality—indeed, makes no real distinction between them.

Ken Wilber's succinct injunction, "abide as emptiness, embrace all form," describes a way of being at the very heart of the awakened life. Here is the unconditional welcoming of all experience as the play of God. There is nothing to run from, no reason to deny anything or to reject any experience. One welcomes the entire manifestation as the divine lila, the blissful dance of consciousness. In the exhilarating realization that this is all the Self, *that everything is you*, it is obvious that all creation is your own bliss incarnate and exists for and as your own enjoyment. One delights in the sensate manifestation while seeing through its transparency. In fact, realizing the emptiness of it all allows one to enjoy the manifestation completely. The knowledge that it is all fundamentally non-existent mysteriously frees one to experience it without fear of attachment.

"Life is a playground for the wise and a graveyard for the foolish," Papaji said clearly to those with ears to hear. It is a graveyard for those who identify with the bodymind and remain sucked in to their egoic movie, for all that is transient and surely dies. Those who see through the apparent separation and struggle of individual doership can participate fully in the cosmic play and still remain free of it.

"If you know it, play in the lila," the master encouraged. "Inside abide alone and yet play in the lila outside. Manifestation is a play. Never forget the "I" is a transient actor, whose friends are bodymind-elements. Identify as That, keep aware, and play the game in lila as you wish, but do not leave the Source."

Play is a natural response of the Self that arises spontaneously when you are free of the ballast of egoic concerns and are no longer weighed down by the gravity of death. All the energy that went into survival is freed up as enthusiasm—from the Greek *theos*—literally, to be inspired by God. Playfulness springs up naturally when the heaviness and stress of doership disappear. In this sense "enlightenment" literally means to "lighten up," to lose one's gravity, and discover the underlying buoyant spaciousness of freedom. It is the ultimate weight-loss program that reveals the lightness of being. The heart bursts with joy, the chest fills with laughter. At the very center of my chest, there is laughter, a causeless eruption of happiness, of release, of getting the joke that the movie is your dream, that you and everyone are and always have been free. "A laugh a day keeps the world away," was Papaji's prescription for world peace.

Yes, it's all funny, and sacred, and ordinary, and utterly bizarre. Life is indeed a playground, a place of celebration, a domain in which to experience and share the original taste—*satchitananda*—the bliss of being awake.

The exquisite tantric vision of life as the dance of enjoyment fleshes out and crowns the nondual realization. Tantra is a way of seeing and experiencing everything as the expression of divine energy. Within the formless unmoving consciousness the Hindus call Shiva, shimmers the pulsing energy known as Shakti. The emptiness is filled with its own dynamic vibration, which gives birth to manifestation. All life is an expression of this inherent union of the divine consorts Shiva and Shakti—consciousness and energy—perpetually joined in ecstatic sexual embrace. The awakened one lives as consciousness filled with the pleasure of its own blissful energy. Grounded in emptiness, playing with energy, enjoyment is the palpable feeling-tone of freedom.

Tantra expresses one's true nature through a full-feeling participation in the manifestation. It is the seamless union of the spiritual and the sensual, a way of being fully open to life and the divinity of all experience. One sees the essentially pure nature of all phenomena: that all feelings, emotions and sensations are transformations of the basic underlying bliss-energy. One is merely an openness that allows this dynamism to flow unimpeded. In such surrendered presence, the energy is experienced as ecstasy dancing and playing within me, and I am dancing and playing with the energy. I am the openness in which the pulsation occurs and I am the pulsating energy that fills me. Freedom dances with itself.

In this total immersion there is no difference between life and devotion. Because all experience is sacred, because everything I smell, taste, touch, feel, hear and see are expressions of the divine, all my experience is heartfelt worship. "Worship of the universal consciousness," Balsekar described in a statement that gives a richer, devotional dimension to his usually cool, non-dual logic, "consists of accepting wholeheartedly whatever comes our way unsought and unsolicited—all physical pleasures and all ailments. It is accepting whatever activities take place through the psychophysical organism. The Self should be worshipped with all of the pleasures that come effortlessly and spontaneously, whether such pleasures are sanctioned or forbidden by the scriptures, whether considered desirable or undesirable, appropriate or inappropriate. . . . All is witnessed without desire, without rejection, without judging."

Such full-feeling experience is devotional surrender. In the depths of the heart I am on my knees in adoration of my beloved. This surrender is so sweet, so blissful, that one easily understands the great Advaitin Ramakrishna's response, when asked why he continued to worship the Mother in the apparent play of duality, knowing full well there is only One: that he would rather eat sugar than be sugar. The One plays the romance of lover-beloved for its own delight. It bows to itself as devotee-lord for the joy of surrendering endlessly into ever-deepening love.

Still, the nondual vision sees through the transparency of archetypal identities and holds the mythological play lightly. The play of Shiva-Shakti, lover-beloved, mother-devotee, all the deities, are but imagined characteristics of the formless supreme. The divine archetype is not ultimate identity. It is still more mindplay, perhaps a more blissful, transpersonal state than the psychological ego, yet it is still a separate identity. To hold archetype and deity as something separate in themselves is to fall into the alluring trap of the realm of the gods where the intense enjoyment of pleasure keeps one attached to subtle form and thus not fully resting as formless reality.

The dream can be so exquisite, promising the most delightful, heavenly pleasures. The allure of the realm of the gods is a great challenge. When the blissful energy gets high, experience is extreme in all directions and temptations become more enticing and attractive. Whatever individual tendencies or desires are still latent are activated and given the opportunity to be satisfied in the most delightful ways. The stronger the bliss the more one wants to hold on to its pleasures. If one follows the tremendous temptation to cling to such enjoyable experience—if you want bliss more than formless being itself—you are caught in the divine playground itself. Papaji used to joke that the realm of the gods is too delightful to allow for freedom, and so even the gods have to enter the human realm to realize the Self. The pleasures of the divine realm are only free for those willing to allow them to come and go without any clinging or identification, and to be at home as the source of all delight.

Living Mystery

When all is said and done, there's no making any sense of it. One can taste it, one can live it, one can be it. Yet try to understand it and we come again to the mystery that can never be known. Nisargadatta Maharaj summed it up so simply: "Love tells me I am everything, wisdom tells me I am nothing, and between the two my life flows." Love and wisdom, everything and nothing, knowing and unknowing. It is all this.

Life flows, an invisible underground stream giving birth to everything. So subtle and imperceptible, it shows up pulsing vibrantly as all creation. Empty and full, intangible and sensate, formless and form—the inseparable faces of the same mystery. It is all this.

Consciousness is simultaneously projecting and receiving the movie of its own imagination, yet awareness remains untouched in stillness. Life arises within the unchanging presence. There is a sense of depth and dimensionality to the appearance, an intimation of the diaphanous infinitude of everything. Creator and creation, the movie and the seer of the movie—dreamer, dreaming, dreamed, and beyond. It is all this.

Abiding as pure presence, living full-feeling enjoyment here and now, the play of phenomena and bodymind experience are welcomed as expressions of Self. Feelings and thoughts come and go, yet they happen to no one. In the absence of an experiencer, no experience sticks or is claimed. Nothing captures the awareness that allows it all.

There is only Self. Within the ocean of wakefulness the individual wave lives out its tendencies. Moved by the whole, nobody is doing anything and it all gets done. Living simply, naturally, one participates in and as the flow of life with an ease that blesses it all. I am That. That is You.

This tender openness compassionately embraces the apparent suffering of its own imagined forms. Untouched by all, love touches all. Lover and beloved—this love is all there is.

The floodtide of words subsides, revealing the pristine ground of silent being, a stillness that infuses all. Only this, always this. What relief. What grace. A huge laugh fills the space of being. If we truly get the joke of this freedom, can we finally rest with Ryokan, the old Zen hermit poet?

> *Why chatter about delusion and enlightenment?*
> *Listening to the night rain on my roof,*
> *I sit comfortably, with both legs stretched out.*

∞ ∞ ∞ ∞ ∞ ∞ ∞ ∞ ∞

PART TWO
CONVERSATIONS WITH ONESELF

These transcripts of my satsang talks, dialogues, and correspondence with lovers of freedom provide a close-up of the process of inquiry by which we can know our true nature. "Satsang," from the Sanskrit, means in the presence of truth or the company of being. It refers to a traditional form of gathering together in silence and intimate dialogue in which the identification with the separate seeker can fall away and reveal that teacher and student, speaker and listener, are the faces of Oneself. Every question is a mirror reflecting the simple presence that you already are. Each response is an opportunity to turn one's awareness back to what is already here, whole and complete and unbounded. Here we face the truth that you are already what you seek, that no effort or development is required, only the seeing through the appearance of separation. In so doing we recognize our conversation as the self-talk of freedom itself.

Being Already Is

Q: It seems as though, instead of actively searching and then thinking that you have found something, it's more in the negative sense of letting go of the doubt, of releasing the belief that you haven't got something. Once those fall away, then what has been there all along can happen.

D: Right. It's already here. If you no longer invest in that belief and doubt, then you realize you are That. If you no longer follow the I-thought, pay credence to it and bow down before it: "Have no other idols before me," remember? That means have no images, no thought. Then you are right here.

So you witness this mysterious capacity of consciousness which is fascinated with its own forms, that is, it's fascinated with thought, and follows thought. And if you are willing to not follow thought, then there's the revelation of what you are. So there's really nothing to do here.

This is what stymies the mind, because the mind is always wanting something to do. It won't rest with that. I'll say there's nothing to do and you'll say "but . . . there's gotta be something to do, right?" I'll say no, being is already. And then there's doing, doing, doing, doing, doing, but there's no doing that gets you to being. (Laughs.) Now to me that's exhilarating, that's joyful, that's wonderful, because who wants something more to do? Do you want one more thing to do on your To Do list? You probably had enough to do just to get here today, right? So this is a freebie, but it's a freebie for the lion. The lion doesn't follow the beaten path, the lion roams the savannah freely in small groups, not in a herd.

Q: And the women do all the work. (Laughter) It's true!

D: In the Self there's no man and there's no woman. So if you don't want to do any work, realize that what you are is prior to gender. You show up in a woman's body, so what. It's just what's happening. What you are is the source of man and woman. (More laughter)

Q: So you only need to be in order to be.

D: Right, you only recognize that you are. It's like this huge, magnificent relaxation, just (breathes in and a long sigh out) because you notice the striving. At the very core of this "I," there is striving. It's anxiety built in to the package. It's always scrambling like a little rat trying to get somewhere. And that's programmed in there, as soon as there's some identification with the I-thought, you are cast onto this endless treadmill of seeking, yearning, wanting, needing, desiring and then the other side of the coin—fearing, avoiding, resisting, running away, and that's part of this egoic structure. It's there. You'll never satisfy it by getting your desires met. I'm not saying that you shouldn't pursue them, just understand that that's not the way home. All that activity has nothing to do with realizing yourself. It has nothing to do with happiness. Or peace. It's just this game that goes on endlessly. As Buddha said, it spins the wheel of suffering.

So this is relief from that. This recognition is freedom, freedom from that "I", from that egoic pattern of striving, anxiety and suffering. And it's the release into peace and joy and wellbeing. So I think that's not a bad end to the movie, huh? If . . . If you're willing to stop thinking you are the star of your drama. Everybody's got their movie . . . it's endless.

Q: Therein lies the dilemma. How do you let go?

D: Who is this "I" that seeks to let go?

Q: The little self.

D: Yes, but what is it?

Q: The unnecessary head (inaudible).

D: Who told you that?

Q: Nobody.

D: You just made it up?

Q: Yes.

D: Well, do you want to continue with that belief?

Q: Nope, I want to stop it.

D: So don't hold on to that thought. See, when that thought is not present, what is here. What is here when that thought is not present?

(Long pause).

Q: Beingness.

D: Good, so beingness is just here, and how is that?

Q: Good.

D: Wonderful, so just be here.

Q: How did we get trapped into all that is not true?

D: Well, you can look at it from the point of view that you're never trapped. Just in this moment, see where that question was coming from.

Q: It was anxiety.

D: Where was that coming from?

Q: From that other self that doesn't belong here?

D: What other self? (Laughs) Whatever money I have here, it's not much, but I offer it to anybody who can show me this "other self," demonstrate this self to me, this "I," this ego, show it to me.

(Long pause).

Q: Well, there are a lot of aspects of the self . . . .

D: When you say the self, what are you referring to?

Q: It's illusion, I think? . . . it doesn't exist?

D: Yes, all these people are describing something that doesn't exist.

Q: Yes, what we think of in others, their personality, is wrong thinking because we don't usually look beyond that and see the real Self.

D: Right, and that's what I'm saying to you. When you say the word "I" or personality, where's that coming from? Where's personality coming from?

(Pause)

Q: I think it's a concept that we have.

D: Right, and where's the concept coming from?

Q: Comes from a lot of places, like our society, and some of our teachings . . .

D: But right now, when you have a concept, where does that come from?

Q: Comes from all these outside places, but it doesn't come from my heart . . . doesn't come from my true Self.

D: Where are these outside places coming from? (Laughter). See, "outside" and "inside" are concepts you have, right. So where do all these concepts come from?

Q: Well, if our true being is purity, then it can't come from that.

D: Who told you that?

Q: Nobody, but I'm trying to figure it out.

D: OK, but I'm not talking about figuring it out. I want you to look directly into consciousness. When you have a thought or a concept, where does it show up from?

Q: The mind?

D: The mind is concept. Where does the mind come from?

Q: I give up.

D: So when you give up, what is here?

Q: The true Self.

D: OK, fine, so what's always here?

Q: My true Self.

D: So where does everything come from?

Q: My true Self???

D: (Laughs). Listen, that's all there is. But right now we're just having an intellectual conversation. I want you to see experientially where everything arises from, where that thought arises from.

Q: From the spring.

D: Yes, from the spring, from the source, from emptiness itself. Everything arises from the same source. Everything. It's like the ocean. Remember this analogy? Let's call the ocean you. And when this ocean moves, what happens? You get a wave, right? That movement of the ocean we call a wave is the arising of form. When this ocean is not moving, it still is, but there's no form, nothing. And then the ocean moves, you get everything, the world of form. When consciousness moves, its waves of thought-activity give birth to everything. So all concept and form arise from this, even the "I," even the ego, everything arises from source and returns to source.

Everything is source. There is nothing that is not That. That's what the nondual is. It is undivided reality, whatever you want to call it. It is you, the reality of everything. And although it takes form as everything, it never ceases to be its own nature. So when you have this idea of being a separate self, that's just an idea from source. Separation is just a concept, it has no reality. When you live as source, it doesn't bother you if some concept arises. And when you attach to the thought, there's the forgetting that you are ocean and you think you're just the wave. That's what human beings do, they think they are just the wave and are attached to this identity of being this individual wave separate from the rest. But the human is just a wave on the ocean of being. That's why "human" is your first name and "being" is your last name. Waking up is the discovery that you are and always have been the ocean. And when this particular bodymind package falls away nothing happens to you in the same way that when the wave dissolves into the ocean, nothing at all has happened to that water. Despite all appearances to the contrary, nothing at all has ever happened to you, no matter what you think.

Q: Even though its an erroneous concept?

D: All concepts are erroneous. By that I mean no thought can grasp or comprehend the formless reality which is prior to word and concept. Still, we talk about it because it's our nature to speak. In the Zen tradition they say that all of the teaching is like a finger pointing to the moon. I used to have a dog named Bonzo, and if I wanted him to fetch I'd say "go get that ball" (pointing with finger), but he'd just stare at the finger and he wouldn't go for the ball. So we're talking about the ball, we're talking about the moon, and we're talking about *this that you are here and now*, so let's not get too hung up on the language. It's a useful vehicle to point you to your own Self, which is only known in the silence beyond all concept.

The ancient Hebrew sages said you could never ever say the name of G-d because there is no name to grasp the beingness. The most that G-d ever said was "I am that I am." And then that was translated as "Lord," which we could call an anthropomorphic projection. This was really the unspeakable reality of being, and that's you. So everything arises from and is being. And everything disappears into being.

Q: And actually all of us sitting here are just waves.

D: You are the waves of the divine. You are the divine. You are God. It's all you.

Q: It's God talking to God. It's happening right now. I love it.

D: That's right. This is all that's going on. And if you bring in the veil of separation, by thinking that I'm just this individual person, talking to this individual person, then it's still God talking to God, but you don't know it. And when that veil of separation is not here, it's still God talking to God, except that God is here, awake to God, and there's peace and happiness and freedom.

∞ ∞ ∞ ∞ ∞ ∞ ∞ ∞ ∞

Q: Can we help this universal power that you speak of, or whatever it is, I'm still learning . . . but can we jump start ourselves a little bit . . . and become conscious of those attitudes, or those feelings, then maybe our ability to be this person who you describe, which is so wonderful, might come a little quicker or a little better?

D: When you say "we," what are you referring to?

Q: I guess myself.

D: When you say "myself," what are you referring to?

Q: It's my presence in this fantastically wonderful universe.

D: Now explore this presence for a moment. I'm not asking you to do anything conceptual, I'm asking you to take your awareness which you're looking at me with, and look at this presence.

Q: It's life. It's experience. It's right here and now.

D: Yes, and what is the experience of being this presence here and now?

Q: Life.

D: Yes, and is this okay?

Q: Yes.

D: Okay, so do you need anything more than this?

Q: Nope.

D: Good. So you're home. You don't have to jump start anything, that's just another concept. You see, if you live in the concept "I'm not it, and I have to get somewhere", then that just generates the whole path. All of a sudden "I've" got a "path," then I have to jump start it. Now I've got to do all these practices, I've got to meditate, I've got to read all these books, you know. That's exhausting, and I promise you that the path doesn't go anywhere. Here you get to abide as the eternal now.

Q: Great concept!

D: (Laughs). What would it be if you just factored the concept out? Then what?

Q: Then you're there. Where you were to begin with. Then you know it.

D: Then you know it. Right, so be it. Okay? And then if you want to read a book, read it, if you want to meditate, meditate. Just see it's not getting anyone anywhere.

Q: Yes. Well, the world will never be the same!

∞ ∞ ∞ ∞ ∞ ∞ ∞ ∞ ∞ ∞ ∞ ∞

D: I was in the health club before I came over here, sitting in a sauna with a friend of mine who does a lot of meditation, and I asked him how he was doing. He said, "It comes and it goes." That it does. We get so attached to the comings and goings of our transient experience, the ups and downs, the ins and outs. There's this ghostly idea, this "I" that gets caught up in its drama of "How am I doing" or "Am I getting there yet?" or "I'm never gonna make it," or some quality attributed to this "I" that is trying to have an existence. That's so exhausting. Don't you think its exhausting? (Laughter)   How stressful does it have to get?

To rest as the presence or the awareness—this that is here, while everything comes and goes—to abide as this that you know very well, that's all. When attention is on the transient, it forgets itself, even though that's not really the case. There's this tremendous tenacity of clinging to this illusory existence, it's really quite a ridiculous thing when you look at it. There's this holding to the "I" and its drama, no matter what its drama is. It doesn't matter whether it's ecstatically joyful or in love or whether it's in the pits of pain and suffering. It doesn't matter what the content is, there's this attachment to that. That's what generates and sustains this illusory sense of separate existence.

When you think about what's called spiritual life, there's the "positive" camp and the "negative" camp. The positive says its flowers and bliss, and God and miracles and crystals, something beautiful, and we're all going to heaven and all these good things are going to happen to you when you get this experience called enlightenment or cosmic consciousness. And then there's this other camp which is the *via negativa*, in which it's not this and its not that, and it's the absence of anything that you can conceptualize. It is the space in which everything can exist but this in itself is nothing, and even if you call it "nothing" you've already said one word too much. And that's the scary part. On that side of the coin the invitation is to give up this "I," to go to death.

That's the essential meaning of the crucifixion—the death of the "I." And even to say "the death of the 'I'" is a little dramatic, because it's not really a death, but the seeing that the "I" doesn't exist. And the seeing that the "I" doesn't exist, that seeing is eternal. It's forever, its now, and that's you. And so it's not as if anything dies. You just realize that you are.

To abide as this awareness which simply witnesses the coming and going of experience and thought is to see through it, is to rest as nothing. Freedom is to abide nowhere, as no one, to not be anything in particular at all. This absence is the same as presence. Just being here and now.

Living in the now means you have no future and you have no past. Everybody knows this: Be Here Now, it's a big book. Then we turn this "be here now" into some doing. That's what the mind does—it needs to do something, otherwise it doesn't exist. So the being, the presence, is truly here now and its not doing anything. It's the absence of the doer. And in the absence of the doer, there's the absence of any sense of trajectory going forward or looking backward.

The sense of time is the way the "I" sustains itself. It's like it has got two mirrors—one mirror is called anticipation which generates an illusion called the future. The other one is memory which generates a picture in the mirror called the past. The "I" locates itself moving from some past toward some future. It's very comfortable in this linear trajectory, which is also the domain of its suffering. To truly rest now is to be no one, just the joy of presence.

∞ ∞ ∞ ∞ ∞ ∞ ∞ ∞ ∞

Silent Awareness

Q: How does one pay attention to oneself? You say be silent, but I have and still don't hear it.

D: In the silence there is no one listening and nothing to hear.

Q: Does direct awakening mean that no one can give it to me, it is already mine?

D: Of course, no one can give you your own Self. It is what you are now. Awakening just means being aware of what you already are.

∞ ∞ ∞ ∞ ∞ ∞ ∞ ∞ ∞

Q: Passing thoughts have stopped.

D: Yeah, and how is this?

Q: It's nice.

D: Yes, it's nice. (Laughter)

Q: For a change. (More laughter)

D: Okay, good, so now can you abide here where there's no thought?

Q: For a little while.

D: No, you can't do it for a little while.

Q: For a long while?

D: No, you can't do it for a little while and you can't do it for a long while. You know why?   Because there's no time in this place of silence. Time is more thought. If you let the time concept go, if you let go of "I'm gonna do this for a little while," then what's here?

Q: (Inaudible)

D: OK now let go of that concept (Laughter).

Q: I feel I see what you're driving at and it makes basically wonderful sense but if you allow your mind to stay clear of thought, which I think is what you're saying, doesn't it impinge on your other senses, your other potentials, if you give no play to anything but openness of mind and almost neutrality on everything, including yourself? Is there some way that that causes or enables us to be even better than we had hoped to be?

D: (Laughter) In the willingness to be silent, the potential that's already inherent within you is unlocked and everything that you need to be and do will show up. Actually, it's already showing up but there's a little monkey wrench in the works, which is this "I" struggling to accomplish something. The "I" is like a fifth wheel on a car—it's unnecessary, and in the human being it causes suffering. There's a big fear that if I'm quiet and simply relax this contraction, that something will happen, some terrible thing, like I won't raise my children, or I'll just become a vegetable, or I'll lose interest in whatever it is. All I can tell you is that, on the contrary, it frees you to be fully who you are and for that to show up here. Okay? Now here's a paradox for you— and remember what I said before about how language cannot really grasp what we're speaking about here—if you're quiet, thought will take place without you, and then you will see thought for what it is, which is an instrument, or a servant of the creative process, rather than some stressor, which it is for most people.

∞ ∞ ∞ ∞ ∞ ∞ ∞ ∞ ∞

D: What's really marvelous about silence is that at first silence seems to be an alternative to thought, it seems to be the opposite of thought. There's this thought, then there's this silent space, and then there's another thought, and then another silent space, and so on. But when you rest in the silence and as the silence, then thought arises in the silence as a natural activity without disrupting it. So there's this background of silence that's always present, and all thought is taking place in silence.

Q: So the void is not an emptiness. . . .

D: Well, the void is empty and it's also full of everything.

∞ ∞ ∞ ∞ ∞ ∞ ∞ ∞ ∞

Q: You stated that in the silence there are thoughts.

D: In silence everything can exist, yes.

Q: So the waves exist in the silence.

D: Yes, the waves arise in silence. What's interesting is that silence is not obstructed or disturbed by the waves that arise within it, in the same way that the ocean couldn't care less if it's frothy or turbulent on the surface, because the ocean in its depth is not affected by any of that. This is what Papaji revealed to me in the very first meeting, that silence is here as a context within which all of this activity—action, behavior, and thought—can exist and the silence doesn't go away. The silence of the Self is here.

It's like the space between us. Everything in this room exists in space and usually we'll look at the objects rather than being aware of the space between them. The space is always here, but we don't even notice space . . . unless you're an architect or somebody like that who is aware of space or dimensionality. But most people don't because the eye goes to the objects. The eye is attached to objects and so it is then unaware of the existence of space in the same way that when consciousness focuses on thought it is unaware of the silence between the thoughts. Space is silence. There's no difference between space and silence. And sounds exist in the silence. You can hear sounds, like the cars going by, but the silence is still here. If your ear is attuned to the silence then the sounds arise in the silence without disruption. And everything is taking place in the silence. The entire universe and all the planets are hanging in this infinite silence. That's the reality of the universe. At this very moment there is this infinite silence, and my voice is a modification, a wave, in the silence. And the silence is source. This is the void, the emptiness, the mother of everything.

Q: Are there any practices that you recommend to go along with this, or is it just as often as possible reminding yourself that you're in the silence?

D: Yes, just be aware of the quiet.

Q So you can be quiet while you're washing the dishes, or you're driving your car.

D: Yes, just be with what is. You can call it whatever you want to. It's very simple. It's who you are. Papaji never recommended practice to anybody because the trap is that then you think there's somebody here having to do some practice. And as soon as you think, "I have to practice" you're already caught in this "I" thing. If there's no practitioner, then practice is just happening. So if it's enjoyable to chant or do ritual, do it. Just remember nobody's doing it. It's the Self doing it all.

∞ ∞ ∞ ∞ ∞ ∞ ∞ ∞ ∞

Q: I have a question for you about meditation which I have been doing regularly. The words for the question will necessarily be a little awkward. During meditation, when I catch myself thinking, I return to my breathing— the tip of my nose, actually. But, when I am thinking, but not aware that I am thinking, where am I?

D: "Where am I?" is a good question, or "Who am I?" too, which, if you follow it, will lead you home to yourself. When you are thinking, you—the Self—are here but you don't know it. When you are silent, not caught in thought, you are here knowingly, awake to your presence. When the Self-as-consciousness focuses on its own thinking, it gets sucked into the thought and lives out that drama as an individual "I." Thought veils awareness of Self, so when you are thinking and not aware that you are thinking, you are totally sucked into the mind-movie. You forget your self-nature and live out the experience generated by thought. The Self—what you truly are—is the source/context of it all, and it is always here, even when you don't know it. When you wake up, it is to the reality that you have been here all the time, that the whole "I"-drama is only the play of your own consciousness, which creates the misperception that you are not home as the Self. You are always here no matter what the experience.

∞ ∞ ∞ ∞ ∞ ∞ ∞ ∞ ∞ ∞

Q: Sometimes in meditation I get bored.

D: Boredom may help to release our grip on the personal story and be less fascinated and compelled by the movie of our imagination. St. John of the Cross referred to this disinterest as the "aridness" of the dark night of the soul, when our experience becomes tasteless, lifeless, has no more allure. We have no interest in anything, and nothing is satisfying. This aridness is valuable precisely because when you see that thought-experience offers you no juice, then you may be more willing to taste the true refreshment of the Self. While we may mistake this listlessness for true silence, at some point one must see that even boredom is a thought-form in resistance to the underlying reality. To truly realize the silence means not clinging to boredom or running from it, not trying to fill it up with experience, but to welcome it fully into awareness. Someone once said that boredom is just a lack of attention. If you pay attention to it, it does not exist.

∞ ∞ ∞ ∞ ∞ ∞ ∞ ∞ ∞ ∞

Q: How to remove the veil so as to see the higher Self always? One clue is that when I am suffering, I am not seeing my higher Self. The veil blocks all sorts of important stuff. Seeing everything as one is a ways off for me.

D: From the perspective of nondual awareness, the essential question to ask at this point is: Who is this "I" that sees or doesn't see the "higher Self?" Who is this "I" that assumes it is not in touch with itself? Who is this "me" that is suffering and feels blocked?

I am not suggesting that you seek conceptual or philosophical answers. Rather I'm suggesting direct self-reflection, a turning of awareness back to this consciousness that keeps saying "I" and an investigation of what this "I" really is and where it comes from. It is a turning to the direct and immediate experience of you, deeper than—prior to—all concepts and assumptions. What are you in the silence free of thought and belief? The basic dualistic dilemma is the concept of some separate "I" that is lost and in suffering. We are thus always looking outside, away from what we already are, as if who we are is not good enough and that there must be something "other" out there which will heal us or save us or that we must attain. Investigate the assumptions of dilemma and separation that you assume to be true, and which then shape your experience consistent with these beliefs. Who are you without the assumptions of dilemma and separation?

In my experience the "higher Self" we seek is already what we are, deeper than the concepts that divide the unity into self and other, subject and object. If we turn to that treasure within we realize "everything as one" here and now.

∞ ∞ ∞ ∞ ∞ ∞ ∞ ∞ ∞ ∞

No Way to What You Are

Q: You were saying there is no practice. I understand that's coming from the side of the realization, but certainly Papaji or Ramana would acknowledge that there's a practice, except that it's quite an achievement to achieve that thought-free state.

D: Papaji wouldn't even encourage the concept of "achievement" or some "state" because its not an achievement in the sense that something is accomplished or created. Its rather what already is. It's being itself.

Q: Most egos are going to have to cultivate being.

D: What would it be like if you were to give up the concept that you had to cultivate anything? Where would that leave you if you really gave that concept up, that "I have to cultivate being"?

Q: Well, I'm not talking about cultivating being itself. We know that being is. But rather, I'm just suggesting that most persons' egos are not necessarily ready to give that up. So there is a process, whether they want to say it or not. That they're announcing that possibility doesn't mean that most people can just jump into that.

D: Of course people can't jump into that. The jumping means seeing through the idea of "people," and seeing through the idea of "jumping." Then what is here? You are here. Egos aren't ready to give that up because ego *is* resistance. All process is resistance to being itself. It is postponement of one's being here and now. It may be true, as you say, that most people don't get this, in the sense that you're saying they're not ready or whatever. That may be so, but for whomever it occurs—and let's just talk about you and me, or us, here—for whomever it occurs, there's the realization that there was no process and no ego. That at best you can say there's a falling away of some illusion, some ignorance, some belief. That is all ego is. It is nothing in itself, and therefore, there is no process for ridding you of what doesn't really exist.

Q: No process in the sense of building up what you've experienced. Falling away is a better description in that sense. What was there was there.

D: Whatever you want to call it, something occurs, there's no question about that! If you want to call that a process, that's fine. My emphasis is on "Who is this seeker?" This was Papaji's grace to me because you know I'd been involved in spiritual practice for many years, a lot of Zen training and Vipassana sitting and all of that, and he said you don't have to do any of that. Just inquire, who is seeking? Once you see that there is no seeker, then you see that there is no one practicing. It is not a question of practice or any attainment. It is a question of no-practitioner. Then practice is just happening within the realization as an expression of freedom.

Forget about the concept of practice for a moment. Just look at this "I," not as an intellectual quest of coming up with some concept but of looking at when the I-thought arises, to actually look at it and see what it is. When I was first with Papaji, I was staying in this really run-down hotel in India and I couldn't sleep so I just kept sitting there saying "Okay, so when I say the word 'I,' what is this "I"? And it became very vividly clear to me that it's just imagination, it's just a thought. And there's this awareness that sees this "I" and this awareness is before the "I" so to speak, and the source of it. And this awareness is just formless silent presence. And as soon as that was seen, there was the immediate recognition of being this silent awareness, and of having always been this presence, except that awareness had gotten focused down on this "I," which is what life is, it's just this focus on the "I". So it was this turning of awareness to itself that reveals this eternal being that's here now, that's free.

∞ ∞ ∞ ∞ ∞ ∞ ∞ ∞ ∞ ∞ ∞

Q: This morning I realized that there is nothing that is not spiritual. Everything is of the spirit. The thing we do is we forget, and that creates the separation. But if we can only remember, then there is nothing else. Now if I can just remember to remember.

D: Actually, there's nothing to remember, because as soon as you hold all that as a concept, as a memory, its gone. What is before the concept? This is very radical. Any concept, any memory is not it. Whether it involves "spiritual," or "God" or anything at all. What is before any concept?

Q Nothing.

D: Yes, but you're giving me a conceptual answer. Abide in the nothing, abide in the no-thought that's prior to any position.

Q: (Pause) There is no word for that.

D: Right. There is no word for that. That's the mystery . . . the mystery that can never be spoken. And so if we attach in any way to the language, then we think there's something to remember. If you rest in silence, what is there to remember? And if there's truly nothing, then abide as that nothing, otherwise the mind will immediately grasp any realization that arises, and say "I have to remember that, I have to get back to that."

Q: It's very hard on the conscious mind.

D: Well, the conscious mind can't work this out. To people who think they have really good minds, this is a big challenge. I was the same way. If you think you are smart, the big challenge is to rest as the source of that mind, not the mind. And the source of that mind is beyond mind. It is mystery itself. This is the willingness to surrender the entire intellectualizing process, to give up, which means you don't follow that thought. You don't follow any concept and abide as silence. In the silence, when there is no thought whatsoever, the silence brims with knowingness, which can never be expressed.

∞ ∞ ∞ ∞ ∞ ∞ ∞ ∞ ∞

Q: You say you have to want freedom above all things. You have to want it bad enough. I always interpreted that to mean pain. When I want freedom, it's painful. I think that impression keeps me from really wanting it.

D: Papaji said freedom needs to be your number one desire because if there is any other desire higher on the list, that is where your energy is going to go. That is how the organism is wired, to pursue its desires. If there is something you want that is more important than freedom, you will pursue that. You just have to decide what your primary desire is and put all your eggs in that basket. Your other desires will become resolved or dissolved by the central yearning for freedom.

Q: There is fear to do that.

D: Yes, fear comes up, the fear of dissolving. But the only thing that dissolves is the sense of limitation. What you are is here. This becomes evident if you are willing to allow this fear to be fully present and experience it unconditionally. Fear is a precious gift—all the emotions are. They are opportunities to bring you to this full embrace. In this case, it would be a full embrace of fear. You simply allow this fear full reign, be present with it and experience it completely. That is all that is needed. It is not fear per se, it is the unwillingness to feel fear that creates the sense of limitation. Your mind has a lot of stories about it. All these stories are false. But the mind continuously gives a story to these sensations that are nothing more than energy-forms. To embrace it completely will reveal yourself to yourself.

Q: Fear is the veil that keeps me from myself.

D: Yes, the mind generates fear as a way to stay in existence. Fear juices up the ego, the sense of separate individuality. But if you actually felt fear completely it would reveal the sham, the illusion of individuality. It would show that fear as an energy comes and goes—like all states—and you are still here. Nothing happens to you. So basically just give fear permission to be and feel it. Ultimately, fear is just a form of your own Self come to reflect itself.

You see that desire and fear are inseparable polarities. They mutually co-generate each other. If you desire something, you fear its opposite. As soon as you gain something, you fear its loss. Whenever I got a new car I didn't want to park it near other cars so it wouldn't get scratched. Immediately the attachment comes up. If you want freedom strongly, then you start to generate that fear and you don't want to go there. If you can really see that, truthfully see that, you don't have to go into either desire or fear.

Q: Oh, that is reassuring (laughs).

D: But are you willing to not go into either? Without holding any position whatsoever. If you are holding no position at all, you are home. That which holds no position is that seeing we were speaking of, the awareness, the silence.

Q: Sounds easier then wanting it.

D: Then be That which neither wants anything nor fears anything, That which allows the entire play to be what it is, untouched by it all.

Q: I imagine I can stay there.

D: Don't even imagine it. As soon as you imagine it, you put this little box around it. You know what I mean? Be the source of all the imagining. It is all taking place within you.

∞ ∞ ∞ ∞ ∞ ∞ ∞ ∞ ∞ ∞ ∞

Q: I can see that my sense of "I" is a just a play in consciousness, and it feels sad. I've invested so much of life in identifying with bullshit. When I stop and just be, I see how it's all meaningless, and I feel sad. What else is left?

D: Sad is okay. You are not honoring the sadness, you are running away from it, still seeking something "else." The sadness comes up as a wonderful invitation to just give up, but you don't want to feel the sadness so you run away from it and ask this question. All you need to do is completely embrace the sadness.

When the awakening is occurring all kinds of old tendencies and feelings are freed up in consciousness. Sadness, anger, confusion, loneliness, whatever, comes up in this opening in awareness. When this stuff comes up we usually tend to judge it and not want to feel it. Yet emotions just want to be felt. If you would allow yourself to feel sad, and not run from it, you would see it for what it is, which is not what you think it is. It is also the play of consciousness. Otherwise, you think "this is not working because I'm feeling sad or confused. I should be blissful," etc. But it is working perfectly.

Watch your tendency to give the feeling a story or meaning. That doesn't quite respect it either. To truly honor this experience is to give it no meaning. You are right on target when you speak of the meaninglessness, but you have to see how liberating that freedom from all interpretation really is.

If you were really willing to feel—just experience what you get without interpreting it, without trying to push it away or hold on to it—you would experience the inherent pleasure of existence. Life gives you exquisite pleasures but if you are too busy trying to control your experience, you cannot receive what is coming to you in the moment. If you think you should be experiencing bliss or pleasure, then you'll feel afraid of the sadness. You'll judge it as wrong, as an obstacle, rather than as an opportunity to experience the bliss. That is the paradox here. If you are willing to feel it, it will take you to the source of all feeling. When emotion is felt fully without interpretation, when the concept of sadness disappears, you get it as the pure energy or bliss of your own Self. That is really the true nature of suffering—beneath and within all the forms of experience is the underlying substrate, the original taste.

Suffering is a function of our attachments and interpretations of life. It ceases to be suffering when you are present in full feeling surrender, when you are with it in its open-endedness without limiting it through your story-definitions, either pushing or pulling it. The intensity of existence, the power underlying all experience, is so off the chart that the only way you can tolerate it is when you don't give it any definition. As soon as you define it, you start contracting and it becomes unbearable. It is experienced as suffering to the egoic mind. In freedom, it is power and joy.

Q: Is it the ego that causes the suffering?

D: Let's forget for a moment that there is something called ego, and just look at the capacity within consciousness called attachment or identification. When that occurs, there is a projection in consciousness we call ego. It has no independent existence. It is just a function of trying to hold on to, or resist, experience. When desire arises and there is attachment, that attachment projects an object that you want and a subject that wants it. Subject and object arise co-dependently, reflections of each other. A needy subject and a desired object are projected as two ends of the continuum of attachment. This duality disappears when you are just with the experience—sadness, or whatever—without trying to hold on or push it away. Then there is no subject or object, just the experiencing happening. No one can enter this place. Here you get it that nothing at all is happening to anyone.

Freedom is an openness to all experience. You see that nothing can harm you because all experience is your own energy. All of that fear contracts you. This openness literally dissolves you so that you experience yourself as the power. That is the lion's roar, the recognition that I am this potentiality showing up as experience.

$$\infty \ \infty \ \infty \ \infty \ \infty \ \infty \ \infty \ \infty \ \infty \ \infty$$

Q: I feel like other people are getting it and I'm not. Like there is something wrong with me. It seems so easy for them. It's hard for me, especially at work.

D: It is a big cause of suffering to measure yourself against other people. Everyone is exactly where they are supposed to be. There is no such thing as being behind or ahead. You are already what you seek and when you look to others you cannot find that which you already are. Sometimes our lives are hard, sometimes they are easy. Frankly, the material conditions or degrees of difficulty in one's life are not signs of your spiritual reality. The individual mind cannot fathom why you are given the life you have. There is nothing wrong with where you are. You really do not have to go anywhere to find yourself because your Self is always where you are. Even in the most difficult work conditions.

Rather than thinking there is something wrong with you, try compassion for yourself, compassion for your suffering. Can you see how hard you are on yourself? That is the main limitation. Self-judgment prevents you from seeing your magnificence and beauty now. If you want real courage, try not judging yourself and just be without evaluating, assessing or measuring yourself against some ideal. In this self-acceptance your already-inherent perfection is revealed. It is much simpler than you think, but you must look in the right place. That means within, to face the Self deeper than your judgments.

∞ ∞ ∞ ∞ ∞ ∞ ∞ ∞ ∞ ∞

Q: If I have this awareness for just a moment, why doesn't it stay? Papaji says you only need to have it for a second. Why doesn't it stay?

D: Who says it doesn't stay? As soon as this "who" comes up, as soon as this "I" says "I had this awareness," then the awareness is focused on the "I," not on itself. As soon as "this one" arises, you say, "Where is that awareness, why doesn't it stay?" The awareness is always here, but when you look for it, that is like awareness looking for awareness. That "I" is just a little cartoon graphic saying "awareness is not here," "I am not there yet," all of it is taking place in the midst of awareness.

Q. But I'm not there yet.

D: That's what you think. You are attached to not being That. Every time you speak that's what you do, you go back to the thought that says "I'm not That." Do you see that?

Q: Yes, I do.

Q: Good, this seeing is the awareness I'm speaking of. This awareness is here and it sees it all. It is aware of thinking, feeling, the body, the I-thought. This awareness is always here. It's just a shift in the focus of awareness. Bring your awareness to this awareness. This precious presence, the seeing itself. Rest as That.

∞ ∞ ∞ ∞ ∞ ∞ ∞ ∞ ∞ ∞

Q: It's easy enough to step back and be aware of thoughts when it is nice and quiet, and there's not a lot of sensory impingement, but what about when I'm engaged in action and there is more at stake. It is harder to step back then. What the hell do you do when it is really strong and things are running real fast and I'm supposed to be accomplishing things? Finding space approaches impossibility.

D: Then just do what you do and stop trying to find space or step back. Relax. Stop trying to stop your thoughts.

Q: It's not about stopping the thoughts. Thoughts can run all they want. But it's trying to see the space behind the thoughts.

D: Relax. Stop trying to do something to yourself in this moment. (Pause) See what happened? It's like all this trying stuff comes up, it just comes up, and that somehow there is some experience here which is not what I want, and I'm trying to do something about it. See the whole pattern?

Q: Yes.

D: So my answer to you is to stop trying, stop in this moment.

Q: Okay.

D: You don't have to try. If you really stop, you'll see you are here. Even when you are the middle of all that activity going on and everything is happening. Just see that thought, which is part of the whole pattern, the thought that says "I have to stop" or "I have to step back and find space." This pulls the rug out from under that pattern. What happens if you stop trying to control it?

Q: There's space.

D: Right.

Q: But, it would be interesting to see this in a real life situation . . .

D: So what is this, chopped liver? (Laughter).

Q: You must have a Jewish background. (Laughter).

D: Can you tell? What do you mean, "real life situation?" What are we, props?

Q: But how do we function if we just stop trying?

D: I said just keep doing what you are doing, but see that you cannot control or stop that experience. This ties into what I said before about unconditionally accepting all your experience.

Q: Right, but unconditional acceptance of experience, I mean, that's a pretty broad brush, because that might mean that if I'm in the middle of this thing and you give me the same line that you are giving me here, even if I can recognize it as absolute truth, it is not going to prevent me from hitting you across the nose, just as it arises, and there won't even be any thought behind it. (Laughter).

D: That's an occupational hazard (Laughter), the chance that people may want to hit me. I'm talking to you about a pattern that comes up, an anxiety about experience and trying to stop it, and that you don't need to try. The trying doesn't help you, it is just more of the same. Papaji would tell people to be quiet, and people would get reactive and say "I can't stop thinking!" and he'd say, "Stop trying to stop thinking." This is where I'm going. Its tricky. I'm saying to release that "aaaahhhh" (clenching) muscle. Ultimately, it means there is no control here, no one who can control this. When you see this, whether you are trying or not makes no difference.

∞ ∞ ∞ ∞ ∞ ∞ ∞ ∞ ∞ ∞ ∞

Q: I've been reading Eckhart Tolle's book *The Power of Now*, and he seems to be saying the more you become a witness to future and past, and try to stay present, theoretically you're supposed to get better and better at it with practice. I find it goes through cycles, rather than a steady improvement. I go through periods where I'm better at doing it than others, depending on the curve balls that life throws at me.

D: What does it do for you to have an idea that there's some trajectory of getting better at it?

Q: Well, I've made lots of progress, not in the sense of "better," but I get a righteous sense there for a few days. But then I thought that wasn't terribly authentic either.

D: I just want to reflect back to you this idea of some evolutionary movement. You see if you're really here now, what is this concept about movement all about? This is a question I have for Eckhart Tolle. He's proposing this movement towards something for people . . .

Q: . . . towards this quest for liberation?

D: Right. And what is it that gets liberated?

Q: Your relationship to the witness? Part of it, but that's not exactly it.

D: But what is this "you"?

Q: Oh, the "you" part.

D: Right the "you" part. This "you" that wants to get liberated. What is this? Let's take a look at it. When you use the word "I" or the word "you," look at it experientially and tell me what it is.

Q: I'm not totally clear on this. I'm just exploring. It's the need that we have to try and identify self to a certain degree, we want some relationship to our being, so is it another form of attachment where we put the "you" on and the "I" on and the "we" on? It's an identity or attachment of sorts to justify our existence?

D: And what is it technically when this "I" or this "you" is being thought? What is it? Here's what I'm driving at. The thought arises and the thought is "I." And then identification arises and there's more thought. So what's going on? We're conceptualizing, we're thinking. Now can you see this thinking taking place?

Q: Yes, there are certain states I can get into where as I become a witness to my chatter, so to speak, sometimes I can drop back and I can actually see or feel this thing that's going on in my head, this exchange of ideas that goes forward or backwards. I can almost see it as a little drama going on. So yes, I can see it sometimes.

D: Okay, so what is the "I" that you really are? These "I" and "you" thoughts that come and go, or this that sees all those thoughts?

Q: When all this stuff is going on, when you drop back, your true being is something behind that, just you, in spirit, perhaps. That's the real you.

D: So is this awareness or spirit here now?

Q: In conversing with you right now?

D: Yes, are you aware of speaking with me right now?

Q: Yes, I can hear you speaking to me.

D: So this beingness is here, isn't it?

Q: Yes, it's in the moment here right now.

D: So I want you to see that there's no going to it.

Q: Oh no, it's right here.

D: Yes, it's right here. I'm referring to what we started talking about, the belief that there's this progressive moving toward it.

Q: So it's actually always here, you're not going toward it, it's actually always with you.

D: Yes, but not "with you." It *is* you. Are you you?

Q: Most of the time.

D: What about the rest of the time? (Laughter) . . . There's this transient flow of experience, and no matter what's going on, you're still here.

Q: This is true.

D: I'm pointing this out to you because otherwise we get caught in the concept that "I'm moving toward myself." I want to reflect to you that you're always yourself, so all you really need to do is to stop insisting you're not. You are here, but you get into this belief that "No I'm not, I have to become myself somehow." Can you see that tendency of mind? It's pretty funny.

Q: Is that why they say half the deal is just showing up, if you show up you're already there?

D: *You are here.* You're here and you're always showing up. Everything that occurs, everything that's showing up here is an aspect of you showing up. Everything. And so even when you're confused and crazy, that's an aspect of you showing up. You're never not here. (Laughter).

Q: So why do we need to take all this stuff so seriously?

D: Somehow or other there's this great desire for drama, which is also a perfect expression of life. But you're right, we don't need to take it seriously. It frees up the joyfulness, doesn't it?

Q: Yeah, we can take it more lightly. We get way too serious about it. It's too hard to figure out when you get to that place anyway, so we can take a lighter approach.

D: Yeah, "Take a load off Fanny" (referring to the song by the Band).

Q: (Singing) "And put the load right on me."

D: We don't have to do that here, Jesus already did it. That'd be a good bumper sticker: "Crucifixion, been there done that." (Lots of Laughter).

∞ ∞ ∞ ∞ ∞ ∞ ∞ ∞ ∞ ∞

Q: This "just being empty here" you refer to, it always brings me to a total, complete dead end.

D: Good.

Q: Here I sit at the dead end.

D: What do you mean "dead end?"

Q: Dead end, nothing, that's all there is.

D: Seems like you are still giving it some interpretation, calling it "dead end" is giving it some meaning. What is it if you are not giving it any interpretation or judgment other than just being here?

Q: I've never done that.

D: That is what I'm asking you. What is your experience when you don't call it a "dead end." If you sit long enough in meditation, you will have "flatness," you will have "boredom," you will have "blankness." They are all just mind states. People think: that's it, it's all over. But they are just more mind states superimposed upon "being here." People somehow think that sitting around bored, not having any experience, being bland, is somehow a high state. But the true high state is not a state at all, it has no definition, you can't call it anything. If you are expecting a "high state," then you will end up calling certain things a "dead end." Because it is not what you think is supposed to be happening.

The mind generates some picture of what it will be like when I get it. We read all those spiritual books of other people talking about their high experiences. We say, "I want it to be like that." "That's really the way it is." The way Swami Beyondananda says. (Laughter). What the mind does is very subtle. If you read Zen, then the mind sets up a Zen realization, calling it "chop wood, carry water." If you read the Hindus, the mind sets up a Hindu realization, seeing deities and visions. The mind creates a clever counterfeit. Papaji used to warn people about the books they read because they predispose us to certain expectations of what will happen that we want to fulfill, and then program the mind to project those experiences. That can lead to the concept of "dead end" because I am not getting what I expected or how I pictured it would be.

Q: I guess when I say "dead end" I'm lying to myself because I know it's not, I'm not extinct.

D: Right on. What is going to be "extinct?"

Q: My investment, what I see as all my work, my investment in this spiritual path will all come to an end.

D: That's right. This huge effort that "I" am making, working really hard, doing a lot of practice, getting better, polishing the mirror. That entire movie goes poof! Freedom is a tremendous disillusionment. I mean that in the technical sense of the word. There is a stripping away of every illusion about what you think it is and will be, including all the spiritual talk, until you come face to face with the absolute mystery of what is here and now. It is here, you are here, and it's easy and peaceful and free.

Q: So it all boils down to a simple act of courage to step into the deep water?

Q: Well, the courage is to see you are already in the water. You *are* the water. Courage is to realize that! Courage is no courage at all.

∞ ∞ ∞ ∞ ∞ ∞ ∞ ∞ ∞ ∞

Q: It seems that truth and I are flirting together but it's not wedding time yet.

D: You can give yourself completely and passionately to your Lover. To flirt all the way actually means losing yourself in the Beloved, giving up the "me" that wants the truth, and then there is only truth. Otherwise, as long as you think there is a "me" and the "truth" and a "wedding time" it will never happen. You are the truth, here and now, so don't postpone.

∞ ∞ ∞ ∞ ∞ ∞ ∞ ∞ ∞ ∞

Q: Sometimes I feel like giving it all up, just wallowing in despair.

D: Despair is a consequence of dualistic perception, the inevitable other polarity of hope. It is an expression of the imagined separate ego that thinks it must willfully carry this burden, and sees no possibility, feels unable to accomplish it. It is your own will that produces defeat. "Give up hope all you who enter here" originally meant "cave in to despair." But here I mean that hope is the last vestige of the illusion that you are not already home. To give up hope is the ultimate surrender that can bring you to the freedom beyond hope and despair.

∞ ∞ ∞ ∞ ∞ ∞ ∞ ∞ ∞ ∞

Q: I just see myself getting stuck in the movie over and over again.

D: Good. Be the awareness that sees you get stuck. Be the consciousness of the action-reaction pattern. This awareness is what frees. There is no working through this, no working it out, no working out of it. There is being conscious of the identification, and in that seeing, there is the wisdom to discriminate between the real, unchanging presence that you are, rather than identifying with the changing forms of experience, emotions, thoughts, that arise like waves on your ocean. I keep seeing this over and over again, that there is no need to do anything. Surrender is seeing the patterns and letting them flow on by, seeing how you get fascinated and sucked into them. This seeing is free of all of it.

∞ ∞ ∞ ∞ ∞ ∞ ∞ ∞ ∞ ∞

Q: Sometimes I feel as if I'm being swallowed up by all this suchness you and Poonja speak of, that I'll drown and never return. And then I laugh because it is such freedom. I know this is all ramblings—but I'm lost and have no idea what to say. And coming fron an Italian background that's says a lot!

D: The feeling that you are being swallowed up by suchness is a great blessing. That's a good way to say it—all that you thought you were is swallowed up by what you are. Yes, drown and never return. Just let that happen and you will know the freedom of that drowning in your own Self. I'm happy to hear you are lost. Be truly lost, have no coordinates, no direction, no background, just here and now. Then you truly are found.

∞ ∞ ∞ ∞ ∞ ∞ ∞ ∞ ∞ ∞ ∞

Q: Understanding is the booby prize . . .

D: Right, you have a very good understanding, but your attachment to it creates a lot of suffering for you. So once you have the understanding of simply being here, forget the rest and just be here now. That is your freedom, otherwise your mind goes on forever spinning out this stuff, right? So just be the awareness that sees all the activity, all that mental activity. Just abide as this presence. Now is your happiness. Now is your freedom and joy.

Q: So why am I so unhappy?

D: Because you're following all your mind stuff, number one. Can you see how fascinated you are with your mind and how it makes you unhappy? And number two, when you ask that question, do you see that's just more of the same? Can you see the fascination with being someone struggling on a path, trying to work it out? Are you willing to give up the agony and longing, the heroic romanticism of the arduous path? We must face this attachment to suffering, and then to getting rid of suffering, and that this getting rid of suffering—the path itself—is part of the suffering. You don't get rid of suffering by trying to get rid of suffering. You see through it to the realization that there is no one who needs to attain some other state, that there never was any separate self. Hope is still suffering. Freedom is utterly hopeless.

Q: I can understand exactly what he's feeling because I do the same thing a lot and just go right into those mental gymnastics that puts me in that uncomfortable place.

D: Right, so see it, or feel it.

Q: OK, when you say go into it and feel it, you mean without any agenda?

D: Yes, because feeling is just an openness, and anything that arises in openness will have to dissipate because there's nothing giving it definition. So you want to see what you're adding to the simple process of being with something. You're adding some interpretation or rejection to it.

Q: I get it, I understand, but sometimes I can be squirming around feeling things for quite awhile.

D: Okay, just be aware of the process. I keep saying just be the awareness that sees and allows the flow of experience, and the freedom becomes obvious. It is. The seer is free. You don't see the seer. The seer can never see itself. The Hindus say—and this is just a story—the entire world is arising so formless being can see itself. It creates its own reflection. The formless projects consciousness, the flow of imagination, as a way to reflect itself back to itself, like a hall of mirrors. And every form is your own formlessness arising as form just so that it can recognize itself, so it can awaken to itself. It's like the entire movie is just this game of forgetting and remembering. That's the game of consciousness. And when you have the eyes to see, you recognize yourself in every form, because everything is you.

Q: So when you ask me who is seeing, there's no answer I can give you.

D: Right.

Q: But I can say I am, right?

D: Yes, you can say that. "I am" is the first movement in the process of creation arising out of source. All creation comes from source through this "I am." But source itself can not be spoken. And that's what you are.

∞ ∞ ∞ ∞ ∞ ∞ ∞ ∞ ∞ ∞

Q: Is therapy useful, can it bring us to freedom?

D: There is a wide range of therapies that have proved useful in their limited domains. Psychological therapies can help us resolve specific issues in our lives, understand the mind better and have a healthier sense of individual self. You can certainly get some short-term relief this way. But in so far as they are ego-based, that is, grounded in the belief in a separate entity who is working on oneself, they still strengthen the illusion of separation, which is the deeper cause of the suffering underlying all specific psychological conditions. The freedom we are speaking of is freedom *from* the illusion of the "I" who is working on oneself, trying to get somewhere, trying to get healthy and balanced. I'd say ultimate mental health is freedom from mind itself.

Q: But can't therapies at least prepare us for freedom, make us ready to receive it?

D: That is a theory we believe in dearly, but I see no evidence for it. Many believe that you must first establish a healthy, balanced ego in the world before you can realize that you are not that limited identity. Get ego all tuned up before you move on, so to speak. This is a neat, logical, theoretical idea, but in fact, if you look at what actually happens, people have awakened from all kinds of states, some of them we would call "dysfunctional." It's pretty messy and doesn't follow neat ideas of the so-called preconditions for awakening. We in western culture especially have these progressive, evolutionary notions, that we are advancing from "less developed" states to "more developed" states, which will eventually culminate in some "realized" state. This is the historical myth of progress, and its psychological version is the belief that therapy can prepare you for liberation, that there is some logical set of steps you must follow, starting with becoming a stable and responsible person. It is all still caught in the belief that there is someone here who needs to evolve. And it is caught in the illusion of time, that over time we can move forward. Waking up is waking up to what is here now, to what is free of the idea of time, to the Self that has always been here and needs no evolution or progress.

Still, I don't discourage anyone from getting into therapy if you wish. It has its appropriate uses. After all, since everything is an invitation to awakening, then therapy could also be. Just as long as we understand that falling off your bike is also an invitation to freedom, or getting thrown in jail or the insane asylum, or having a business disaster, or your spouse leaving you. Everything in the movie exists to reflect truth back to you, to reflect the perfection of what is and the fullness of your true nature just as you are. So do what you wish, just see through the doer, see through its needs for development and its heroic drama of progress.

∞ ∞ ∞ ∞ ∞ ∞ ∞ ∞ ∞ ∞

Living Life

Q: I can see that living the life that you present is beautiful and has got a lot of merit, but to do it to the ultimate, to be good at it almost leads you to a monk-like existence. (Laughter and "No, no" in the group) You have an everyday life, too. Papaji worked many jobs, didn't he?

D: Papaji worked for a living after his awakening. He supported his family, including being a mining manager. Work and life in the world is no obstacle to freedom. My work and active participation in the corporate world has taken off over the past ten years. You see that's just an idea that you have, that it will be a certain way, that it needs a monkish existence. Better to be without that idea and just see what comes. Are you willing to experiment? Are you willing to be a true scientist, which is to experiment with this and see how it goes?

Q: I'd love to.

D: Good, then just be this consciousness and see. Alright? Because I promise you that in this simple awareness you will discover you, and then it will be a big joke because all the concerns that you have are just mind, they're just fears. They're part of the egoic structure, which is in resistance to this. It generates an entire survival mechanism that's intended to support the body-mind package, and it does a good job of it, but it also has a lot of weirdness in it. Part of its survival mechanism is that it doesn't want to go out of existence. And so it clings to its melodrama, it rebels, it creates this fear—fear that you'll have to be a monk, or something.

Q: Are you saying you go about your daily chores . . . but the point is to go about your business always with this overlay of involvement with eternity, or whatever you call it? Whatever those names are. (Laughter).

D: (Laughing) You don't need any names.

Q: Yeah, that's good, no names, no concepts.

D: No concept at all. You see it's simple. The mind loves complexity because it keeps it employed. Because it is deathly afraid of unemployment, it creates all this complexity and it's afraid of the simplicity of this approach. If you don't cling to any notion, if you have no intention, if you have no desire, and you have no goal, in this moment you recognize this being that you are, and from this beingness everything flows, everything gets taken care of, because it's all getting taken care of anyway except you don't know it. Now you know it.

When you live as source you see that all activity, all work—whether you work or not—is all flowing through you. It's all just happening. It's the source doing everything. The Self, God, the absolute, is doing everything. Just abide as this emptiness through which all activity occurs. That is what this realization is. You still do what you do but it's not "you" doing it. It's just the One, which is you, so the language gets in the way here a little bit.

Q: I think most people have a sense of responsibility and they think it's this separate self that has to manifest whatever the responsibility is, and if we could convert that idea to the realization of letting this flow through then we wouldn't have to worry so much.

D: Exactly, you wouldn't have to worry at all because, if there is any responsibility here, it is the supreme power taking responsibility and doing x, y and z. And it has nothing to do with "you", that is, the separate self sense. The illusion is that the "I" is doing things, whereas in reality it is always the Self doing everything. So there's no conversion needed.

∞ ∞ ∞ ∞ ∞ ∞ ∞ ∞ ∞ ∞

Q: What makes you want to do anything if you're not striving?

D: Well, you'll just have to find out what inherently moves you. I've seen this incredible mystery take place. Action takes place all by itself. It doesn't need any motivation from this 'I', this illusory ego. The totality is humming along, living itself out absolutely perfectly. And it will do with you what it will. But when that occurs there's the realization that you are That, living itself out. From my experience, the potentiality that I was born with as an individual wave and which life is an opportunity to experience and fulfill, that potentiality is fulfilled in this awakening. The particular characteristics or qualities you were born with are freed up to flower in this. It could be something in particular or it could be just sitting in a cave somewhere. I watch in pure amazement and gratitude as I play out this life, as if living out a dream come true.

∞ ∞ ∞ ∞ ∞ ∞ ∞ ∞ ∞ ∞

Q: I was just reading a quote the other day where Plato had referred to spiritual practice or spiritual philosophy as "the art of dying while still alive."

D: Very nice. Papaji's phrase was "how to be asleep while awake," or "be awake while asleep"—same thing. He used this analogy: When you go to bed at night, what has to happen for you to go to sleep? You get into bed and you have to let go of your life. You can't be thinking about all that stuff right? And you have to let go of people, even if you have a person lying next to you. If you're somehow focused on that person, you can't get to sleep. So you have to let go of that, and you have to let go of any thought, because you can't sleep if you're thinking. And so it's that entire experience of being dead to everything, that's real sleep, that's total rest. I'm not talking about dreams, because dream sleep is just more mind. So it's that same dying in life.

∞ ∞ ∞ ∞ ∞ ∞ ∞ ∞ ∞ ∞

Q: Is it easy to be in the world in this consciousness? How do I be in the world that is always defining me?

D: Yes, of course, you are here. There's an awareness that the "I" you thought you were is just a concept, and what is here is *you*, the presence. This presence is not defined. Yet you live in the world that is defining you, calling you "woman," "daughter," "employee." Everyone has definitions. So how to live in the world that does this? Well, you play the game. I am no one, and I show up here as an actor in people's movies. Circumstances and relationships are like magnets that pull the formless into some form. With my kids I'm their "daddy" when I'm with them. When they are gone I'm no one. When I go down to Corning I'm a "coach," and play that game. You know who you are and you play these roles. The roles are soft and flexible for me, even though they may be hard in the minds of others. They arise when they are appropriate and fall away when they are not. I call this "situational identity." Identities come and go within the no one, free of all identification.

There is no problem in this. It is the very nature of the formless to show up as form. The ocean makes waves. It plays roles, that is, the totality is playing all these roles. One of my teachers once said, "It's not the roles that give us pain, it's the preservatives in the rolls." When there is identification with the role, there is the whole range of suffering. Then you live out the drama as the individual. When you know who you are and you are simply playing the role, no problem.

∞ ∞ ∞ ∞ ∞ ∞ ∞ ∞ ∞ ∞

Q: So with the knowledge or presence of Self, then there is the choice, one has the choice to engage in life at any level. Or is there no choice?

D: (Laughing) You beat me to it!

Q: We are all in this room. We get into our cars, I go to my life, you go to your life. What is that all about?

D: It is just happening. It is the way the totality is manifesting in this moment. I'll be anthropomorphic here: let's call it the "will of God" that you get up, walk to your car and drive home. Every breath is the pulsing of the totality. Once you see through the illusion of separation, you see it is all the ocean. What moves the waves? The waves made a decision to rise and fall? No way. It is the ocean doing it all. The waves don't have any independent existence or causality. So if "I"—the wave—decide to stand up, it was the ocean that made me have that decision and made me stand up, because "I" am not a separate category. There is only That happening. So it's not as if there is choice or not. *There just isn't any chooser.* Choice happens, decisions are made, thoughts occur, and that is all streaming through the bodymind process. It just happens.

Q: And it streams through each bodymind process uniquely.

D: Yes, uniquely. It is all a magnificently rich diversity. Every stream is living out its particular destiny, conditioning, programming, inheritance, values, preferences, choices, all of it streaming through.

Q: So there's nothing we can call free will?

D: Free will is a concept. So long as you believe you are the individual doer, then you talk about free will. Once there is the realization that ego is fiction, that the separate "I" is just a concept, then you see free will is just a concept. There is an endless debate in western philosophy about "free will vs. determinism" that has gone on for two thousand years. But the whole debate is caught in duality. Beyond that duality, no concept applies, neither free will nor determinism. It's all just happening.

∞ ∞ ∞ ∞ ∞ ∞ ∞ ∞ ∞ ∞

Q: I'm afraid that if I'm free, I'll do whatever I want. What about my commitments, my work, my family?

D: People often express the concern that if they truly give themselves to freedom, that somehow they will become dysfunctional or their lives will fall apart or they won't do the right thing or they will abandon their children or not make a living or no longer care about others and do terrible, immoral things. This is all fear. It may be the reflection of strong desires that you have never allowed yourself to face. But whatever the content of the fear, it is a tool of the egoic resistance to dissolution, the refusal to give up control. When it fears going out of existence it projects all kinds of unwanted, scary scenarios and outcomes which it then seeks to avoid. These are all excuses. The point is not whether these projected scenarios will happen or not—you never know what is down the road—but to rest as your own Self from whom all action flows.

∞ ∞ ∞ ∞ ∞ ∞ ∞ ∞ ∞ ∞

Q: If I am the Self then I do not have to care for what I eat or how money will be provided?

D: Since the Self is doing everything, you don't have to "care" (that is, worry) about money or eating or anything else. The Self is taking quite good care of you and will always do so. As Ramana said, if you are meant to work, you will work. If you are not meant to work, you won't. Just follow your nose and do what makes sense. As long as you still identify with the bodymind package, then act as if you are responsible for what is happening, even if the Self is everything and is doing everything. Once you realize you are the formless source of it all, you won't ask the question about money and eating.

Q: I'm simply speechless and do not know what to say, except sometimes it is so difficult to be present and open to what you are saying when I'm in the daily stuff of living, i.e. getting a job—or are you saying that is my bliss—the daily goings on of life?

D: Good to be speechless. At first it seems difficult to be present because you still think it is something you have to do. But being is being. When you see there is absolutely nothing you need to do to be what you are, then being is seen to be already present. See how mind makes this all into effort. Then you will see that ordinary life truly is your bliss.

∞ ∞ ∞ ∞ ∞ ∞ ∞ ∞ ∞ ∞

Q: We can choose to play in the movie?

D: It's all just flowing along. And when one is awake to it, that's when the playing of it can be experienced freely. When one thinks one is the player, then one is caught in that identification. So the play is taking place and we are all being played. The one life, the one reality, the one presence, whatever you want to call it, is playing its tune through us. It's playing all the parts in this play.

Q: And we don't have any choice whether we play or not play because we're all just flowing along with everything else. Where does your will come into this?

D: When you see that there is no "I," then you see that there is no chooser. There's no one to make any choices, no one to have a will. It's all just flowing along. This is the freedom of being that which is not touched by all of this, which is just flowing along. Now the "I" thinks it makes choices. I choose to stand up, I choose to sit down. But that was just how the consciousness moved in that moment. In this sense it is all the "will" of the totality, although, of course, it has no will.

Q: Your mind had no effect over your body in terms of motor skills to make you stand up or sit down?

D: My mind did have an effect over the body, but the mindbody is just an expression of this presence that is doing everything. When you nodded your head, it was just in that moment that consciousness nodded your head.

Q: And this consciousness has no individuality, it's just manifesting in a zillion different particles and pieces?

D: It manifests as individuality, but individuality is not a real division . .

Q: It's all connected in the primordial soup of it all?

D: It's all one, its never divided. In India they call it Advaita, which means not-two, never been divided. It's not even like it's "connected." It's not like there's something here and there's something there and then you join them. It's that they were never divided to begin with. So the one that is, is enacting itself through all form and then the game is that the form forgets its true nature and thinks it's this individual "I" making choices. And the waking up is the waking up to the fact that I am/you are this presence which is the source of the entire dance, and that the dance is dancing itself.

Q: So once you have a real good hang of that, then the idea that you can control anything or make any effort to try to control anything seems utterly pointless. You just allow it to orchestrate itself.

D: Yes. It's all playing itself out, and there's absolutely nothing to worry about. And this is where it gets scary for people because they don't want to let go of that control. When you abide as this awareness that simply witnesses this whole thing playing out, that's freedom. And this thing has its momentum, its got it's program it's living out.

Q: So there's absolutely no point in worrying about what's going to happen tomorrow, it's utterly pointless.

D: Zero.

Q: So just groove on the moment here, and forget about tomorrow.

D: Be here, open your heart and enjoy.

Q: That sounds very groovy, but what about getting the kids to school and paying the rent or any of those kinds of things. If I were really to indulge my total liberation in this moment I wouldn't do much of anything.

D: Well, let's try it. (Laughter) Because right now you're speaking from an anticipation of . . .

Q: the chaos . . .

D: You think its going to be chaos, we have all these thoughts like if I really got it I'd run away from home, leave my spouse, make love to millions of people, quit my job, get fat, whatever, we have all these ideas about that. That's what the mind does as resistance to simply being in this moment.

Q: But how about the days when I just decide to check out and do nothing and then I pay the consequences the next day?

D: That's what happens, there are consequences in the movie.

Q: You also have to be comfortable with the consequences of just being in the moment.

D: Yes, of course. I had those expectations and concerns too, but what I came to see is that life goes on and it's just astounding, life goes on and whatever does happen, you see its perfection.

Q: So tomorrow morning I get up and decide that I'm just going to be in the moment and meditate and exist in myself and . . . (laughter) . . .

D: Why wait? What is this "tomorrow morning" stuff? You get no breaks here, this is it. Why not just do it now and see what comes?

Q: Well, I feel very good with it right now.

D: Why leave this "feeling good" with it? You see what you're doing? You're going "Uh oh." And then anticipation comes up, you get worried and then it ruins your experience of the now.

Q: That I see, I understand that.

D: Good, you get to see that we pee in the soup . . . (Laughter) . . . we pee in the pool. I want you to see it's a simple little mechanism in consciousness that disturbs. It's like a perturbation in the now.

Q: Am I the only one struggling with this?

D: No, you're just speaking for everybody. (Lots of laughter) . . . You're at the slippery slope here, where consciousness is always pulling the rug out from under the position it just had. But this presence, this awareness, has no position whatsoever.

Q: So don't even try to get a handle on it.

D: Right, see the inherent desire in consciousness to get a handle on it. See you have a very strong drive to understand. That's okay, that's just the way it's programmed.

Q: Yeah, I'll have to get rid of that . . .

D: Just learn to love it, just learn to love the particular flavor of your weirdness.

Q: Yeah, I grovel in this stuff.

D: Whatever. Because you do a good job at it, just enjoy it and don't worry about it because it doesn't mean anything (laughs).

∞ ∞ ∞ ∞ ∞ ∞ ∞ ∞ ∞ ∞ ∞

Q: So does it matter what we do?

D: Do you mean if I pollute the earth, does the earth get polluted? Yes, that happens, there are consequences to our actions.

Q: Does that matter?

D: If it's your values, then it matters to you.

Q: Does that matter to the presence of your being? So your being doesn't react to that, so it's okay with your being?

D: Yes, presence has no position whether the earth is polluted or not, has no position as to whether you die or not. It's the source of everything that arises—everything that happens arises from the source and is an activity of the source.

Q: So whatever goes on in the universe, as far as the source is concerned, it's indifferent?

D: It has no relationship to this. It's all just happening.

Q: Let us say that there's a man beating a child with a whip that will kill him, do you think that either Papaji or Ramana would intercede, or simply be present wth the act.

D: They might have interceded. Papaji was a very active person, but whatever they would do would be whatever the consciousness does in the moment. To intercede or not is just whatever the programming does.

Q: Is there any right use of will in this, or not?

D: Will is a concept based on believing you are an individual. When you realize there is no individual you realize there is no individual will. It's all just the activity of the totality. As long as you're talking from the point of view of the individual you have all these issues. I'm not talking from that perspective. I'm making no statement here about morality. If you have morals then I'm not saying you shouldn't follow them. The upshot of being free is not that you're not going to follow your morals. You won't know that until you simply rest as presence. We cannot answer your question now. You will know the answer by simply being in this moment and you'll see what shows up. And so I say abide as the beingness, and the answer to your question will be evident. Otherwise it's all just concept.

∞ ∞ ∞ ∞ ∞ ∞ ∞ ∞ ∞ ∞

Q: How do you deal with difficult people out there? Do you just ignore them?

D: You deal with "difficult people" by dealing with your own "difficult person," by coming fully face to face with "I," the sense of ego and personality that you have identified with. You must see clearly this "difficult person," all the beliefs and self-images that it holds, the attachment to its desires and fears and all the play of mind that generates its experience—your difficult experience and dysfunctional behaviors. Once you are fully aware of this, and fully unconditionally accept this, your sense of who you are shifts from the content—from being the "difficult person"—to being the context, the loving, accepting awareness in which it all takes place. From this space you relate to the difficult people around you.

In truth, you are only relating to yourself. Everything you see, all beings and all forms, are manifestations of the only One that you are. So there is only One relating to itself. This realization frees you to respond appropriately to the "difficult people" you think are "out there" because you will see them all as you. So, how to do you relate to yourself? That is, what you find "difficult" about people's behavior, their emotional reactions, their thinking, is likely what you find difficult within your own mindbody and its behavior. It is a seed of your own potentiality that you have not fully realized within yourself, and thus, it is projected out in others and you react to it in others. Your reaction to them is the way you react to yourself. When you see this projection, you can return your attention to your own functioning. When you are aware and accepting of yourself, you will have an appropriate response to what is "out there." Or perhaps it will disappear out there, or the false distinction between "out there" and "in here" dissolves. In any case, it will no longer be a dilemma or question.

∞ ∞ ∞ ∞ ∞ ∞ ∞ ∞ ∞ ∞

Q: How do I maintain awareness and not get drawn into the story? Especially when maintaining awareness means allowing and not reacting out of old ways or no longer meeting the demands, expectations, and/or obligations which another has placed upon me, which seems to be making this person become very critical of me, having negative interpretations of me.

D: Actually, you don't really have to "maintain" awareness. Awareness is already here. It is what you are, the reality underlying everything. Just be quiet in this moment and see what is already aware. This seeing is always present. Just become aware of the awareness that is already here and now. When awareness turns to awareness, all there is, is awareness.

The more you dwell as awareness you will see that everything happens from this source consciousness, that your responses flow from the silence. If you truly want freedom—freedom from the "I" and its story—let the Self shape the flow of your life and what happens. Everything comes from the silence, so be quiet and the decision will flow from there. No need to force yourself into a decision you are not in a position to make.

It is true that awareness brings about changes in your responses to others and they may get confused and not understand where it is coming from. So it would be good to let this person know as best you can what is happening with you and the changes in your view of those "demands, expectations, and/or obligations." They may or may not get it, but it is the best you can do. Then at least they will be better informed to make their own choices.

The most precious relationship is when the individuals are committed to being free together, to being awake together. The great invitation is to enjoy the no-relationship of satsang with your intimates. See your friend as the same Self you are. True relationship is no-relationship. Then see what comes.

∞ ∞ ∞ ∞ ∞ ∞ ∞ ∞ ∞ ∞

Realization

*Q : This "noticing of reality" in your case . . . did it seem to happen in a particular moment, or over a period of time?

D: Both. There have been many moments in my life where there was this recognition. I remember when I was a little boy about 12 years old or so walking to the movies on a Saturday morning. Everything simply disappeared and there was this sense of presence. And in this sense of presence there was a recognition (even for a 12-year-old boy) that, "This is it." And then ordinary consciousness seemed to refocus itself and that was that.

There have been moments like that throughout my life where this, that is always here, was revealed. I would say, though, that I realized it as more of an ongoing background of my own existence when I met Papaji in March of 1992. It happened over a ten-day period of having met the master and sat with him, during satsang and in his house at various times. It just crept up and pulled me to it, so to speak, until there was this clear recognition that this is what I am. There was an awareness that this is always here, that this presence—the words, as you know, don't do it justice, they never can—or sense of stillness or peace is always available.

There's a sense of timelessness. Time really stopped for me then. And I continued to function—I had a watch and all of that. You know it's just numbers going around in a circle. This became very forcefully present in '92.

Even when ordinary consciousness returned, so to speak, when just the day-to-day experience is present, it doesn't obliterate this timelessness. They don't invalidate each other. It seems like this presence allows for everything, including unconsciousness. It allows for all thought of any kind including body-consciousness. It allows for ordinary existence to take place within it. And yet, what I think is the greatest liberation of all is knowing that ordinary existence and all its ups and downs do not really touch this place. Nor do you ever leave it, although you might think you do.

After the awakening in '92, there were many more times of awakening, some of them in India with Papaji, others just occurring spontaneously in everyday life. I think it's important for people who are getting all kinds of ideal pictures of what we call realization as an event or an experience to know that after that very momentous transformation in '92, I had a real roller coaster of experience for a few years. There would be extraordinary times of transcendence and bliss, alternating with all kinds of very intense uncomfortable experiences and mental tendencies arising.

I had moments of fear, worry, doubt, arrogance. They were all coming up in this space of consciousness that had been opened up. They were taking place in the midst of this realization. This is really very difficult to describe because it's not an either/or thing. It's a real trap to get into "there's only the purity of emptiness" you know. There is this emptiness and in the midst of this emptiness there's a lot of stuff that seems to be going on.

But, what's also interesting is that it didn't matter how many awakenings there were, each time it was the same. Each realization was the same realization. It was the recognition of *being* this awareness, of being this spacious presence. Rather than identifying with all that comes and goes, I was and am this truth, which is the ground of it all. It includes everything. It includes emptiness and the realization of being nobody at the same time as it includes being this very specific bodymind process called Dasarath, living out some kind of mysterious destiny. It's all of that.

[* Excerpted from an interview with Quidam Green Meyers in the book *Wide Awake: The Miracle of Spiritual Breakthrough*, published by The Book Tree.]

∞ ∞ ∞ ∞ ∞ ∞ ∞ ∞ ∞ ∞

Q: What is really to be gained by this whole spiritual quest? Sometimes I wonder.

D: Good wondering. There is really nothing to be gained, just that the silence that is always here is revealed. As soon as there is a thought that there is something gained, then there is loss. Gain and loss go together. It is not an experience to be gained, not an experience to be lost. There is no holding on to it. Typically the "I" seeks to own it or claim realization as its possession. I had this experience. Then there is the fear of losing the experience, worrying how to get back to this experience. That entire process is mind, taking place as a superimposition upon the reality of the natural state that is always here. There is no getting or losing enlightenment. Anything that is gotten or lost is not it. Be alert to the way mind tries to coopt this and turn it into an object. The consciousness that sees it is free of all of it.

∞ ∞ ∞ ∞ ∞ ∞ ∞ ∞ ∞ ∞

Q: Would you describe this realization that you are pointing us toward?

D: Its impossible to describe realization fully because the reality of who one is is beyond all concepts. The best I can say about it is this: You—I, the Self—are being-awareness without boundaries or limits. Everything is arising within you: time, space, mind, body, senses, the whole world, is arising as your own imagination, all of it a three-dimensional, multi-sensory, holographic projection of this single underlying reality. You are the real, unchanging essence-source-consciousness and you imagine the whole world, including your individual bodymind identity. Because it is imagination, it doesn't mean you don't experience it. The senses are an aspect of the hologram, just as in a dream you can have "real" sensory experience and it is still a dream. Sensory experience is fully valid within the world of form—you think, feel, speak, listen, etc., just like everyone else, yet it is not a measure of the absolute reality which is deeper than the senses. You cannot taste, touch, see, feel, or hear your own Self, yet you abide as the space in which all this is happening. Bodymind and the world come and go, yet you are eternal and unchanging. This is your true nature, and what is called "enlightenment" or "self-realization" is the waking up to this. The knowing is revealed naturally in no-thought. When you are quiet, it is apparent.

∞ ∞ ∞ ∞ ∞ ∞ ∞ ∞ ∞ ∞

Guru

Q: What is the role of the guru in all this?

D: In the Indian nondual tradition they say the guru is the "dispeller of darkness." Papaji often said that the function of the guru was to clear away your doubt. He doesn't give you anything new, because you already are the Self. He just allows you to relinquish your doubts. In giving up the belief that you are not already That, the pre-existing presence is revealed. One day we were sitting at Papaji's table having tea and cookies and he said, "Okay, ask me all your questions now, because I don't want you to have any doubts." He systematically answered my questions and continually asserted: No development, no progress, no practice, no attainment, no purification was needed. He said he never gave anyone anything to do. He was the end of the do's and don'ts. He then asked me what else he could do for me, and when I asked him to support my teaching work, he said, "I'm not going to give you a certificate." He gave absolutely nothing. What a precious gift!

There was no floor to stand on around him. Papaji was a doorway to infinity, and no one could go through that door. That is, on the other side of the door there is no Dasarath or Papaji, only the undivided truth itself. The guru is that open doorway to your own Self. The presence of the master, the very field of awakened consciousness itself, is enough to reveal this.

∞ ∞ ∞ ∞ ∞ ∞ ∞ ∞ ∞ ∞

Q: Is a guru necessary for awakening?

D: If we are speaking narrowly of the guru as an enlightened person, then this is clearly not so. Many people have awakened without a direct association with such an individual. If, however, we understand the guru to be a *function of consciousness*, not a person, then it can be seen to be a fundamental element in realization. In this view the guru is an activity of the Self, your own being, that plays an imaginary game of hide and seek with itself. Having imagined yourself to be asleep, hidden in the bodymind, you then show up as guru to awaken yourself from your individual dream. This is the grace that launches you on the search for self-realization, that puts you on the spiritual path. The very seeking itself is the pull of the guru, the magnetic force within you calling you home. When the seeker is ready, the Self may manifest as an external guru in one's life. The outer guru in form is a projection of one's readiness and desire for liberation. While it may seem like we choose our teachers, in the wisdom of the totality, the guru chooses you. The guru is the executioner of the individual self-sense, and plays whatever role is necessary—friend, parent, master, guide, lover, etc.—to free you from your limited identification and reveal that guru and student are one.

I should add, too, that the guru need not take human form. In truth, all life is the guru. Everything is a form of your own Self and an invitation to realize that. The guru can show up as any being, object, circumstance, whatever form it takes to arouse you and turn your attention to yourself. The guru has shown up as a still pond in the moonlight, a bird in flight, a fall from a tree, even a cockroach.

Q: What about all the obvious abuses that teachers have committed on sincere and trusting students? There are so many stories of sexual abuse, lying, and taking advantage of unsuspecting disciples.

D: That is all part of the movie of appearances. From the dualistic perspective, we could say both teachers and students project all kinds of co-dependent needs, desires and idealized archetypes on one another. The innocence of the student lays them bare to exploitation and control by manipulative or misguided teachers. Perhaps students, especially idealistic westerners who haven't had a lot of experience with gurus, naively impose all kinds of moral standards of behavior where they don't apply. We could also say that the abuse is a powerful opportunity for disciples to see their own fixations and dependencies. All of it is grist for the mill for those willing to have the liberating insights that such experiences might bring.

From the nondual perspective, once we recognize the deeper, impersonal function of the guru, no matter what the outward appearance, we may better understand Papaji's seemingly ruthless quip to people who complained about their teachers: "Everybody gets the guru they deserve." The individual has only the dimmest idea of what one has to go through in order to know oneself, nor does one have any control over the circumstances or timing of one's realization. Awakening may come through bliss or pain, it may come through loving, gentle care or through ferocious and seemingly insensitive treatment or abuse. All of it is an invitation to see the whole play as your own Self. In that seeing, we can only bow to the Self-as-guru in gratitude for playing it so perfectly.

∞ ∞ ∞ ∞ ∞ ∞ ∞ ∞ ∞ ∞

Q: What is the difference as far as Mother Meera and Sai Baba are concerned? Because Mother Meera says she is really higher than the human being, she's something higher than all of us.

D: The Self as guru shows up in many ways to awaken itself. And it awakens in every form imaginable. If you look at the entire movie of manifestation as an opportunity to realize your nature, then because the Self shows up as multiplicity and every individual is unique, it provides an infinite number of unique ways to realize yourself. So you'll have Sai Baba, you'll have Mother Meera, you'll have Muktananda, and you'll have Zen and Tibetan and all the different traditions because every tradition is a doorway, with a certain cultural framework and orientation for certain individuals who get it that way. So no way is for everybody. The particular version that we are speaking about here is not a mass movement. It's for the very few. And you discover for yourself. Jesus said just lay down your burden. Give it to me. This was the Christian way to say it . . . like, take a break, it's all done. And when you read the *Bhagavad Gita*, Krishna said the same thing. If one immerses deeply in whatever tradition, then the same invitation is present beneath the surface diversity of forms and approaches.

∞ ∞ ∞ ∞ ∞ ∞ ∞ ∞ ∞ ∞

Mystery Movie

D: I think it's so appropriate that we're here in the theatre. The movie is one of the classic images that Ramana used to describe the mystery of consciousness. He was talking in the early and mid-20th century, using the technological metaphor of a movie screen, that your true nature—that is, consciousness—is the substratum or screen upon which all images are projected. Like when you watch a movie, you have this continuous play—this dance of light and form and sound—the infinite variety of thought-forms that play on the unchanging screen of consciousness. You come in here and you can watch an action movie, or a thriller, or these hot, lusty sex movies, or goofy cartoons, and the content doesn't matter to the screen. Just as the screen is never touched by the images that show up on it, your true nature is never affected by the experiences that arise within you.

Ignorance, or the cause of suffering, is the identification with the movie, the belief that you are limited to these experiences that are continually arising and disappearing on the screen of consciousness. We identify with all that. In the same way that you sit down in the theatre, if it's a *good* movie, you get sucked in. You *want* to get sucked in, that's why people go to movies, they want to forget, they want to come in here and get sucked into the drama. This is the mysterious power inherent in consciousness to imagine form and then get sucked into it, to delude yourself into taking your own movie of consciousness as real. So if the hero is about to fall off a cliff, you're tense and about to fall off a cliff, and if the lovers are making love, you're turned on and making love. And we know from mindbody studies that this act of consciousness is triggering a flood of neurochemicals that are flowing through your neurophysiology, generating actual physical sensations. The nervous system is operating, the glands are activated and the hormones are flowing, the muscles are being driven as well by this entire play of consciousness that is taking place. The whole organism is obeying this consciousness. So everyone is sucked into the movie of thought which is actually playing you like an instrument. And people have totally forgotten that they are the consciousness that is projecting the whole show.

Freedom is the awareness of being That within which all of this arises, and which is never affected by any of it. This is what you are now, this is what you've always been. In the great nondual teachings, there's nothing whatsoever to be done about this movie, but rather to be the Seer that sees it. There is nothing you need to do about fixing the movie in any way. The movie is the play of your own imagination, and you're always the awareness free of it all, you're the freedom within which the movie plays out. The movie comes and goes, and you are always here. So enjoy the movie. (Laughs).

Q: Why do we play this movie? Why not stay as consciousness?

D: (Laughs). Abide as consciousness and find out. We get this intense fascination with the drama. That's why we go to these movies. Think about the movies we go to—like horror flicks. Why are people going to horror flicks? They just like to be totally terrified. We have this intense fascination with drama and suffering. We try to suck the life out of experience, like nursing on the teat of appearances. It's like a programming in the organism. People used to ask Papaji: "Well, if it's so easy why isn't everybody awake and free all the time?" And he said that they are too fascinated with the movie, too attached to their own dramas.

When awareness sees that, the seeing of it is not caught in the movie. Freedom is here, the truth of your being is here, this sense of presence and clarity is here, you have always been here. To be free is actually the simplest thing, and what's difficult is this holding to all this stuff. You somehow think the holding is going to accomplish something. Just seeing that is liberating. There's nothing to do about it. You don't have to extricate yourself from it, just relax. No need for effort, no need to strive, just be. And in this being, it all just shows up. It just does itself.

∞ ∞ ∞ ∞ ∞ ∞ ∞ ∞ ∞ ∞

Q: To me its one of the mysteries why humans were put into this material world, which makes it so difficult to know the source, and to be a part of the mystery, which in itself is a mystery, that somehow it seems like there has to be a reason, that I am constantly trying to figure it out. Do we really have to do this?

D: As long as you're operating from a dualistic framework that says there's "us" who are separate and then there's the "mystery" that put "us" here in the material world, there's never any real answer to that. Because all you get is a lot of human beings who believe they're separate, spinning more and more explanations of some "other."

Q: Well, even though you know you're not separate, still the materiality is not a mystery. See what I'm trying to say?

D: What I'm asking you to do is to come back to what is this "I" or this "you" that thinks it's asking this question, because if you delve into *what you are*, the answer will arise. When you say "I", "what am I doing here?" what is that "I"?

Q: The "I" that stands behind the materiality of the form. The "I" is not the form.

D: What is the "I"?

Q: Well, it's the eternal beingness.

D: Okay, so if you are the eternal beingness, rest as that eternal beingness and you will answer your own question. Because the beingness knows. Because the individual self sense *can't answer it.* What I am talking about is something experiential, not an intellectual concept. If you abide as this conscious presence that is within or behind the form, which is implicit in everything, which is the source of all thought and all explanation, and the source of all materiality—because all materiality is arising as an expression of your own nature—then you will see this delightful dance of mystery happening and everything will be obvious. Because you are the answer.

Q: But you don't know that all the time.

D: Again, you're identifying with the individual mind. I'm talking about what you *are.* You see the radical challenge here? You say, "You don't know it all the time." The individual mind doesn't know it all the time because it clings to thought, because "all the time" is a thought that divides you from what is now. If there's no clinging to any story—any thought or concept of time—the mystery of what is occurring in this moment is revealed. When there's attachment to thought, the human being will spin a million stories, a million explanations as to why this is all happening.

Q: Oh, we do, we do.

D: Right, so see it arising as simply the play of your own consciousness. If you want to give it a point—and this is just a story, too—the point is that you forget in order to remember. It's for the joy of remembering. Remember we talked last time about how you can hit yourself over the head with a hammer for a while for the pleasure of it stopping. And so the one-being-that-is plays hide and seek with itself, it projects itself as the many for the joy of realizing its own oneness. So the one-as-many wakes up to itself. And the waking up is the realization that you are and always have been this undivided being, this consciousness that imagines itself into existence as all of us. What a relief. (Laughs).

Q: But if there isn't some validity to the sleeping consciousness, so to speak, then there could be no waking up. You see the duality is necessary in order to experience the realization.

D: Sure, that's right. The duality is created by the One as its own play. But you know that the duality is nothing. Ramana used to say that the sage sees only the Self in all things. It's not that you don't see form, but you see that this form is you, that all form is you, that there is always the unity, there's no separation there and that everything is the form of the one Self. If you see reality in everything, you don't buy the objectivity of separation. Separation is just a concept, duality is just a projection of the unity.

Q: Now, when you're in the silence, you know this.

D: Yes, knowing is here.

Q: Then you come back, as it were, then it has to be translated into a thought.

D: As soon as you conceptualize it, it becomes this separate thought, rather than the unconceptualized knowing. So that's why I say "be quiet" (laughs) and abide as consciousness. You know we talked about this analogy of the ocean giving birth to waves. So the ocean is consciousness. In its depths it is unmoving and unchanging, while on the surface it is moving and changing— those are individual thoughts. So live from the unchanging depth and allow the thoughts to arise. So we can tell our stories here. I can tell you this myth of consciousness and you can tell me this story about how humans have to go through growth, which is fine. There's nothing invalid about that, but abide as the consciousness that sees this as story and that dwells in the presence of freedom now, okay? That's all. And enjoy it. Everybody's got a story.

Q: And there's nothing wrong with that, it's just a way of trying to express that which is inexpressible and that's valid.

D: Yes, because in some sense, that's what we are, we are expressions of the inexpressible. Every word, every action, every gesture is an expression of the Self, yet no word can capture it or grasp it. And when we speak to each other, that's what we're sharing. That's what love is all about. We can talk about this being as consciousness or we could talk about it as love. God *is* love, not like God loves, but God is love itself. And so how does this formlessness be love? It expresses itself as multiplicity and bursts into form, it gives birth to itself as form and then it communes with itself through communication, which is satsang. And that's what this love is.

Q: It communes with itself through the form.

D: Yes, through form, because without the form, there's no communion.

Q: Well, there has to be expression, and the only expression is through the form.

D: Right, so that form is the way the formless expresses itself and then love is the way it relates to itself, so to speak.

Q: Also this form can distort the reality. Can it not?

D: You could say that all thought is a distortion of formless consciousness. But mind is only distortion if you're coming from attachment to thought. When you rest as awareness then it's not even distortion, it's just your own play. All of this is just the play of your own love.

∞ ∞ ∞ ∞ ∞ ∞ ∞ ∞ ∞ ∞

Q: How do you differentiate emptiness from nihilism?

D: Nihilism is a concept, and emptiness is freedom from all concepts, all thought, all interpretation.

Q: So it's freedom, it's beyond everything and nothing, to no concept at all, nothing.

D: Yes, it has no concept. Like, experientially, if you're here and you have no thought, you're not placing any interpretation on anything. What's here?

(Pause)

Because it only matters experientially. We can talk conceptually, and I'm happy to do that, but the proof is in the pudding of silence. Have no thought. Because in that emptiness, the mystery of reality is revealed. But it's not a concept. Whereas nihilism will have some definitional statements about "nothing exists" and "blah blah blah." But this is not that.

∞ ∞ ∞ ∞ ∞ ∞ ∞ ∞ ∞ ∞

Q: I am pretty foggy on how to regard the whole enchilada of reincarnation and ancestors, etc. What can you tell me that would be of help here?

D: I have never been attracted to theories of reincarnation and ancestor stuff, since in the nondual approach, it is like a fifth wheel—basically unnecessary to the direct realization of who you are here and now. I have had a few experiences that one might call "past lives" but I'm not very interested in them. In my own experience, and the teaching coming through Ramana Maharshi and my master Papaji, past lives may seem to happen, but they are just as illusory as this life. That is, all identification with a separate self—whether "this one" or in some past—is just attachment to the "I"-thought which sustains the experience that you are not the absolute now. The "past" is just mind, as is "future," which are projections of consciousness in this always-already now. So freedom is now, free of all identity and time. And the play of "lives," be it in the past or future, is just the play of consciousness. In this sense all "lives" are the same—call them real, call them illusory—it is all just one case after another of mistaken identity.

Past lives may be interesting, but to dwell on them keeps one bound to the wheel of birth and death. Who has the courage to see through the entire wheel, that is, to be nobody with no story? Or shall I say, you can enjoy the whole movie purely as story for the sheer entertainment of it without taking it seriously or getting sucked into it. With the price of movies these days going up, it is not a bad deal for a night out.

∞ ∞ ∞ ∞ ∞ ∞ ∞ ∞ ∞ ∞

Q: Sorry we have to leave satsang today.

D: If you don't make it a place or a time of day, you see you never leave satsang. Wherever you are is satsang. It is home. It is the unmoving space within which all movement takes place. You come to Ithaca, go to Corning, yet you never move, never go anywhere. You never leave home. Put no limit on satsang and you realize your limitlessness.

∞ ∞ ∞ ∞ ∞ ∞ ∞ ∞ ∞ ∞

PART THREE

AWAKENING
WITH PAPAJI

The word 'guru' means 'that which removes ignorance, that which dispels darkness'—the darkness of 'I am the body,' 'I am the mind,' 'I am the senses,' and 'I am the objects and manifestation'. That person who has known Truth himself and is able to impart this knowledge, that person who gives this experience, he is called 'guru'. —Papaji.

A real teacher has no teaching. He merely apprises you of the fact that you are no different from himself, the Self! You are already that! You are already free! What is there to teach? . . . The ultimate truth is that there is no teacher, no teaching and no student. —Papaji.

I have had many profound and influential teachers in my life, yet I considered none of them to be my guru until I met Sri H.L.W. Poonja (1910-1997) in India in 1992. I had no inkling of what the guru was all about until I came into the presence of this magnificent examplar of freedom who was in the no-nonsense business of igniting awakening in those around him. Known affectionately by his many students around the world as Poonjaji, or more intimately, as Papaji—literally, dear father—in his presence my true nature was self-evident.

Papaji's life was totally dedicated to being free and sharing freedom with all who sincerely wanted to know the Self. His message, in the tradition of the great *Advaita* (nondual) sages, was simple and direct: There is only the Self. You are that eternal mystery that is the source and essence of all. And being That, there can be no path to what you already are. In most spiritual lineages there is the complicit assumption by both teacher and student of the unenlightened dilemma that must be solved by teaching, practice, or movement toward a goal. In sharp contrast, Papaji pointed to the immediacy of the Self here and now. If there was any injunction at all, it was simply to be, to be aware, to be silent. In the silence of no-thought, your freedom is revealed. His fundamental teaching was "no teaching, no teacher, no student." The master demanded of those who came to him the courage to cut through all spiritual drama to the raw truth of our common identity. He offered an empty mirror in which to see yourself to be that same undivided emptiness prior to all individuality, thought or spiritual work. He didn't teach you anything, didn't give you anything new to believe or practice. Papaji insisted that any indication that you are not already the Self, and that you must somehow move toward it, did not come from the guru. This was just a subtle trap for both teachers and students to get caught in. As long as you held yourself to be a student and he a teacher, you did not know your own self-nature.

Papaji was not only awake himself, he had the extraordinary power to transmit that awareness to others. In his presence literally hundreds of people were given a taste of the silence of their true being. He demonstrated the purely functional definition of the guru as the awakener. No awakening, no guru. Some teachers are empowered by the Self to awaken others. They are the guru. Others may be realized, but without the power of transmission. Papaji himself said that grace had given him that power. "If the Self picks you out . . . " he noted, "it gives you all the power that you need to do the job. That power is like a powerful perfume that attracts people who are interested in freedom. When it has attracted you, it destroys you." The guru is above all the destroyer—the executioner of the individual self-sense—who plays whatever role is necessary to free you from that limited identification.

When I first heard of Papaji I was both attracted and resistant to that powerful perfume. After twenty years of spiritual practice and working on myself, I was fascinated and captivated by the prospect of freedom here and now. Yet I was also fearful of the uncontollable force that had begun to pull me into the unknown. The tension between my yearning for freedom and my fear of surrender, between my devotion to truth and my arrogant resistance to selflessness, played itself out through a series of dramatic ups and downs during five years of frequent visits with the master in India. In the midst of these intense fluctuations Papaji showed me the unchanging peace of the Self within and beyond all experience.

During that time of transformation, I entered the mystery of the guru—the guru both as a masterful human being and as a phenomenon of my own consciousness come to remind itself of its unconditioned being. I describe here specific episodes in my experience with Papaji that shed light on the process of awakening and how the master worked as a force of freedom. The guru's activity showed up in the details of our interactions, sometimes so seemingly ordinary, sometimes shattering all sense of what I thought was real. Papaji appeared in many guises: the loving, kind master, patient and affirming of my true nature; the ferocious slayer ruthlessly intolerant of any self-indulgence; and the impersonal presence indifferent to the whole drama. Each of these widely different forms was an appropriate response to who I thought I was, and a clear mirror reflecting the invisible truth of who I am. The words that follow only begin to convey my gratitude and praise for the guru.

Guru Prep

Everything is your guru: rocks teach you Silence, trees teach you compassion, and the breeze teaches you non-attachment. You can have many gurus and lecturers and psychologists, but the Satguru is One. —Papaji.

Although we ordinarily think of the guru as an enlightened individual or saint, the essence of the guru is best understood as a *function*, not a person. The guru-function is an activity of your own Self, the underlying source-reality which plays a game of hide and seek with itself for its own delight and entertainment. The guru is an expression of grace, a way that consciousness finds itself after hiding within its own manifestation. Having imagined yourself to be asleep, you then show up within your own dream as guru to awaken yourself from your individual slumber. The grace may begin with the stirrings of yearning for your own forgotten nature, which launches you on the search for self-realization. The search itself, the very desire for freedom, is the pull of the guru, the magnetic force within you calling you home. When the seeker is ready, the Self may manifest as an external guru—a projection of one's readiness and desire for one's own Self. The guru need not be a human being. It can take whatever form truth requires to arouse you and turn your attention to the Satguru within, your own being.

Before meeting Papaji I had my first glimmers of the guru through psychedelics in the 1960s. Drugs literally blew my mind. They opened me to a new world of experience that seemed radically different from ordinary awareness, yet was also an ancient, familiar reality I had always known. My experiences on pysilicibin mushrooms, peyote (mescaline), LSD and cannabis brought moments of peace and bliss, where the sense of separation disappeared and the boundary-less awareness beneath the surface of everyday mind was revealed. These were unmistakable tastes of an underlying reality that I never thereafter doubted, even after I came down into ordinary consciousness. During these trips I also had vivid flashes of what seemed to be past lives, of many years as an ascetic yogi meditating in caves in India and Tibet. While I considered myself an agnostic rationalist, and was not given to psychic phenomena, I could not invalidate the detailed visions that came during those trips.

Like so many others of my generation, drugs opened a new world of understanding and experience. They showed me the possibility of an ultimate fulfillment and self-realization in this life, and gave me the inspiration to pursue it. The trips became a sacred ritual, begun in meditation and filled with awe and thankfulness. They launched me deeper into a study of the spiritual literature and techniques that would allow me to experience that awareness without the ups and downs, and physical side effects, of drugs. As I read through the world wisdom literature I recognized my own experience in the descriptions of the mystics and sages. While I burned the psychedelic candle intensely at both ends through the '60s and early '70s, hallucinogens gradually became sporadic, occasional events into the '80s as my spiritual practice strengthened and my body could no longer handle the physical wear and tear of the stronger drugs.

For over two decades I sought to rediscover those transcendental experiences through intense spiritual and transformational work with a wide variety of teachers——yoga with Swami Satchidananda, meditation and spiritual community with Gil Locks, intensive Zen training with Joshu Sasaki Roshi, Vipassana retreats with S.N. Goenka, Joseph Goldstein and others, the est Training and advanced courses with Werner Erhard and his trainers. Throughout those years of practice I was visited occasionally by glimpses of nondual awareness, though nothing equaled the intensity of the psychedelic experiences.

Although I gained precious insights from my teachers, I considered none of them to be my guru. I stayed somewhat aloof and never quite gave myself fully to any of them or their teachings. I was especially attracted to teachers who said a guru was unnecessary, and to approaches that emphasized a kind of spiritual self-reliance. I believed I did not need a guru, meaning in my view at the time, someone to surrender to and follow, some one to put all one's faith in. So I admired J. Krishnamurti and Bhagawan Sree Rajneesh (Osho), and was drawn to the Zen and Vipassana meditation traditions that allowed for my iconoclastic leanings.

Yet behind the egalitarian façade lurked the demon of pride that would bow to no one. Democratic self-reliance masked a multitude of sins and generated the clouds of my self-deception. I had had a lifetime of stubbornness and arrogance. I was driven by the need to feel special and unique, fueled by a fear of being ordinary and getting caught in the quicksand of pedestrian existence. Spiritual life became the domain in which I sought to raise myself up and escape, adopting an elitist higher-than-thou stance that implied I had attained a certain spiritual understanding. I had also been a rebel much of the time, in resistance to my father and other authority figures. I would only accept authority if it had some power over me or I wanted something from it. Yet no matter how much I might protest that this was all an indication of my underlying independence and spiritual maturity, I also dimly suspected that it concealed the arrogance of the "I" itself and its dream of a separate identity. The refusal to surrrender to a guru sustained the painful sense of separation from my own Self. There was no way I was going to surrender until I realized what was truly in it for me.

The Pull to Papaji

You do not find a guru by running around the world, looking for one. You find him by having an intense desire for freedom. If that desire is there, then the guru will find you. —Papaji

"When the student is ready the master appears," an old saying in spiritual circles, is vividly demonstrated in how Papaji did, in fact, find me. My desire for a guru was first ignited in the late '80's when I read Nisargadatta Maharaj's *I Am That*, one of the great modern classics of the nondual teaching whose radical depths have touched a whole generation of spiritual seekers. I was taken by the majestic power of Nisargadatta's realization and his simple injunction that one need only focus awareness on one's own being to realize freedom. While that was fully consistent with my program of self-reliance, what caught my eye was how the sage's realization came swiftly as he faithfully followed the guidance of his guru:

"I was a simple man," Maharaj said, "but I trusted my guru. What he told me to do I did. He told me to concentrate on "I AM"—I did. I believed. I gave him my heart and soul, my entire attention and the whole of my spare time (I had to work hard to keep the family alive). As a result of faith and earnest application, I realized my self within three years."

This made a powerful impression on me and whipped up the flames of my yearning for freedom. Realize myself within three years! I was in a hurry, and it seemed so possible. Yet while I could see the role of the guru in one's realization, I was scared to come that close to the Self, to give myself to truth in such an intimate way. So in its unfathomable wisdom, the guru began to come to me.

In 1989-1990 my oldest and dearest friends began to tell me about a great master they had met in India. Sri H.W.L. Poonja, they wrote, taught that freedom is available here and now. There was no need to work on oneself or change your life in any way. Rather, simply see through the belief that you are someone engaged in practice or self-transformation, and wake up to who you really are. They noted that many people, including some of the leading western meditation teachers, were visiting Poonjaji, that he was already in his eighties, his health was not good, and that I would be foolish not to visit him while he was still alive. My friend enticingly told me me: "You could go all the way, or at least drop some considerable pounds" and urged me to consider visiting him in India. Their strong urgings brought up my inherent resistance and competitiveness. My stubborn streak resented people telling me what I should do, as if they knew more, were higher or closer to truth than I was. Yet as my resistance arose, the guru came to me from another side as well.

Throughout the 1980s I was meeting regularly with a perceptive spiritual astrologer for guidance on my work, relationships and spiritual life. Throughout the decade we had focused on self-reliance, working on myself through transformational disciplines, and developing my persona and effectiveness in my work and family. In 1989-90 he pointed out that the chart indicated clearly that it was time for me to have a devotional relationship with a teacher. He said the next few years would be a time of great spiritual renewal, of profound transformation of consciousness, personality, and way of life for me, and a very rare and propitious opportunity to be with the guru. The chart also revealed that my spiritual orientation was precisely the nondual *jnana* (wisdom) way of Papaji and his master, Sri Ramana Maharshi, whom I greatly admired. He said I should definitely consider going to India, which itself would be a spiritual retreat for me. I felt the same indignant resistance to this information that I did to my other friends. I was doing just fine on my own and the thought of an intimate relationship to a guru got my bristles up. Beneath the arrogance I definitely noted the subliminal fear of surrender.

By 1991, as the guru closed in on me pincers-like through my friends, I was beginning to realize that after two decades of spiritual practice, all my emphasis on transformation with its self-reliant focus on working on myself would no longer be necessary. I understood that freedom was beyond all individual effort and volitional activity, and that it was time to give up. Self-realization was intimately tied in my mind to surrender to a guru, whoever that was and whatever that meant. While the fear was still there, I began to relish the mysterious adventure of discovering the guru.

I had found David Godman's edition of the teachings of Sri Ramana Maharshi, one of India's greatest sages in the 20th century and a magnificent exemplar of the Advaita realization. I had always been attracted to Ramana since my first contact with him in a course on the spiritual philosophies of the East at Yale thirty years earlier. Since that time I had kept a copy of his teachings and felt a mysterious kinship with him. When I heard that Ramana was Papaji's guru, that Poonjaji had his full self-realization in the mid-1940s in the Maharshi's presence, I felt an inexplicable bonding with the two of them. On the cover of Godman's edition is an exquisite photo of Ramana with his tender, compassionate eyes penetrating directly into the viewer. I remember very clearly feeling the Maharshi's face begin to glow in the center of my chest. I also began to have dreams of Poonjaji, as if he were reassuring me, calling to me from within. I recognized that I could not do this by myself, that it was all out of my hands and I needed a teacher to pull me home. As I lay awake at night I prayed for the first time in a long time: Will my teacher please show up and guide me? Are you my teacher, Poonjaji? Come to me.

Sri Ramana Maharshi

At the same time I had heard of other Americans who had been with Papaji in India and were speaking and writing about their awakenings there. As I spoke with them and read their accounts I was deeply inspired by their experiences with the master and realized just how much I wanted that intimate relationship with a guru. Their moving stories became models that inspired me to begin writing my own notes on the process of awakening that eventually led me to Papaji.

I was encouraged to face the fear within me and trust that I could surrender fully to truth. At first the possibility of visiting Poonjaji in India brought up the worry that I would enter into some kind of slavish obedience to a master who would tell me to give everything up, and that I would do something impulsive. I didn't want to run off and drop everything, including my consulting and training work which I had worked so hard to develop into a successful business. I had tried a version of that in the '70's and saw no need to do it again. My friends had helped me to understand that my drive for material security and business success needed to be focused within, on the realization of the Self. While it was time to want freedom above all things, I was reassured that Papaji and Ramana taught that one need not make radical changes in one's life to be free. All that is required, they affirmed, was a shift in knowing who you are, regardless of the circumstances that you find yourself in.

I sensed that I had somehow entered the magnetic field of the guru. Life began to take on a movie-like quality in which I observed the whole process running on automatic. I began to feel a subtle gravitational pull so delicious and reassuring, as if an inner power were taking over. I felt totally taken care of, exhilarated, in love. I experienced something I can only call a rush of destiny, as if Papaji were pulling me home. All I needed to do was give in to this pull.

I was excited to hear the master had an extensive correspondence with many of his students. On September 21, 1991, I wrote him:

> Dear Poonjaji,
> Your devoted students. . . who are my dearest and oldest dharma friends, have shared your Being with me. I feel open to you and have a strong pull to come to India to see you in the last half of March and first days of April next year. I sense that this is a propitious time to re-establish my relationship with a true teacher—someone who can help me yield to the inner gravitational force that I feel is pulling me home to live awake as my True Self. Such a familiar, mysterious presence, so close and yet seemingly so far.
> I have been on this path consciously for at least twenty years, during which I have read many spiritual books, studied with different teachers in various traditions, and have had experiences of bliss, momentary awakenings and temporary dissolutions of mind/ego. Yet the mind is still strong, the sense of attachment to individuality still prevails, even though I feel the deepening of surrender and the greater presence of conscious witnessing of this impersonal, empty process. It has become clear that "I" cannot do this by "myself"—deep surrender and great trust are being demanded.

I asked if he could teach me to be awake in the midst of my life and work commitments as they were. I also mentioned that in the past I tried to be a spiritual teacher, but it obviously wasn't the right time, and suggested that perhaps my destiny would allow for that in the future.

To my astonishment, three weeks later I received Papaji's handwritten response of October 5:

You are invited to go here whenever you have convenience. Whenever the desire for freedom arises in a certain mind, it has to be given preference to be attended to right at the same moment, lest this flame may not at all show itself. That is the instant one has to dive within you to find out the Source of this Inner Consciousness. Ask a question to your Self: "Who Am I?" Hold on to the "I", look for, from where the "I" rises from. Proceed further, make no effort, don't carry alongside any intention, ideation or notion.

He reassured me unequivocally that there was no need to change my life routine; that realizing the Self would in fact transform my experience of my life. "First you will find your own Self and later you will find the Self seated in all beings. You have to find happiness by your Self and later you will be compelled to have compassion towards all beings. It is your nature spontaneously. You will love all beings." I needed quite a bit of reassurance that I could be awake and continue to master the everyday details of practical life. I was plagued by the notion that freedom meant being swept away into some realm of consciousness where I couldn't handle life, where my business would fall apart and I would stop earning money. My model here was mostly based on my drug experiences, especially the peak of acid trips that I identified with enlightenment, where I dissolved into transcendent bliss and couldn't hold anything together.

I now knew unquestionably that I *must* see Poonjaji, that he was my destiny. I knew that full commitment and surrender to living awake was what the trip to the guru was all about. As I made my travel arrangements I felt like I was walking the plank, going to my death.

In March 1992, on the quincentenary of Columbus' fateful voyage, I too headed to India. In meeting the guru face to face I also came upon a vast new world.

The Lion King

Guru sees only the Self. You are my very own Self. I am your very own Self. This relationship is no relationship. Your Self and my Self, what is the difference? I am speaking to that Self which you truly are. I am speaking to my Self. Others may be preachers from some sect, they may give you some dogma, but a guru gives you his own experience, and this experience is timeless consciousness, nothing else. Guru does not give you any teachings, any method, or anything that is destructible, impermanent. One who does this is not a guru. You are not to follow anyone. You are a lion, and where a lion goes, it cuts its own path. —Papaji.

When I met Papaji in March 1992 his life had changed radically. For the previous half-century, after his awakening with Ramana Maharshi at Ramanashram in the early 40's, he had been a loner, a peripatetic sage traveling from place to place throughout India, Europe, and the Americas. With the exception of some of his travels in Europe and the Americas where he might have larger attendances, he met mostly with small numbers of students in intimate, informal satsangs. Students would spend time with him, living in closed quarters, traveling together. Papaji didn't want large crowds, didn't want to be visible. If these conditions changed he might move away suddenly. He was opposed to settling down for long, owning property or setting up an ashram or any organization. He had no interest in a lineage of successors or some codified teaching. He was critical of the swamis in India who had large ashrams and charged money. He never expected payment for what he saw as the activity of grace itself. He told us many times that he vowed "never to lay a brick in the transit lounge," in the world of impermanence.

By 1991-1992 Papaji was in his early eighties and his various physical ailments, which made it difficult for him to travel, kept him grounded in Lucknow with an occasional railroad trip to Hardwar or Rishikesh to cool off during the brutally hot Indian summers. As some well-known western teachers began visiting him and magazine articles on him came out, word spread rapidly through the West of this great guru bestowing tastes of enlightenment. When I showed up there were at least 100-150 people—many of them westerners—attending his satsangs. Some of the older students, who had been accustomed to the small, intimate gatherings with very direct interactions with him, had already begun to grumble that the old days were over. Yet while the size of the gatherings may have expanded, the awesome silent power of the master had in no way diminished.

I was attracted to the fact that for Papaji everything was naturally integrated into everyday life. He didn't encourage us to separate from our daily existence to live in ashrams and caves or have a protected spiritual life apart from work, family and daily responsibilities. Papaji had no ashram, lived simply in a small, plain house, and met with his students in an ordinary neighborhood on the outskirts of the city. No idyllic rural ideal here. We all arrived at satsang on bicycles, motorcycles and scooters, in taxis or noisy, polluting tempos. It was a busy, dusty scene outside the satsang house with pigs rooting about noisily in the garbage and water buffalo lumbering down the road leaving steaming paddies in their wake.

The master's daily satsang—sitting, teaching, dialoguing, telling stories, joking with his students—could not have been more integrated in everyday life. As we spoke together, the din of honking traffic and street noise, laughing, shouting schoolchildren, vendors hawking their wares, and barking dogs were always in the background. There was nothing romantic or especially "holy" about it, yet after a short while everything became extraordinarily beautiful and sacred, bathed in silence. Papaji joked: "When you can see those pigs as God, as your own Self, then you're home." That was his gift, to reveal purity and freedom in the midst of what is.

There was a simplicity and ordinariness to Papaji's life. He would go to the market, personally examining the vegetables and picking out the best ones. He loved to take walks and feed the mangy, undernourished neighborhood dogs. He had the most contagious sense of humor, giggling often in satsang and breaking up the most solemn moments with laughter, puns, and his uncontainable happiness. His laughing jags that would have us all in hysterics openly shared the joke that you are already free. The great sage was also an impassioned sports fan, having been quite athletic in his youth. He especially loved the game of cricket and when there was an international match he might cancel satsang so he could watch it on TV. One rare day when we had all gathered in the satsang hall, the master arose from his white satin-like guru chair and had a TV set placed on it. Papaji sat down on the floor with all of us and announced we were going to watch cricket. When about half the people in the hall left, he turned to us who stayed and said impishly: "They think this isn't satsang!" For Papaji every day and everything was satsang. There was no division in his life and he invited all of us to share the undivided reality of freedom.

The message of this towering Indian Brahman was simple and direct: This is it, you are it. You are reality. You are truth itself, happiness, bliss, the ultimate mystery that can never be described. This is who you are here and now. Although the enigmatic nature of reality had been debated and argued for millenia in the Indian philosophical tradition, for Papaji it was quite simple and experiential: Just be quiet, face your Self and realize your being as eternal, limitless consciousness. In the silence the inconceivable mystery is revealed for what it is. Rather than discuss it philosophically, the master pointed directly to it, so that we might come upon it fresh and unmediated. Papaji continually joked about the impossibility of describing the mystery. He would sit up in front of the satsang hall and announce: "I have been waiting sixty years for someone to describe this. Would someone please come up and speak about it?" Papaji's life was a constant invitation, a challenge, a demand, to know oneself and to share that freely with others.

It was obvious that he taught purely for the purpose of our awakening here and now. He encouraged no dependence on himself or on any practice designed to attain some future goal. He uncompromisingly refused to indulge in any developmental thinking or tolerate evolutionary ways. There was no progress towards something. He said that he was here for those who have had enough of working on themselves and were willing to be free here and now. He was here to give the final push to the courageous ones, the ones who would be fully Self-reliant in the ultimate sense. You are an emperor, he told us, not a beggar. Don't come here begging—to guru or to God—for the treasure that you already have and are. You are home.

Papaji sat majestically in satsang like the great Lion King. Be a lion, he declared. The lion travels alone or in small prides. They roam where they will, unlike the sheep that obediently follow huge herds, being led to the slaughter by teachers and preachers. You must walk the trackless emptiness alone, cut your own path. He wanted us all to wake up and roar: "I am That!" He attracted those who made their own path, who didn't travel in herds. Many of the people drawn to Papaji were old hippies and others who had lived on the fringes of society or outside the law. He was not the master of those who sought rules to follow. He was here for those who had had enough of "do's and don'ts." He said he didn't give us anything to do or not to do. Freedom was beyond all boundaries, laws, rules, all roles and identities, even, ultimately, the most hallowed guru-disciple relationship.

His fundamental teaching was "no teaching, no teacher, no student." Who had the courage to see through all the spiritual drama to the raw truth? There is only the mystery itself, only consciousness, only freedom. In this there is no separation. As long as you held yourself as a student and he as a teacher, you were missing it, still caught in duality, caught in the spiritual circus. Hearing this I knew without a doubt he was my guru—delightful paradox!—the guru of this rebel, this loner who would never surrender to anyone. He was my very Self.

Many of his students were attracted to him as I was, precisely because his promise was freedom with no strings attached. His greatest joy was for you to realize yourself and return to your life and share it. He loved to tell stories about people who would come all the way from Japan or some far off land, sit with him for a few minutes, get it and leave. He was thrilled by that. He wanted you to know the absolute availability of truth and that once you've tasted it, it would take care of everything for you. Papaji was available to anyone who came up before him and sincerely called for freedom. I never saw him turn away a sincere seeker.

In his presence we knew what it was to be with the Buddha, to be with Christ. He embodied the mysterious guru tradition of the ancient Indian Vedic sages who sat in satsang with their pupils in the forest transmitting the Upanishadic wisdom. He was the very gift of grace, a massive blessing from reality. In his presence was a pure reflection of the Self, an empty mirror in which you could see your own true face.

In the Indian nondual guru tradition, going back over a millennium to the great interpreter of Vedic wisdom the Adi-Shankaracharya, the purpose of the teacher is to remove the ignorance of the student. The guru not only shares the transmission, the guru removes all doubt. All the disciple need do is follow the words of the guru. Papaji said faith in the guru's words was enough. In referring to the role Ramana played in his own realization, Papaji said: "That is the role of the true teacher: to show you and tell you that you are already That, and to do it in such an authoritative way, you never doubt his words." Papaji saw this as his main function as well: "To remove your doubt that you are not Brahman [the absolute reality] and by doing so to allow you to see who you really are."

Like his master Ramana before him, Papaji radiated a profound stillness that engulfed one. It is uncanny how hundreds of individuals were touched by this emptiness. Merely to be around him was enough. There was a gravitational field of silence surrounding him in which the mind stopped, and the silent mystery was realized to be one's own nature.

The definition of the guru as awakener was vividly manifested in the many remarkable awakenings of Papaji's students throughout the master's long career. In his biography, *Nothing Ever Happened*, David Godman painstakingly detailed Papaji's hands-on approach with his students and their marvelous stories of realization. Papaji was notorious for working on people with the full intent of transmitting the direct experience of Self. His longtime companion Meera described Papaji's guru function clearly:

"Master told me on several occasions that it was not his mission in life to have an ashram and be surrounded by hundreds of people. Instead, he had somehow been selected to give the final kick to seekers who were ready for a direct experience. The right people would be sent at the right time and master's 'inner voice' would simply direct him to the place where they were. Master did have an ashram, but it was an invisible one. It was not on any map, but those who had a desire for freedom would find that their footsteps would be directed towards it."

Papaji himself said that he had the power to awaken people. He claimed that the guru's words were sufficient to temporarily stop the mind, and if the student were attentive enough, committed enough, pure enough of heart, that would sustain the tranmission:

"When the guru, who is consciousness itself, speaks, there is a power in his words that can transmit an awareness of that consciousness to others."

'When you hear the word of truth directly from the mouth of a true guru, that word will directly enter the Heart of the one who is hearing it. This word from the guru will dissolve there and itself become the Heart of the listener."

"Here in satsang you have to listen to my words with full attention and full devotion. If you do, they will work, and if you don't, they won't. It's as simple as that. As you listen to my words, you have to keep your Heart open, not your ears. When the word is uttered it must enter your Heart, not your mind."

Papaji had discovered a secret method for fixing his gaze, staring into people's eyes to open their consciousness: "When I look into a person's eyes, my sight enters their Heart. When this gaze enters their Heart, their mind stops and they feel peace."

"When people sit in front of me, I pull their minds back into the Heart. I give them a seat within my Heart, and there I speak to them. This is not ordinary speech. It takes place on a different level. When I put people in this place and speak to them, their minds become quiet. They experience a profound peace, and become attached to this peace. When these people leave Lucknow, they take this peace with them wherever they go."

Papaji was also certain that this process did not take any time at all. Just a glance from him, just a few seconds in his presence, was enough: "A glance of the guru is compassion and removes the darkness of those who really want to be Free," Papaji declared. "In the proximity of the teacher it doesn't take time or practice. Instantly, light is here, like you touch the switch and the light is on. Only your honest and sincere dedication is needed." And again: "One satsang is quite enough, when you come with a definite purpose. If you have a burning desire for freedom, that is enough. It can happen immediately."

Papaji also knew that while many people might have a taste of eternity through him—lasting from a few moments to a few months or more—for most of them it dissipated because there were still thoughts and unfulfilled desires or mental tendencies (vasanas) to which people remained attached. He frequently said that all one needed to do was remain in peace—in the silence of no thought—but "people have other things on their minds." They are too attached to their dramas, too fascinated with their lives to abide as silence.

"I can give this direct experience to anyone for a short time, but it is not within my power to make the experience stay. One who has been granted this experience by the guru has to guard it himself till the end of his life."

"I found that although I could give people these experiences [silence, awareness of Self], I couldn't make them stick. When I stopped pushing, the mind just came back again. So now I don't do it anymore. I have come to realize that if the mind is not free from all vasanas, it will always reassert itself later."

Papaji gave up this intense practice sometime in the mid-90s, probably by 1994, at about the time his satsangs had swelled with many people and began to take on a more festive atmosphere with much singing and dancing. "No one can stand the silence of the guru," he noted. "The mind or the body is always looking for an excuse to run away from it. Here too, no one can sit in silence. That's why I ask some of the girls to sing and dance."

It was my great good fortune to arrive at the master's feet while he was still engaged in the intense practice of confronting his students verbally and actively transmitting consciousness of the Self. I was definitely calling for a kick-ass guru, and my beloved Papaji knew exactly how to do it.

One Gracious Stare

One gracious stare of the master is enough to remove the darkness of a billion years of shifting from womb to womb in the world process. —Papaji

Papaji offered me that grace in my first satsang with him in India, March 23, 1992. As I sat in the crowd, I experienced the master as a vast vacuum whose magnetic force was pulling me into itself. He told us we had been suffering for 35 million years and asked if we had had enough. I felt like he was speaking directly to me. Something collapsed within me and I felt the full weight of this truth. A silent "yes!" swelled up—yes, this is it, yes, it is all over. There was nothing whatsover to do to be the Self that is already free. I saw that even "surrender" was just the recognition that it is over, the release of the volitional effort to do something. Papaji was the most absolute reassurance that there was nothing whatsoever to be done but be what I am.

I went up and sat before him. Papaji was very friendly and welcoming, bantering with me about New York, where he had lived on one of his visits to the States. He was laughing and joking throughout the whole conversation. Sitting before him I asked him again, as I had in my letters, how I could live free and awake in the midst of a busy life. He laughed and said there was no problem with that, that I only needed to give him five seconds of my time here and now, a full five seconds without thinking or mental activity of any kind, and he would take me somewhere that would last a lifetime.

"Out of these five seconds," the master told me, "you are not to give anything to family or the world. Are you sure these five seconds belong to you? And let nobody trespass into these five seconds. Are you sure that you will be quite honest and not allow any trespass whatsoever it is? I will take you somewhere else in these five seconds, not only in a day, in a total span of eighty years. Just five seconds in a total human span of life. Eighty years is quite good, isn't it? I don't think anyone has any complaint, if you steal five seconds for you out of eighty years, isn't it? Now, these five seconds are yours. Are you going to spend it now?"

"Yes," I replied.

"Here and now?" he re-emphasized.

"Yes."

"Don't give these five seconds to anybody whatsoever, neither to past nor to future, okay?"

I paused, then asked if I could be "here and now" all the time. As soon as I asked that, I realized what a dumb question that was. Now is all there is.

Papaji laughed. "No, no just five seconds. I want you for entirely five seconds now."

"Right now," I got it.

"Yes, right now. Because you have come here now. Five seconds. Mind you, nothing should trespass into these five seconds. Start. I count. I will tell you where you are going. I have a stop watch. . . . (laughs) Tell me where your mind is going because I will see under your eyes what you are doing. I will know very well. And ask your questions. . . and don't waste time, you see. So you tell me, during this five seconds, my mind is going here and there. Tell me. You wanted time, I will [give] you the shortest time, five seconds in a span of eighty years . . . . This much time is needed for freedom, liberation. Just five seconds. I am very liberal to give you all this. I don't give that much time. Everybody knows. But I am very liberal because I lived in New York. You are very friendly to me (laughs)."

As I sat there silently he continued: "Don't allow any thought even to stir during this five seconds. Not even a thought should rise. Yes. Yes, that is the condition and I have to wait for five seconds and see your reaction."

Being very literal-minded, I took him at his word, and sat there quietly, staring for a while into his eyes. I could sense he was focusing intently on me with tremendous love, that he truly wanted me to get it. His gaze, fixed deep within me, was boring into me. I felt utterly open and receptive. As I closed my eyes I had no sense of anything happening.

After a few minutes he asked me what I was experiencing. I knew there was nothing I could say to describe this emptiness, and I told him: "I'm just sitting here." I felt a bit smug as I said it, as if I were giving some clever zen-like answer.

He got very stern and told me: "Wait, again. I told you . . . don't make a mistake. I will again tell you, you have to spend five seconds, and you used the word "I am staying here," isn't it? . . . I told you five seconds with no trespass of even "I am," you see? This "I" has not to arise during this five seconds. If five seconds is too much, I will reduce the time. . . . No thought should arise from anywhere, you see. Five seconds are going to be your own time. It should not belong to time at all. It should not belong to past or future, or even present, you see. That's all, five seconds. I call it."

I realized the radical nature of Papaji's demand—to give up all thought, all self-concept. I then sighed, closed my eyes and experienced silence, light shimmering in darkness, and a sense of bliss and deep peaceful wellbeing. After a few minutes he again asked what I experienced, and when I described it he said, laughingly:

"That's all, you've done well. You're an honest man (laughs). This is all. This is all you have to do. This is enough. This will recall you. You can't forget it so easily, I am very sure of it. All the rest you will forget or you must have forgotten. Your boyhood experiences, you must have forgotten. Your childhood experiences, you must have forgotten already. But this is going to stay with you, and this is going to help you all the time. And this is the only help where you can depend very safely. This is a raft (laughs) which will take you on the other side of miserable ocean. And you can only use this when you don't make any effort. It is here. So when you try to make effort, you will not see it. That is how it has happened. It was already there, but I only avoided your effort, no? (laughs). I avoided your relationships, and efforts, and thought process. And you sighed (laughs). You sighed only because I removed the thought process, thoughts, thinking, and effort, that's all. When you think, and make use of any effort, you don't see your self-nature. It is always, everywhere, there. The only way is to keep quiet and you are there. Keep quiet, simply keep quiet. Then it will reveal. You can't hold it. It has to reveal its revelation. It's revelation, not gain (laughs). It has to reveal when you are in love with it."

Papaji jokes most of the time, and I figured he was putting me on. There were no dramatic energy experiences, no psychedelic visions. The peace and wellbeing were familiar experiences I had had on retreats before. I was surprised that he kept insisting I had it. I was confused and uncertain about what was going on. It all seemed too simple, too easy. There must be more to it than this!

He then asked me if I had any questions for him. I asked him how I could run a business, be an active seminar leader and consultant and not think? I understood it intellectually, having read all those books about active non-action or effortless effort in my years of Zen training. I knew how to be quiet and surrendered in a meditation retreat (and even for a while afterwards), but not ongoingly in my job. Now it was time to live it. I asked the master how I could make decisions, phone calls, give seminars without thinking.

He said all the work comes from the abode of silence where I had just been. This is home, this is the Self, the source of all energy for work. All doing comes from that no-thought in which there is no individual "I" doing anything. If I were just quiet, I would see that the Self, the supreme power, is doing it all.

"Whenever you are doing work, you see, all the work you are going to do is coming from not-thinking only, you see . . . . And that you do not know, where this work, the power of work, is coming from, the instinct to work, the energy to work. I tell you, when you work, any kind of work, you need energy to work. . . . Do you know where the energy to work is coming from? Go back now to energy and you will see it is the same place you have been in this five seconds. Always, whatever you are doing. Now you will know. Before you did not know. Then if you know that is there, you will not be arrogant. It is the supreme power that is making use of me as an instrument. Then you are free. No bondage. You are free, and you will be always. You can live better in the household, better householder, better husband, better father, better friend. Only you have to know where it is coming from."

Papaji again asserted strongly that I had it and would not lose it: "So this you are not going to forget. I am very sure you can't forget it. It has a hold on you. Only one glimpse is enough, you see. You've got it. I'm sure you got it, no?"

By this time I was beginning to see through the ancient confusion. I saw that only doubt stood in the way, that there was some doubt saying that "I don't have it," and that was the only obstacle to recognizing the simplicity of my being here and now. Papaji must have seen that uncertainty because he kept pressing me, emphasizing that I had it, asking me if I was sure. I felt like he was playing with me, yet he was also deadly serious in inviting me home. How could I continue to deny it when this magnificent master was insisting that I had it? I gave in to the tremendous force of the guru and dove in. "I've got it," I declared, "And if you're sure, I'm sure." We all started laughing.

At first it felt like a forced declaration of faith, yet in the moment I said, "I got it," I felt a tremendous release. Exhilaration came up, happiness came bubbling up. There was a great sense of freedom. I really am free! The energy came up into my head and I felt stoned, giddy, stunned. He had demanded that I own it. In the face of the master's relentless insistence, I acknowledged it myself, which was like diving through the veil of doubt and confusion.

Papaji laughed heartedly: "If you are not sure, you tell me now. This is the time. Yes, strike when the iron is red."

By then I knew I had to seize this entirely. "Right, I'm sure."

Again, the master continued: "Now the iron is very red, and hammer is in my hand. Hammer is in my hand, iron is red, now I know where to strike."

"That's why I came," I told him.

"That's why you came (laughing). Give it a good shake!"

Totally open in his presence I offered myself fully: "Strike me."

"Good," he said. "Welcome."

In that brief encounter, perhaps thirty minutes on the clock, Papaji had done his work. He had opened up the space of truth and forcefully confronted my doubt, the two key functions of the guru. I felt the tremendous exhilaration of having been welcomed to my own Self. My body was trembling with energy, as if I were in shock. My mind was stunned in no-thought, yet bubbling with celebration of this new freedom. I had no idea what was going on. I didn't know what I had or what I had lost. I just felt free. Though I knew nothing, this nothing was everything. Silence, Papaji said, was the raft across the ocean of suffering. He told me that glimpse of stillness was everything. It was here and it would not go away, that it had a hold on me. All I needed to do was turn to it to realize that I am home. To be quiet, to make no effort, was the entire teaching.

During the next ten days, as I followed his simple advice to be quiet and turn within, a profound stillness revealed itself. It was literally deafening, as if I were underwater. All life was taking place in this all-pervading silence. Thoughts flittered in and out like faint echoes without disturbing the quiet. It was clear that there is no "I" separate from this, that I am this conscious emptiness within which all thought and experience arises and passes away. It felt like I had entered a sacred realm and was being given everything I needed by my beloved master.

In the Guru's Web

[The guru's] function is to tell you, "I am within you," and to give you the conviction that you are Existence-Consciousness-Bliss. . . . Every True Teacher tells you: "look within, there is no difference between yourself, Self, and guru. —Papaji.

Somehow, Papaji had awakened me to being-awareness, and my devotion and gratitude were overflowing. I felt completely at home with the master, tingling as if I were with a new lover. I wrote him frequent love notes: "My mind flip flops between the bliss of silent no-thought, and sweet thoughts of you, Papaji. I am so in love. The Self is Love."

As the days passed Papaji continued to play the role of the dispeller of doubt. Though the silence was vividly real, my need for reassurance was still strong, fueled by old, romantic expectations I had of the nature of "enlightenment." I had come to expect a dramatic occurrence similar to my psychedelic experiences, filled with light and visions and carried off to a world of blissful trancendence in which I would be incapacitated for everyday activity. By contrast, the simple silent awareness filling me in Lucknow was way too ordinary. Every once in a while a question would arise: Is this really it? Will this go away? As the subtle flickers of doubt arose, I kept turning to Papaji for affirmation.

I took full advantage of Papaji's gracious hospitality to his students by spending much time in his house. One day we sat at his table alone having tea and cookies and spoke at length together intimately. I was honored and grateful for the friendship he extended, treating me so familiarly, and patiently reassuring me. He told me this would be my opportunity to clear up any doubts once and for all, that I should ask him all my questions and express any concerns so that he could deal with them. And in response to my questions he affirmed: There was no need to grow or to be healed in any way. There was no development or purification, no advancement by stages toward some imagined goal, no levels of consciousness. He strongly emphasized that all sense of progress or levels or stages of attainment were just more mind, all of it illusorily projected on the Self here and now. In the master's presence I felt a total reassurance that there was no need for any effort at all. This is it, he reiterated, it is all done.

We also discussed my suspicion that I was part of an invisible lineage. I mentioned how I had felt that Papaji and his guru Ramana Maharshi were somehow merged within me. I asked the master if he were Ramana, if there were any difference between them. He said they were the same, that there is only one Self, only one guru. I drew on paper a set of concentric circles, with my name in the smallest circle in the middle, surrounded by expanding rings marked Papaji, Ramana, Shiva and the formless Self at the outermost edge. I included Shiva, one of the primary Hindu deities and a representation of nondual consciousness, since I had had many intimations of Shiva within me during the 1980s and had learned that my astrological sign, Taurus, represented Shiva in the chart. Also, Arunachala, the mountain that Ramana lived on or near his entire life and that he worshipped as his guru, was considered to be a manifestation of Shiva. Papaji confirmed the drawing of the lineage, and said that there was no difference between them. However, he reversed the names on the rings, putting the Self in the center and "Let" (as I had called myself at the time) on the outer rim. I didn't catch it at the time but it was the beginning of Papaji's subtle warnings of my still unconscious tendency to dramatize my experience and put myself in the center.

I was so exhilarated, after our tea I wrote Papaji:

> You offer a gift I already have.
> You are the truest of friends!
> I awaken from the dream that never was.
> Here's the deal: an "I" for an "eye" makes a seer.
> A small price to pay for eternal Freedom.
> The eye of Awareness devours its-self and is never hungry.
> The only diet (duet, do-it!) that works.
> A truly effective spiritual weight-loss program.

My friends had told me I might drop a few pounds. As the days progressed I felt as if I had been released from the force of gravity itself, my body was so light and spacious. While Papaji's grace was the key element, Indian food also had its effect.

The next day I went to downtown Lucknow with a student very close to Papaji who was an old India hand. I was impressed that he not only hung out with the master, he also chewed pan with him. Pan is the red beetle nut concoction Indians chew that stains their teeth and sidewalks crimson. He was very helpful in explaining Papaji's severe nondual approach. At one point when I began to describe "my way," he said sharply, "no way," an insight that penetrated deeply and I saw again clearly that no one was going anywhere. A longtime Buddhist practitioner, he also quoted the *Heart Sutra*: "Form is emptiness, emptiness is form." While I had known that intellectually for many years, this wisdom incarnated for me as the day progressed. He took me to a funky Nepalese restaurant where we had chicken that looked like it had died of starvation—mistake number one. Then we went to a filthy chai shop for tea and my favorite dessert, *gulab jamun*, which was delicious, though covered with huge, insistent flies—mistake number two. Then he bought me a chaw of pan. Despite his warning, I swallowed some juice, and immediately felt movement in the bowels and got terrible diarrhea, which lasted into the next day.

Up most of the night, I was visited by a simple, penetrating awareness, which I tried to put into words in a letter to Papaji. I saw how I had been identified with the stream of mindbody experience—thoughts, feelings, body, actions—that I usually called "myself." Yet here it dawned so clearly that I am the awareness that sees all of this. This wakeful context—spacious, intangible, untouchable—is not bound or affected in any way by the thoughts or experiences that arise within it. This is home. It is only a dream of mind that one is not home. It was like you are in your own bed, dreaming you are lost and trying to find your way home. When you wake up you see that you have always been home, just dreaming in your bed. What a relief! In this emptiness there is no one in bondage and no one to be liberated. There is no God or world. Everything is just the play of imagination, all arising within the matrix of pure potentiality. "Nothing is happening," I wrote Papaji, "nothing has ever happened, nothing ever will happen."

I intended to give the letter to Papaji after satsang the next morning. I wanted to keep it private, and not follow his usual custom of reading letters out loud in front of the whole satsang. I was a bit intimidated by the boldness of the insights, and hoped to discuss it with him in private. I had written "not for satsang," on the envelope that the satsang managers had suggested earlier that I do if I wanted him to look at it later.

Near the end of satsang Papaji caught my eye and asked me if there was anything I wanted to talk about. We chatted some about the States, our mutual friends there, and how happy he was about my work supporting people in organizations. I felt so warm and acknowledged. It seemed as if he were expecting me to share something with him, so I told him I had a letter for him, but it wasn't for satsang. He said he had no private life at all and that it was all satsang for him. With a devilish glint in his eye he said he wouldn't read "not for satsang" letters, that they were all garbage, and would be deposited in the "DLO" (dead letter office). He definitely seemed to be playing with me, and I began to suspect I was a puppet in the guru's hands. I sheepishly asked him to read the letter now in front of all the people. He seemed pleased, with a knowing look of mock innocence as if he had maneuvered the whole scene and knew exactly what was coming.

Papaji read the letter aloud and called it a "faultless description" for which he had no comment. "This makes me very happy," he told me. "Somehow, you have tickled my heart." He emphasized the part about "nothing has ever existed, nothing will ever exist." He said it was a secret so sacred that he didn't even speak about it, and told me not even to use the word "enlightenment" to describe it. Most teachers, he said, just talk about bondage and freedom, ignorance and enlightenment, not what is beyond all of it. He said he knew of only three sages who had had that experience, one of them was so old he couldn't name him, but that I would know who he meant.

Years later, when I read Gaudapada's commentary (*"Karika"*) on the *Mandukya Upanishad*, I felt an immediate kinship with him and realized that Papaji was probably referring to him in this scene. Gaudapada, an Indian sage who wrote and taught around 500 AD, is considered to be one of the formative teachers of the Advaita Vedanta tradition. His profound interpretations of the Vedic wisdom influenced the first Shankara who systematized and revitalized that approach some two hundred years later. Gaudapada was uncompromising in his insistence on the illusory nature of the world and the *ajata* (non-creation) principle that "nothing has ever been born and nothing has ever died." This was precisely the stand Papaji had come to, and while he rarely spoke of it in satsang, it was his "ultimate truth" which he emphasized in his private interviews with David Godman for his biography. In the book David pointed out that Papaji was in full agreement with Gaudapada, and considered Ramana and himself to be in his lineage.

I was stunned speechless by the master's response to my letter, and wondered if he were just given to dramatic hyperbole. Obviously more than three people have had this realization. Perhaps he was just playing with me, as of course he was always doing with everyone. Still, I basked in his affirmation. It was so important to me to have my experience confirmed by the guru, who, for whatever reason, was fulfilling my desire to be unique and special beyond my fondest dreams. A few days earlier Papaji had mentioned that sometimes God would fulfill a desire just so you could enjoy it and let go. Here he was offering the pedestal I had always yearned for. He congratulated me in front of the whole satsang, had me sit next to him, and held my hand throughout the rest of the session. He invited me to come to his house that afternoon to discuss where I had found this "booty," this precious treasure.

I told him I felt like he had done it all, that he had gone fishing for me and pulled me all the way to India. I had fallen into the guru's net and the whole play had been orchestrated by him. Papaji laughed and said, "I have very good friends in New York and Brooklyn." He had the look of a cat that had just swallowed the canary, a playful look of puckish accomplishment. I could see that he was teasing me, that it was all a joke to him, that there was really nothing he said or did that I could hold on to.

I sensed the deeper, invisible reality of how the guru had attracted me home. I saw the whole network of people leading me to him, and how all of that—my friends' urging, the astrology readings—were the surface manifestations of the inner Guru operating. I was indeed drawn to him, as if he had pulled all the strings, like a magnificent Wizard of Oz of freedom.

After satsang we rode together in the van to have lunch at his house. As we sat down to eat I told him I had diarrhea and was concerned about eating. He said adamantly, "At my table everyone eats." I still resisted. He asked me if I wanted my diarrhea to be over. When I said yes, he replied matter-of-factly, "It's over, eat anything you want." I did, and the diarrhea was gone immediately and never came back. What a slam-dunk! I was awed by the guru's power.

After lunch we sat in his bedroom alone and he asked me how I came to know the secret and where it came from. I told him that it didn't come from anywhere, that in silence the knowing just is. He told me: "This freedom will continue. You will do your work." He then abruptly dismissed me and sent me back to my hotel. I was a bit disoriented, expecting more conversation. The people in his household told me everything changes quite suddenly around Papaji. The guru's words reverberated within me: This freedom will continue. I will do my work.

On the way back to the palatial Hotel Carlton, I looked out the window of the tempo—one of those noisy, polluting motor scooter jitneys that fill the streets of Lucknow—and experienced a deep peace, untouched by the noise, pollution and chaotic rush-hour traffic. The sutras kept chanting: form is emptiness, emptiness is form. I could see all the people and that hectic Indian city arising like a mirage in the midst of vast emptiness. The next morning I wrote:

A poem for you Papaji, upon awakening this morning:

> So simple and ordinary,
> Both presence and absence.
> Form is emptiness, emptiness is form.
> Great peace deeper than life itself:
> Nothing can compare to this!

> The mandala of form floats in the space of Being.
> Taking a tempo (chariot of time) through the streets of
> Lucknow back to the Carlton,
> Where has all the noise and pollution gone?
> As No-One rides home to the Emperor's palace.

At satsang the next day Papaji read the poem and emphasized the balance of emptiness and form, absence and presence. Some of us are attached to form, caught up in the world. Others are attached to emptiness, caught in seeking to de-manifest and avoiding life experience. It is all of the above: nothing and something, absence and presence. Hold no position; embrace it all. The Self is both, and neither, and beyond.

On my last morning in India I awoke to gentle, floating bliss, to Papaji's shining presence and reassurance saying: yes it is all done, yes this freedom continues. Yet flickers of doubt came and went that it would disappear. At Papaji's house to say goodbye, we stood together in his garden just before departing. As I anticipated leaving him and returning to my busy life in the States, my concerns arose that this consciousness would go away. I can remember the compassionate look he gave me when I foolishly asked him how I could hold on to this freedom. "Don't try," he replied. "Make no effort. There is no holding onto it." He put his arm around my shoulder and said he would write to me. "I'm very happy with you," he said reassuringly. "You'll see."

My Master, My Father, My Self

Because you do not understand the language of the Self, the Satguru manifests as the outer guru. If you think you have a body, you need a Teacher with one. —Papaji.

Those precious moments with the master revealed to me the magnificent, inexplicable mystery of the guru. As I got close to Papaji I sensed his transparency and saw through his form to the emptiness within and beyond him. It was as if everything we usually call physical reality is just an appearance projected in an intangible immensity. His physical presence was an open doorway—like a black hole—to an infinite emptiness in which nothing or no one could exist. No one could make it through that opening. To pass through was to disappear, to realize that you are that immensity itself. In this vast stillness neither student nor master exist. They are both seen to be transparent forms of the only Self, the one Satguru, indweller and essence of all.

I began to live the joyful enigma of the master-disciple relationship. On the one hand, I felt so close to the unique individual form called Papaji. I was swept by waves of gratitude to him for the gift of awakening. At the same time I realized that no one was giving anything to anyone.

It's no accident that most of his students call him Papa or Papaji—literally, dear father. Soon after meeting him I began to sense that Papaji was my real father. It was very clear that in the movie of relative appearances, he engendered my awakening. He fathered me. Not only that, on a number of occasions in satsang I had the unnerving experience of seeing my biological father's facial expressions in Papaji's face when he looked at me. There was no mistaking how he held his mouth in a kind of knowing smirk with one corner turned down. I immediately felt that I was in the presence of my spiritual father. I felt completely safe and trusted him as a son in his father's embrace.

I was drawn even closer to Papaji as my guru when I discovered that he had continued to work for a living to support his family after his realization in the mid-1940s. I was inspired that Papaji continued to function effectively in his work down to the most minute, practical details, working in business and as a mining manager with responsibility for production quotas, delivery times, and a large payroll of mine workers whom he managed. Like Ramana before him, he didn't counsel seekers to leave their work and explicitly insisted that no such change in living conditions was required for realization. One need only abide in silence, or inquire "Who works?" to see through the illusion of doership to the Self doing all the work.

In verbal conversations and subsequent letters, Papaji told me how pleased he was that I was helping people in the workplace. Ironically, when he asked if there was anything he could do for me, and I asked him to support my work, he replied somewhat tersely: "I'm not going to give you a certificate." As I came to realize later, Papaji's support of my work was much more intangible and powerful than that.

Entering the Stream

The Teacher will not be recognized by the diamonds on his head or by the number of students he has. Know the Teacher to be the One whose presence gives you Peace. —Papaji

Ten days in Lucknow with the master had parted the clouds of mind to reveal an inner expanse of peace. At first I thought that the silence was just another experience that came and went. But as I turned more fully to it, it became clear that this stillness was the unchanging context in which all thought, identity and experience—everything that I used to think I was—arose and disappeared. This peace, this emptiness itself was my true self-nature.

It is so difficult to describe this awakening because it involved everything all at once. A threshold had been crossed in which I could no longer take the separate "I" as real. The crucial shift in consciousness was from thinking that I was an individual seeking an experience of enlightenment to realizing that I am the presence itself that was already home. The I-thought continued to come and go, yet it was obvious there was no permanent or independent reality to this "I." The sense of being a separate, individual identity was seen for what it is—a constellation of tendencies in space that only *seemed* to have shape and substance. There is no actual big dipper in the sky, merely some lights that the imagination connects into an illusory pattern. There was really no egoic subject here, only the stream of mental patterns occurring in space, and this space is home.

The joke was obvious: there was no one who was unenlightened, there was no one who got enlightened. All those concepts—bondage and freedom, ignorance and enlightenment—were just the play of consciousness. It is all the imagination of the Self. The whole bodymind process—indeed, the entire world of manifestation—is only an appearance in, or modification of, this all-pervading source consciousness which is apparently giving birth to waves of thought, feeling, experience, action. Tendencies and momentary identifications arose, the whole gamut of human experience continued to happen, yet it was not happening to anyone and none of it had staying power.

My experience of time changed radically. I found myself living in a timeless now that has "continued" until this very moment. Days come and go without any sense of time passing. While the clock continues to move, memory and anticipation still operate, planning and scheduling go on as usual, the work gets done, programs and meetings occur, yet it is all just happening on its own in a mysterious process unfolding now.

For the first three months of my awakening the underlying essence of my daily experience was a simple quiet joy and wellbeing. Emotions and sensations, ecstatic moments of transcendence and bliss, would come and go, dissipating back into the peace that remained beneath the surface. There was a sense of spaciousness in my body. Without the gravity of strong ego identification, the ease and lightness of physical experience was exhilarating. I was amazed at how Papaji's simple assurances were so accurate. The Self really was doing it all. In the silence of no-thought I witnessed life happening effortlessly on automatic.

Guru's grace had swept me into the unknown. I definitely had no idea what I was getting into. Any expectations that it was going to be all peace and joy, however, were soon punctured.

Dance of the Vasanas

Only when you possess or attain something does the concept and fear of losing it arise. Only Self can not be lost.. . . . This 'losing' starts from the ego wanting to be the 'doer' and wanting to proudly own Freedom.. . . So do not achieve anything, just get rid of all the notions that have been dumped on you for lifetimes. —Papaji.

The Beloved will not leave you, even if you see this Beauty for only a second. It is the mind that carries this fear and tension, but it is not true. Don't worry, IT will have a permanent hold on you. You think you have lost it, but it is not lost. If you have this glimpse for only one moment it is finished, but if you put your attachments over it you can't see it even though it is still there. —Papaji.

It was a well-known pattern among Papaji's students to have an intense taste of the Self in the master's presence, and then to "lose" it in varying degrees, especially if one left Lucknow. Papaji often pointed out that when the space of freedom is opened up, all the vasanas—ancient tendencies of mind, conditioned patterns, desires, fears, attachments of all kinds—invariably arise to be seen and then leave you. If one identifies with or attaches to them, the momentum of ignorance and habit pulls consciousness back to the old patterns and the suffering ego drama begins all over again.

Papaji gave clear warnings and guidance on being with this eruption of tendencies: "The avalanche of vasanas which may happen as you approach the summit is notions, intentions and ideations. . . . Hidden tendencies arise to leave when you are quiet so it is a good sign when vasanas arise. Do not be dismayed because they are Self. Let vasanas arise, they do not exist. . . . They are transient imaginations, and even the "I" to which they occur is imagination itself. Abide as substratum and allow circumstances to come and go. Stay quiet with no intention or notion, not even to inquire for freedom, and don't utter the word "I". Then the gods and demons of the vasanas will vanish."

Within a few months after meeting Papaji my vasanas arose with a vengeance. While for the most part I rested as blissful silent awareness, I was periodically visited by intense storms of doubt, worry, fear, desire, arrogance, and confusion. These were familiar conditioned patterns I had experienced throughout my life that I had previously considered integral aspects of "myself." Now, although they were taking place within me, I saw them as just tendencies streaking across the sky of consciousness like shooting stars. They would flare up with great intensity and then disappear into the endless night. When they were here they could be quite powerful. When they were gone it was as if they didn't exist. I seemed to have no control over the weather. Most days were clear, some days cloudy, a few were stormy. Every once in a while I felt thrust onto a roller coaster of experience, in which the ecstatic highs were so spectacular that any departure felt like a crash.

The fleeting doubts I experienced in Lucknow continued to come and go. Thoughts like "I will lose this" or "This will all go away" occasionally buzzed like annoying mosquitoes in consciousness. I realized that my fear of losing it in one form or another had underlay my whole life. I had experienced it in the past as the anxiety of not succeeding, not making it, not getting the work done, not getting to places on time, all driven by the fear that something would go wrong and cut me off or take me away from it. I now saw how this doubt comes from the intuition that the "I" has separated from source and is trying to get back. It has turned its face from its Self, like a ray of light turning away from the sun, looking into the darkness, feeling like it has to generate its own light and seeing that it is fading. In the wake of my awakening in Lucknow, this doubt arose very clearly as the fear of falling from the peace and bliss of the Self and coming back down into suffering. Doubt took on a kind of imposter complex, the belief that I hadn't really made it at all, that it was all a sham and I was just deluding myself. This thought would arise in the midst of the realization and take over my consciousness, clouding the knowing with doubt.

My most vulnerable times were in the early mornings. I would sometimes wake up filled with anxiety and the fear of losing it, trying to hold on, trying to remember what freedom was. In those moments I turned to Papaji for dear life. I wrote him fervent, passionate letters, pleading with him to confirm me, to reassure me again. I would focus on Papaji's reminder to be quiet and relax. I could hear his reassuring voice: "You are the emperor, you are this treasure. Do not try to hold it." I could see the beggar mind trying to hold on and to remember all his warnings about not clinging to bliss, peace, or the unmanifest. Then I would remember: there is nothing to remember! All feelings and thoughts are okay. The manifestation is also okay. The truth is still the truth. Trust Papaji. Then the worry would pass, and the emptiness would be revealed once again, as if the clouds parted to show the sky is still here. I had never left, no matter what the experience seemed!

It was obvious that attachment to the highs created the lows. I would attach to bliss, to peace, to disappearing into emptiness. Then whenever ordinary experience would arise, I would interpret that as loss of Self. Self, of course, cannot be lost because it is not an experience of any kind. Rather, it is the context in which all experience takes place. Yet I would forget this and get swept away until it became clear that all experience takes place within the emptiness that is always here. Experience is not a measure of being the Self. I got it that even if I "lose" it, I'm still It, that everything comes and goes, bliss comes and goes, confusion comes and goes, forgetting and remembering come and go, and presence is still here.

Papaji often reminded us that only purity of heart and total vigilance—a continual abiding as silent awareness—would keep one from getting stuck all over again. In each moment there is the opportunity to get involved in the tendency or simply allow it to come and go and keep focus on the Self. A thousand times a day I was faced with this simple choice.

I followed the two methods Papaji and Ramana regularly counseled: silence and inquiry. When thought arose I would simply let it go and return to the quiet. Thoughts of all kinds continued to come and go. At first I was concerned it was a disruption of silence. As it continued I realized that even when thought is here, it is just a projection of the source consciousness, so that there is really no obstruction to freedom. Silence is always here. It is the space between the thoughts as well as the emptiness within the thought.

Other times, I would inquire, "To whom is this thought occurring?" and immediately the thought would fall away and the underlying selflessness was evident. Nothing was happening to anybody. When fear or doubt came, it was followed by the self-inquiry that asks: "What will go away from whom?" Instantly, the empty peace revealed itself. Inquiry arose naturally and spontaneously, as if it were doing it by itself. It was as if the magnetic power of the Self would not allow consciousness to wander too far into the "I" drama. By continually recalling awareness to itself, the subject-object split dissolves into conscious presence. I was amazed at the simple power of this approach, that no matter how active thought was, the clarity was always available beneath the surface.

All of these tendencies were variations of what Papaji called arrogance, which is the attachment to the "I" and its claims of independent existence and doership. The ego seeks to reassert itself by claiming freedom for itself and proclaiming its own enlightenment which is then reduced to a concept, a possession of the "I" which thinks it has attained some "enlightened state." This attainment itself becomes the illusion and the trap—a counterfeit freedom. Once realization is made into an object that has been attained, doubt and fear of loss inevitably arise. When claims of enlightenment arose, they were followed by the inquiry: "Who is enlightened?" and then came the knowing that there was no one to claim any state, nothing to hold on to, nothing to lose.

Because the energy I was experiencing was so powerful, because the bliss was so intense, any holding became extremely uncomfortable. It often had the familiar feel of a bad acid trip in which the energy would take me over even as I would be witnessing the experience. There were automatic, unconscious patterns of grasping and contracting that arose and seemingly sought to recreate themselves. The holding arose in the stomach, began to form a contraction or knot of energy. When there was holding or desire, the "I" reappeared. I saw that any identification with experience sustains the I-thought and creates suffering. By breathing, relaxing, simply allowing the sensation to be, it dissolved back into the peace. Waves of confusion would arise and often make me so dizzy I would have to lie on the floor until they dissolved. They would pass as quickly as they came and then exhilaration would return. My nervous system felt like an instrument being played by some manic-depressive musician. I could see how strongly these patterns sought to re-establish themselves, as if they were living out some inherent momentum to exist.

Yet no matter how overwhelming the experience, it could not fully blow away the underlying silence. Even my allergies, which had devastated me in the past, could not overwhelm the Self. As I wrote to Papaji in June '92: "The Joy and Peace are almost constant, no matter what else is happening. I had a severe allergy attack last week, much sneezing, itchy eyes, runny nose, very tired and sleepy, and even in the midst of all of that, the remembrance of being *Sat-chit-ananda* [being-consciousness-bliss] kept bubbling up. The body/mind was miserable, and yet I am free and blissful. So odd! "

It was odd to know who I am and yet still be swept by the whole range of human experience. I would get blinded by the hope of an ultimate purity, and tried to identify with some permanent emptiness in which no experience existed. It took me a while to get how it all came together so paradoxically. Yes, emptiness exists, and yes, experience arises within it. It was all seen to be happening without an experiencer—all of it just energy flow, streams of consciousness. Intense experience might momentarily take me over, then pass. Over and over again the peace returned, like a gentle snow fall on a moonlit night that blankets everything in stillness.

Explosion of Devotion

Find out how you can devote your mind and your physical activity to the Satguru twenty-four hours a day. Then there is no chance of any thought disturbing you. Prayer and devotion is better than keeping the mind quiet because the mind troubles you more when you try to keep it quiet. Let it run to the Lotus Feet of the Teacher. —Papaji

A great wave of devotion to Papaji surged up in me after my return to the States. I was intoxicated with the awakening that I saw as a gift from the guru. My letters overflowed with gratitude: "We are One, dear Papa, One Self, One Light, One Consciousness, One Joyful Blissful Love. Thank you from the depths of my Heart for your overwhelming Grace. Reveal your will. My joy is to serve. Such a sweet joy to be alive. So much gratitude to you, beloved Papaji. What did I do to deserve this?"

I felt Papaji's presence and invoked him often, whether in times of gratitude or intense doubt and worry when I called to him for reassurance. My love flowed in tears of joy, meditating on him, and sensing his presence near me. It opened the floodgates of devotion within me.

Papaji himself loved the devotional (*bhakti*) approach. For many years, before he awakened with Ramana, his spiritual practice had been singing to and meditating on Krishna. Even after his realization of the nondual reality, Papaji kept a soft place in his heart for the devotional play of lover and beloved. Like so many other Indian sages, he knew that the apparent division into such roles was just the One seeming to divide for the sheer joy of loving itself and recognizing over and over again its prior, undivided unity. When I met him Papaji still welcomed devotional expression. He loved the chanting and devotional songs, and in his satsangs in '93 and afterwards there were more times of singing and dancing.

"When I look at people singing and dancing before me in satsang," Papaji revealed in his biography, "I don't just listen to their words or look at the movements. I look to see where the singing and dancing are coming from. If the words and movements come from the mind, then to me it looks and sounds ugly, even if the person performing is a skilled, accomplished professional. But if the singing and dancing come from the Heart, from the place of no-thought, then the performance is always beautiful to me, even if the singer is out of tune or the dancer clumsy."

I too had the bhakti spirit, having spent many years singing to the Beloved. The wellspring of devotion had first been tapped at the Yea God family in early '70s, where we would sing for hours in love and praise of God. Later my devotional streak had been submerged in Zen and Vipassana training and the Advaita approach, but it came up from time to time in communal gatherings in the '80s.

In Lucknow I had wanted to sing to Papaji, but was too intimidated or self-conscious to do so in front of the satsang. A few weeks after my return to the States I could no longer contain the bursting of my heart and poured out my love to him in an audio tape of devotional songs and bhajans. I was so in love and swept away in devotion for Papaji. I had no idea of the impact the tape would have.

Almost a month later a friend from Lucknow left a message on my answering machine telling me that Papaji was singing and dancing again. I was thrilled and vaguely wondered if my tape had something to do with it. Shortly after that, I received Papaji's letter of April 25, 1992, describing how he had played my tape in satsang:

> Dear Let,
>   Let there be Let,
>   and there is Let.
> Today's Satsang is Let Satsang. I read your letter and later played the tape of your recorded song. Everyone went MAD & DRUNK and asked for photostat copies, that I did at once to be distributed tomorrow. How have I enjoyed both Let and letter. I just kept quiet and later 3 people came after satsang to tell me that your physical form disappeared, only there was holiness of Light. I could not speak a word & returned quietly into the room. Having met Let my heart is now content who wanted someone to speak about unspoken, unknown, unheard of love. . . .
>
> A copy of your letter is being sent throughout the world, to the people who have known the Secret, ever known to all Beings.

I was stunned by the impact of the tape, and deeply thrilled that the master and others were so touched by it. It fed my deep need for adulation and affirmation that seemed to keep surfacing no matter how much acknowledgment I was receiving. Still, as much as I wanted it, it was almost too much for me to accept how deeply Papaji had received my love. I wrote back:

> My Beloved Self, My True Being. I was thrilled to hear you enjoyed my letter and tape of love songs to you, and that you shared them in satsang. I want the entire universe to know of my devotion to the One Truth that we are. This Great Love is uncontainable and demands to be shared. Dear Papaji, you are my master, my Heart, my very Self. Let us be One forever. Hold me to you. Let me do your will. Let my teaching unfold to reach those it is meant for. Let my voice be your voice.

I felt that we had entered a deeper communion of guru-disciple, that for the first time I began to feel the inner sanctum of that mysterious relationship. I sensed that Papaji was taking me into his domain, and using me to share the transmission. He told various people to speak to me when they got to the States and I would address their doubts. A number of Papaji's students who were giving satsang invited me to co-lead satsang with them.

Papaji was continually with me in my seminars and corporate trainings. I carried his photo wherever I went, and as I traveled from hotel to hotel I would immediately set up an altar. I would put his photo on the podium when I was speaking so his smile and penetrating gaze were constantly fixed on me as I went through my work. Wherever I was, be it a hotel or corporate conference room, Papaji was there, always with me. He would be so alive and present, great energy, joy and laughter would fill me. Sometimes, in the middle of a session, I would have to go out of the room or to the men's room and laugh hysterically.

Through Papaji's grace my teaching work flowed just as he had said it would. In the midst of a busy seminar schedule I simply witnessed the talking and action pouring out of me spontaneously and effortlessly. I wrote him that "I am having a great time being this automatic instrument, laughing and joking with them, being funny (not as funny as you). Will you give me that great humor and lightness you have?" Papaji responded May 5, 1992:

> Your letter of 25th April shows you have been very busy after your return from Lucknow, with seminars, showing them how to keep peace while active. I am sure you have known the secret of how to meet with people, yet not keeping any connection with anyone including your own Self. All the activity is ceaselessly being done through the Awareness-Being by itself.

I felt as if I were completely in the embrace of the master who was taking care of everything.

Unscheduled Visits of the Master

The Guru's Grace can do anything! —Papaji.

Every once in a while Papaji would come to me in dramatic ways, especially in dreams. I wrote him of a vivid nocturnal visit in the summer of '92:

> During the night of June 25 I had the most extraordinary dream. In the dream I knew that I was free, and yet I was reluctant to admit it to others. I finally shared it with my friends and students, and then came to see you in India. I was afraid that you would not confirm me, but, rather, that you would say I was deluded and arrogant. Of course, in the dream you affirmed my freedom completely and very matter-of-factly. I felt such incredible relief and floated in pure consciousness. In the morning I

awoke from the dream in the same state, knowing with certainty that I am empty awareness. I realized that the dream was about recognizing that I did not need to be affirmed. I saw that my need to be affirmed, to be recognized as 'enlightened,' was just more doubt.

In response Papaji sent me a tape of the satsang in which he read the letter aloud to the satsang. At the section on the dream, Papaji paused and, on the tape, told the people in satsang: "He thinks this is a dream." That was his only response to the letter. In other conversations Papaji said that when one dreams of the guru, that is a reality deeper even than the ordinary waking state, that the guru communicates in dreams and that these are to be taken as real. The guru is truly with you. If so, it seemed the master kept coming up with surprising ways to reassure my persistent doubt tendency.

Papaji's most extraordinary visit came in the waking state. I had written him on October 8, 1992, describing the confusion and suffering I had been experiencing, and that I was planning to visit him again in Lucknow in January '93. I asked him: "Hold me to you, my dear Self and master. I would love to receive a word from you."

Papaji fulfilled that promise beyond my wildest expectations. Earlier that week an old friend K called to say she had a special friend coming into town and wanted me to meet her. She was very insistent that this was something I must not miss. The night after I wrote Papaji I went out to K's house and met her friend G, a spiritual teacher and healer, a very light being clearly immersed in consciousness. She had the feel of an angel, a deva. She was sweet and quiet, and I felt an easy connection with her.

I soon noticed that G and K were there to do some kind of esoteric spiritual work on me. G took the lead, with K's assistance, and performed an unusual ritual that she said would transform me. She lay on my body, her chest flush with mine—we were fully clothed—while K touched my feet. G said she was releasing energy within me; that she was planting depth charges in me that would go off later. She gave some hint that turbulent times were coming for me. Afterwards, G and I sat facing each other in meditation. I asked her who she was. She said that she had many names, that she was the absolute, the infinite. At that moment she turned into Papaji.

The master appeared sitting right in front of me, glowing with a strange yellowish, almost chartreuse light. It reminded me of a psychedelic experience. I looked directly at him and saw, yes, it was Papaji without a doubt. He was right in front of me, laughing, looking at me with great love. I realized again that I am in the realm of the divine and I saw the mysterious reality of the guru behind it all. All form is the guru, everything is a manifestation of the Self. Papaji is always with me no matter what I think. That evening was a special gift of the guru.

Then it was G again sitting in front of me. She was tender and loving. She told me: "You must remember who you are: pure being. You just are. No matter how hard it gets, remember: you are, you are love. See through all forms, see through illusion, remember the truth. Allow yourself to love and be loved. It brings you out. You deserve to receive all the love the universe has for you. This is your life: to share love and flourish in this joyful loving play." She told me that January was a perfect time to go back to India.

Guru India

The Presence of the guru is Satsang. So make the best use of the Teacher's physical presence because the nature of this Grace is to enlighten and stop the cycle of birth and death. —Papaji

Papaji and India were inextricably fused in my consciousness. In a sense they were both forms of the guru for me. On my first trip I remember distinctly that when the plane touched down in Lucknow, I had a sense of being home, that it was all somewhat familiar. I have no doubt that if reincarnation exists, I certainly had spent much time there before. It was easy to assimilate, not strange or foreign to me. Even though my usual creature comforts were missing, and technology was not as reliable as in the west, I easily slipped into the flow of Indian life.

On my second trip in January 1993, I felt even more at home there and began to experience its power. I realized that India is less of a geographical reality than a domain of consciousness. Everything about it encourages awakening. India wears away at ego identification like a relentless grinding machine, pressing against all survival concerns in a constant challenge to surrender.

I arrived in New Delhi to find all domestic flights to Lucknow canceled for at least two days and no clear idea of when Indian Airlines would be flying again. I immediately ran around in taxis and tempos to the bus and train stations trying to find a ground route to Lucknow. Unable to find a connection, overwhelmed and exhausted by the chaotic traffic, noise, suffocating dirt and pollution of the capital, I finally gave up and checked into the Centaur Hotel at the international airport and collapsed. Remembering Papaji's injunction to be the emperor, I settled into that luxurious oasis and let the manager arrange my trip to Lucknow, which he did very graciously and efficiently, booking me on the Avadh Assam express train to Lucknow the next day. Once I stopped trying to fight India I quickly again slipped into the awareness that I was being totally taken care of, that I needn't do anything; that it was all being done. Sleeping at the Centaur brought deep remembrance of Papa's grace.

Indian trains are my favorite way to travel within India, and despite an occasional train wreck, they are pleasant, efficient and reliable. The second class, two-tier, a/c coach I took to Lucknow became a temple of grace which quickly revealed the loving, playful communion with the guru. Two young Indian businessmen in their thirties took bunks facing me. They were taking their aging father somewhere. He was sick, frail, and could barely stand, dressed like a sadhu, wearing only a white cotton dhoti. They said he had a bad heart. For a while he lay asleep on the upper bunk facing me. The old man woke up, chipper and happy, his eyes glistening. He began talking in an animated, singsong way, then began gesturing dramatically. As it went on and on without ceasing for hours, I realized he was probably reciting the *Ramayana*, the great Hindu epic story. Everyone in the compartment was riveted. I was drifting into nothingness and felt his voice like poetry in my heart. I gradually realized the blessing that was occurring. The energy was so light and evanescent. It was a big deja-vu, like a dream relived. The train moved rhythmically across the vast Indian plateau, its soothing sounds carrying me through Mother India to the master. This is the guru—the sadhu chanting, the people listening in rapt devotion, the gentle rocking train, the vast expanse of India. I felt Papaji's presence. Yes, God is doing it all.

Devoted Disciple

This is the only devotion: that you must be dedicated and devoted to your own Self. . . . If you want to be a devotee, have full devotion to yourself. — Papaji.

My arrival in Lucknow in January '93 was the return of the devoted disciple. Papaji welcomed me warmly and again allowed me to spend much time in his house for meals and tea. While many of Papaji's satsangs were cancelled, it didn't matter. The presence was there anyway. I was filled with sweet devotion for Papaji. Earlier I had wanted to have a real dharma dialogue with him. I felt like I had been holding back, protecting myself by silence. As I was filled with inexpressible mystery, all I wanted to do was sing to the master in satsang and celebrate freedom.

"It is easy for me to speak with many people," I wrote him, "but around you I get tongue-tied. As soon as I want to speak with you, Papaji, I am aware of the impossibility of expressing it, or it seems arrogant. Singing makes it easier.

"May the Silence sing its song of love? The inexpressible is so unbearable it creates itself as something for the sheer joy of it. Let me sing; let my heart sing praises unto thee. Though the truth be wordless, it must express its mystery. My Beloved Silence, I am your Song. My Joy is to sing at your feet. Here it is all complete."

I sat up front near Papaji where I could drink him in and exude my love to him. The master sat like the great Lion King, observing the fervent celebration and music jams we had, often asking some of the musicians to play together.

Yet as my devotion came up, I struggled with the question of my relationship to Papaji. I saw that there were many devotees who served him very closely, whom he favored in some way, who lived in his household and spent much or even all of their time with him. Did I want this depth of intimacy? Did I need to surrender more? Or was real surrender letting go of that desire, letting go of "Papaji" and "Let" and seeing through the dance of form? He had already revealed the formless reality of the Self and showed me that "no teacher, no student" was the naked truth. I knew that there was no need whatsoever to be around the form of the master once I knew the guru was within. So why was I attaching to the physical form?

This creeping attachment to Papaji was born of the doubts I had been experiencing throughout the past year—the doubt that while I had moments of awakening and bliss, there was still no "permanent enlightenment." The realization seemed to come and go, the "I" thought and body consciousness always returned. I was still holding to the thought that I wasn't fully home, that there was more to go. I kept thinking that being closer to Papaji would somehow burn all that away and make the realization stick. I wanted to be part of the inner circle and hang out in his house. I thought that would assure my enlightenment, although, in truth, it was just more ignorance and desire which caused me much distress.

The Freedom Trap

Freedom is a trap! A man who is imprisoned in a jail needs to be free, doesn't he? He is trapped in the jail and he knows that the people outside are free. . . . Once you believe it, you are caught in the trap of wanting freedom. You should be out of both these traps—neither in bondage nor in freedom—because these are only concepts. Bondage was a concept which gave rise to the concept of freedom. Get rid of both these concepts. Then, where are you?
—Papaji

Near the end of my stay in January 1993, as I saw my days with the master dwindling away, I became increasingly concerned to experience "permanent freedom." I appealed to Papaji to help me once again: "Last year you gave me a powerful taste of freedom," I wrote him, "and each day brings moments of awareness as the formless indescribable Self. Yet since this comes and goes, there must still be some doubt or resistance that I am truly free. Please remove this resistance to unbroken awareness of my ongoing freedom."

I was increasingly preoccupied and spent much time earnestly discussing this "ultimate freedom" with my satsang friends. One day at tea a friend came over on his motor scooter and said he was going to Papa's house. Everyone encouraged me to go and clear it up with with the master. They reminded me that Papaji urged his students to come to him when they were burning and to deal with him directly. I hopped on the back of the scooter and felt myself being swept along to his house, like I was being ushered over to ask this burning question. I was nervous. I didn't feel ready, but I had to do this.

At Papaji's house I stood a bit hesitantly at the open doorway, seeing him sitting there in the living room talking with a group of visitors from New Delhi. I interrupted, feeling very impolite, but I dove in, came right up to Papa's feet and told him I had to talk with him, that I must ask him a question. He smiled and happily said yes. Papaji relished these kinds of events, when the fire was burning.

I explained that last year he gave me freedom, that I had had many glimpses of awareness and the experience of nobody home. But it came and went. Now I wanted it to be final and continuous. How could I make it final? What was the next step? He laughed, and said "Good question, very good question!" to all the people. He was truly enjoying this.

I asked him what my resistance was. He said: "Identification. You have identified with freedom as some thing. Once it becomes a thing, an identity, it can only come and go. Anything that you attain you can lose. Anything you can identify with is not you, just a concept." He asked: "What is beyond identification? What is beyond freedom and bondage, beyond enlightenment and unenlightenment? What is beyond concept, even beyond 'beyond concept'?"

I was sitting right in front of him, a few inches from his face. He insisted that I answer. At first I tried to give an answer. But my mind was boggled. I couldn't think of anything and no words came out. I was frustrated, realizing that it could not be expressed. I began to wave my hands and arms in strange movements trying to describe the inexpressible. I was flapping my arms like a big bird and making strange sounds. It was all I could do. He started laughing. I started laughing. It became a big joke. We were just sitting there looking at one another, laughing hysterically. It felt absurd. The question was gone. Papaji looked at me and said: "Last year I gave you freedom. This year

I take it away." The meaning was so clear: living beyond all concept, beyond identification, no enlightenment or unenlightenment, no claims, no one to make any claims.

In joy and gratitude I bowed with my hands together in prayer. I was on my knees and fell forward into Papaji who was seated in front of me. He took my hands and brought them to his lips and kissed my hands. I collapsed into his embrace and we hugged. It was such a warm, gentle, loving hug. I felt his huge arms around me, his big hands were gently massaging my spine as he murmured something in my ear. I was holding him in deep love. I looked directly into his eyes, our faces inches apart. I kissed his forehead and face, he kissed my face and was giggling, mumbling something. I could barely breathe. I was telling him he was my father. I was overwhelmed in love and gratitude. I was completely empty, the mind had stopped, the body was trembling.

Somehow the scene ended and I wandered out of the house and into the empty lot across the road. I was filled with a vivid awareness: I am infinite, I am the formless potentiality, the mystery of conscious being that arises endlessly as all forms, as all worlds. I am all pervading. I see the faces of all the people and every face is me. I know with certainty that all there is, is me, that I am both emptiness and presence, that I am the source consciousness which is the only reality. I never have form or name, yet everyone and everything is me. Out of my void nature I project the movie of name, form, universe, and this is always my projection. This is home. This is certainty. There is no dilemma here, no confusion, no question of "I" or "not-I". It is all clear and a totally inexpressible mystery. Yet . . . still a question arose in this floating awareness: Why possibly do anything? How could I work as a consultant in this dream? Then the awareness answered: It is all my projection. Just live as source, it is all done.

There is Only Papaji

The guru has no body, visible or invisible. Do not depend on anybody, which are just fingers pointing to the Truth. The guru is your own Self. — Papaji.

Later that afternoon I returned home and sat in the patio: I was Papaji. I felt inside his face and being. I felt his head, his bones, like I was in his body. I felt like I was intangible consciousness manifesting as his face. His presence was everything—indescribable vastness and all manifestation simultaneously. The entire universe was my projection. I floated as pure consciousness, wandering about, hanging out with friends, sharing this ecstatic reverie.

I was pulled by a yearning to be with Papaji, wanting to share this experience with him. The next day I went to Papa's house, but his household staff said he was not seeing anyone. I left. I lay awake most of the night in reverie, feeling one with Papaji, seeing through his eyes. The need to be with him was so strong. The next day I waited by his house until he came back. Papaji let me in and I sat at his feet while he read letters and talked to people. As I sat there quietly I was aware of a wordless transmission coming from master. This was the beginning of many times when I would just sit silently near him and the realization simply arose on its own as the grace of the guru.

Papaji told me that yesterday, five minutes after I left his house, he sent his attendants out to let me in. He asked me why I hadn't come back last evening. He said he woke many times in the night waiting for me. Why didn't I just jump the fence, he asked, with "such a thing." I said I was too polite to come and disturb him. He knew it was powerful, he wanted me to share it with him. He said that when I had something so beautiful to share, I should always just come in no matter what the household said. He asked me to come back that night. He wanted to talk to me alone.

I came back in the evening. At the gate one of Papaji's household said he was not seeing people. I walked right past him and told him Papaji said to come and I'm going in. The master was at the table alone writing letters. He seated me at his right elbow where I sat silently for over an hour as he wrote or talked to people. I read over his shoulder the letter he was writing to a swami in New Delhi. He was saying: "It is not Brahman or Atman or realization or enlightenment. It is beyond any identification whatsoever." The last line he wrote touched me deeply: "I can't express it very well." As I sat again there was a sense of Papa's silent grace working in me, bringing up the realization of mysterious freedom. I was filled with bliss and started to laugh. The laughter was a great power cleansing from within. Everything was so clear and funny. Let was gone. There was just presence, a mysterious knowing filled with joy. It was all so simple.

I wrote Papa a note and passed it across the table to him: "Let is dead."

He wrote below it and passed it back: "To live as Eternity."

We continued passing notes back and forth like school children playing at their desks. I was thrilled sitting at the master's table playing this profoundly silly game.

I wrote: "Mystery."

He wrote: "Secret."

I wrote: "Impossible."

Papaji laughed, and said, "Yes, congratulations." Putting his arm around me, he said, "You have accomplished your mission for coming to Lucknow."

He was very happy, we felt so close, laughing together. I had a clear sense it was all over. I rubbed his chest. He asked me to come the next day at tea time.

That evening, intoxicated with mystery, I wrote a song for Papaji that I sang at the following day's satsang, my last one before I left for the States.

> *Mystery, Mystery*
> *Always here*
> *Yet never to be known.*
> *Infinite potentiality,*
> *Seemingly projecting,*
> *Always home.*
> *Beyond any place to land,*
> *Beyond the "I"*
> *Beyond the "Am"*
> *Beyond, Beyond the Mystery*
> *Secret Mystery.*

Dasarath

> *The Self is the charioteer. Find the charioteer seated in your Heart and you will be at Peace always. . . . The Atman charioteer will not make a mistake. Surrender the reins of your senses to the Atman.* —Papaji.

It is a traditional activity of the gurus in India to give spiritual names to their students, names that reflect some aspect of one's true nature. Papaji seemed to enjoy giving Sanskrit names to the people who spent time with him in satsang. Typically, though not always, he would only give a name when the person asked for one. In our very first meeting in March 1992, Papaji had made an issue of my name. When I told him my name was Let, Papaji first laughed, then his expression became mockingly stern and he said pointedly: "Get rid of that name." Punning on the British meaning for "let"—to rent out an apartment—he said that some tenants had been living inside me for thirty-five million years, and that it was time to keep my place vacant and not to "let" out my space anymore. I understood he was referring to the "I," the illusory ego that had been living within me, that I must be empty and not allow anyone home but the formless presence.

This command was so sudden, it sent a jolt of fear and confusion through me. It felt like going too far too fast. I couldn't leap into a new name, especially not some esoteric-sounding Sanskrit name. I liked my name. In a note I defensively explained to him the dual spiritual meaning of Let. One was the act of surrender, to let go, let it be. The other was the dynamic principle behind all manifestation, as in "let there be light," the first word in the act of the creation. That all seemed sufficient to me. Papaji didn't mention it again in 1992. Though he did address me as "Let" in letters, during my next visit in January 1993 I was perturbed that he often called me "Davidson." It seemed so distant and formal. I was a bit confused and irritated when he called me that.

In January 1993 friends close to the master told me that he had said he would like to give me a new name. Again, my resistance came up. I liked "Let." I didn't want to be one of the crowd with a weird Sanskrit name. It was like a leveling; I would no longer be unique. I began to worry that holding on to the old name was holding on to ego. It seemed like I was refusing full sur-render, and hence, avoiding final freedom. I didn't like that interpretation. I felt anxious, put in a corner, and felt Papaji pressing in on me. One night I got sick, a flu-like sore throat, fever, aching body. I slept fitfully, worrying in strange fever dreams: What is the importance of a name? Is "Let" the past? Is it resistance to Papaji, a refusal to surrender? Would a new name bring me closer to him? Would it finally dissolve the ego mind?

I wrote Papaji: "What is left to do to fully surrender? Is my name "Let" an obstacle? Is it holding on to the past, to old identity? Do you have a name that would express this inexpressible nameless state beyond all states?" In truth I still didn't really want a Sanskrit name, but if it would bring me home, I'd do anything. I asked him on a couple of occasions at his house if he had a name for me, but he never answered. When I asked him why he called me "Davidson" rather than "Let," he said, cryptically, "You know." I asked him if there was there anything he would rather call me, but he didn't say any-thing. I'm sure it was obvious to him that I didn't really want a new name, and Papaji only gave you what you truly wanted. Still, the power of the guru was working subtly within me.

After the passing of notes about "Let is dead," the whole issue of my name seemed beside the point anyway. Knowing that I am the nameless One itself, "Let" was as good as any other arbitrary name to move through this dream with. It really didn't matter what name I had. I was floating free with-out worries or doubts when I visited Papa to say goodbye on my last evening in Lucknow. It was the custom for people who were leaving the next day to spend their last evening together with him. I sat near him, quiet and fulfilled, enjoying his playful banter. Just as Papa was getting up to leave the room, one of the women asked him about the meaning of her Sanskrit name. Papaji delightedly sat back down and got out all his Sanskrit dictionaries and made a big production out of discussing her name. As he was doing so, I got an unexplainable, uncontrollable urge to ask him about my name. It kept welling up from deep within me until I couldn't resist any longer and blurted out:

"What about my name? Do you have a name for me? I can see you don't like 'Let.' What would you like to call me?" I was amazed as I watched myself ask these questions, as if I had no control over them.

Papaji laughed, and with great relish said that he had been wanting to give me a name, implying that he was waiting for me to really ask for it. He then playfully discussed different names, and, it seemed, teasing me and testing my reactions. Then he put the book down, closed his eyes and was silent for a few minutes. When he opened his eyes, he wrote a name on a small card and gave it to me: *Dasaratha*. "This is your name. It just came through from the Higher Power." He said you can take the "a" off and just use "Dasarath," and you can be called "Dasa" for short. Papa said: "No one has this name," meaning, I imagined, that it is a rare name in spiritual circles and is not given often. Dasarath, Papaji explained, lived seven thousand years ago, was a well-known enlightened emperor in Hindu mythology and the father of Ram, one of the most popular deities of India. If people asked the meaning, Papaji joked, "tell them you are the father of God." Dasarath, he explained, literally means "ten chariots" in the Sanskrit (*das* = ten, *aratha* = chariot). The chariots are the senses, he elaborated: the five physical senses and five inner or mental senses. Dasarath is a *jivamukti*, a free being who drives the chariots of the senses and remains completely free of them. They are your instruments and you are never caught in them.

I immediately loved the name and grasped its significance for me. The name seemed to answer the question of how I could live and work awake in the world as the free consciousness that rides the senses through life. "Dasarath" elicited a regal image of dignity and power, a sense of abundance and freedom. The entire universe is my domain and I fly through my own projection on the chariots of the mindbody process. I could use all the mental faculties and senses as my tools. It was an exhilarating image of liberation and the skillful means to show up fully and effectively in the movie.

The name seemed to place me fully in the groove with Papaji. A few days later after my return to the States I wrote:

> Now you come through me, or whatever it is that we both are, comes through this form. At certain times I get the distinct sense of your presence, the special flavor of your energy, facial expressions, voice. People say that they sense you coming through me. A friend who has only seen you on video was astounded, said I looked like you and she sensed you. I went to the New Alexandrian bookstore for incense and was drawn into the back office where two friends were talking. Looking at their picture of Ramana triggered a sense of intense presence. I sat

down and your energy came so intensely it forced us all into deep meditation. All of us were aware of the intense blessing that occurred. It felt to me like you were giving them a gift through me. All this is the illusory play of consciousness, of course, yet my experience is of being an empty instrument of this power that moves and speaks through this form called Dasarath. You are truly my father. You brought me to life by revealing my eternal nature. I and the Father are One.

Shortly thereafter I received this from Papaji, dated February 10, 1993:

> My dear Dasaratha,
> I am very glad to have read your fax. Nataraj also wrote to me about the conversation he has had with you on the phone.
> I am glad you have already begun with your seminars & workshops, this time blended with wisdom and a divine message that would pour through your tongue to the listeners. I like this way, that spiritual understanding can function into the daily routine, so that those totally attached to the world may not be afraid of spirituality.

Arrogance & The Teacher Trap

Teaching is the last trap of the ego. If a teacher is not realized, his teachings just spread confusion. —Papaji.

Pride and arrogance is doership and this causes trouble. They have never paid you, so be humble. Anything that you 'do' conceals Self with the arrogance of doership. Arrogance is not recognizing this timeless moment, arrogance is 'I am the body.' Remove arrogance and enlightenment is instantaneous. 'I am so-and-so' is the first arrogance, and 'this is mine' is the second. Look at it! —Papaji.

As opportunities to share the wisdom came up, one of my most powerful tendencies surfaced fully into consciousness—the yearning to be a guru or "enlightened teacher."

The teaching impulse was a mixed bag of sublime inspiration and base motives. On the one hand I had been blessed with insights that I genuinely wanted to share. I had always been good at words, able to communicate a clear vision, and to support people to work through their confusion and questions to greater self-awareness. I had been teaching for many years: first as an academic historian, later as a personal growth seminar leader and spiritual teacher, most recently as a corporate consultant and trainer. Besides these formal roles, I "played teacher" often in informal situations, trying to show up as the "wise one," the one with the answers.

It was more obvious to others than it was to me that these natural gifts were serving an egoic agenda. Beneath the noble surface my teaching was an instrument of arrogance. I had always had a proud streak, thinking I was better, smarter, or higher than others. I was driven by the need for self-affirmation, needing to be admired or acclaimed by others. "Look at me." "See how great I am." "See how high I am."

Arrogance is a fundamental egoic tendency that defiantly asserts a separate identity and tries to shore up its illusory solidity. It is the willful rebellion of the "I" against its source and its unwillingness to surrender to truth. In Judeo-Christian parlance, it is Lucifer's rebellion against God and the desire to carve out one's own domain (which is hell). This identification with being the separate "I" is the root cause of suffering. Arrogance is the rejection of freedom and the refusal to be the Self. It is the wave's ignorant denial that it is the ocean.

I noticed my arrogance going in two directions simultaneously. On the one hand it was an ultimate self-inflation, in which the "I" claimed and clung to enlightenment as its own possession. Ego creates "enlightenment" as its prize or accomplishment. This is the way it holds on to itself, by puffing up to what it believes is its ultimate state. On the other hand, when doubt came, I backed off from fully claiming my divine nature, and kept calling for affirmation to "finalize" the realization. Papaji said it was arrogant to entertain all those questions and doubts, that it was a rejection of the truth that I am already free. Doubt itself is arrogance. That is, doubt and arrogance arise together, mutually creating and sustaining each other, as the two polarities of the egoic denial. To give up questions and doubts is the end of arrogance.

In truth, any self-image, regardless of content, is arrogance. Usually we associate arrogance with an over-confident high self-image. But even low self-esteem is arrogant since it still feeds the illusion of being a separate, solid subject in the world. Arrogance—and doubt—disappears when there is no "I" making any claim either for worthiness or unworthiness, for enlightenment or unenlightenment.

Teaching served my arrogance. It fed my desire to be right, to seem higher than others, to be holier-than-thou. Teaching embodied a know-it-all quality that was there beneath the camouflage seeking to demonstrate that "I had it." It was a way to get attention, approval, recognition, a way to impress people and feel a sense of accomplishment. It could be a come-on for sex as well as a way to distance myself from others and avoid real relationship. Talking was an art form for me as well as a subtle manipulation, perhaps my most well developed tool in ego's bag of tricks. I used the intellect to survive, to win, to control people or get my way. As I entered spiritual life in the '70s and '80s it co-opted all the spiritual information I was digesting and set its sights on becoming the guru. I learned to share the dharma and to hold myself as a wise teacher. I was not conscious enough to see how the authentic drive to share awareness was mixed with arrogance.

In my awakening with Papaji, the teaching tendency was reactivated as a desire to give satsang. It was a way of announcing that I was awake and of being recognized for it. While I truly loved to share with people and support them to wake up, it also seemed that sharing the realization made it more real for me. And beneath it all there was some subliminal sense of being a mini-clone of Papaji. I wanted to sit in the guru-chair just as the master did. Seeing that a few of Papaji's students had already begun to give satsang in the States and Europe, I dreamed of doing the same. I held a few small satsangs for my friends and clients in Ithaca, and in the late summer co-led satsangs with friends in the Bay area and Seattle.

Papaji often said he saw all of us who came to Lucknow as his "ambassadors" or "messengers" to the world. He wanted us to realize freedom and return to our countries to share it so that others could know who they are and discover the peace and happiness of the Self. He occasionally asked some of his students to give satsang. While Papaji never directly asked me, he knew I was leading satsangs and saw some of the videos. He also sent people to speak with me about satsang-like matters.

At that time there was some stress for me in giving satsang, as if I felt the effort of trying to prove myself or show off. I was aware of my desire to be an "enlightened teacher" and troubled by the undertone of "look at me, I got it" which lingered beneath the surface of consciousness. For someone who had supposedly realized identitylessness, I was secretly pleased to be a "somebody" in spiritual circles. While I was acutely aware of this contradiction, the guru tendency was so powerful that it just seemed to come up and take over.

At least some of my old dharma friends saw the egoic tendency more clearly than I did. A close Zen friend said that I had a "zen-stink" about me. I later got what he meant on reading Zen Master Taisen Deshamaru's vivid warning: "If we achieve satori, and the satori shows, like a bit of dogshit stuck on the tip of our nose, that is not so good." While I caught a whiff, it wasn't enough to get it off my nose.

I found myself caught in a vicious cycle of doubt and arrogance that fed each other. Doubt led me to seek affirmation through satsang. Yet I was aware that giving satsang was a kind of bragging and so I held back from sharing fully. I didn't want to be seen as arrogant and so bent over backwards to not continue the arrogant pattern. It felt best to follow the safe way and not speak about it. I expressed my confusion in letters to Papaji, asking for advice: "Was it arrogant to want to give satsang? But isn't doubt and the fear of arrogance really arrogance itself, more holding back or resistance to being myself? Your whole teaching says it is ok to claim that I am that I am. This is my direct experience. Is this not so?"

Papaji never responded directly to my questions. He was much more subtle. He just sent me the audio tape in which he read my whole letter to the satsang in Lucknow. I noticed that as he read the letter aloud he pointedly changed some of my language to read in the past tense: "the awakening I had in Lucknow" so that it didn't sound as if I were still experiencing it. He was trying to tell me that I was speaking as if I still had it, that I was making claims for an experience that was no longer present, but had become a memory I continually invoked. I noticed that, but I was too deluded or resistant to absorb his subtle hint. On the tape, just after Papaji read my letter, another student also asked him if he could give satsang in Boulder. Papaji simply asked him, cleverly punning: "Are you bold enough?" I took this to be Papaji's answer to my request to give satsang as well. Was I bold enough? Was I free enough? Papaji wasn't about to say. The demand was for me to get clear of the self-deception I was caught in. As long as there was any "I" and its attendant doubt or arrogance, it was better not to talk about freedom. Yet, not taking Papaji's hints, I was too blind to see the pit I was about to fall in.

Mercy Killing

The guru is the butcher of the sheep ego. —Papaji.

The same pattern of doubt and arrogance in my desire to be a teacher showed up in my wanting Papaji to affirm my "enlightenment." I was driven by the need for his acknowledgment, which I thought would give the awakening some permanent reality. I chronicled the endless details of my awakening in lyrical, passionate letters I wrote to him, all of them describing precious mystical experience, yet still in the service of this illusory "I" that called out: "Look at me, see what I have attained."

At its depths, the yearning for recognition is the purest desire—the burning necessity to know the Self. It is driven by the subliminal knowing of the truth, yet somehow that knowing is veiled by ignorance and doubt. As Papaji said, the function of the guru was to remove doubt and point directly to your true nature, which he offered to everyone.

Of course Papaji had been acknowledging me all along. He told me a number of times during my first visit that he was sure I "had it." He confirmed the awareness expressed in my poetry. He told me how pleased he was with my teaching and how I was reaching people. In January '93 he told me my mission to Lucknow was over. He even came in dreams and confirmed my freedom. Yet I would not fully accept this. The doubt was so deep, the longing for affirmation was so unconsciously on automatic that I kept wanting it even when I was getting it. I saw this absurdity, that in the very midst of this underlying awareness, these doubts and yearnings played out their senseless, mechanical dance.

By the summer of '93 this pattern was peaking. Consciousness had been flip-flopping between realizations and doubt, between great joy and worry. I had become ensnared again in attachments. I was looking forward to my trip to India in August as an opportunity to share my consciousness with Papaji and clarify it. Papaji always invited—sometimes dared—people to come up front with him in satsang and share their awareness. I wanted to be able to sit close to the master and speak as equals. Just before leaving for India in August I faxed him that I was looking forward to being with him "to discuss the undiscussible, to express the inexpressible." Talk about setting myself up for a fall! Little did I know that I was walking right into a ferocious lion's den.

In my first satsang with Papaji in August '93 I came clean and admitted that I had been stuck in attachments the past few months, a very difficult admission for me in front of the whole satsang. I confessed that I wanted to give up the arrogance of trying to appear "enlightened" and to release the burden of holding up some image of myself as a high teacher. It all troubled me. Besides, it was an exhausting and impossible effort. I told him I thought I was dead when I left Lucknow in January, but the corpse had stirred. I asked my beloved master for a mercy killing.

I felt exposed and vulnerable, admitting this to Papaji and the whole satang. When he said my mind wasn't expanded enough, I was humiliated and embarrassed. All my attempts to appear high and enlightened were unmasked here. I blew my cover entirely. Everyone could see that I was still stuck. I was ashamed of myself. Papa was both sweet and stern. While he lectured me gently and told some funny stories about attachments, he definitely heard my request for a mercy killing.

I was immensely relieved that I had revealed myself and placed myself in the hands of the master. The days with Papaji floated by in peace and joy, laughter and tears. Above all, my commitment was to keep quiet, to let others be wise. There was nothing to know and nothing to say. I knew it was foolish and arrogant to try to describe it. There was no need to announce it or seek confirmation. The Self needs no affirmation.

Yet the vasanas were so deep and subtle. Even though I had given up the teacher role, I found myself thinking again that now—at last!—I could hold satsang back home and discuss all my learning! The teacher trap was still there, the desire to show up enlightened and seek affirmation was still there. I noticed these impulses bubbling up, and kept relaxing them. Yet I had no control over the playing out of fate.

On my last night in Lucknow I had dinner at Papaji's house. After he went to bed I sat up late at his table speaking with an American woman who had been teaching in India. I was only vaguely aware that I was bragging, telling her of all my spiritual experiences and great insights. It was late when we left Papa's house, a slight rain coming down as we started walking down the dark road. I walked about ten yards when all of a sudden I fell into a deep ditch on the side of the road, scraping my knee, feet and toes, and finding myself up to my armpits in murky water.

The Indians who pulled me out told me it was a sewer that had been left uncovered. I looked at myself bleeding from multiple cuts, dripping with disgusting filth. I had always been repulsed by the open sewers in India and concerned about contamination. My skin crawled with the thought of being covered with excrement and urine and God knows what else. The most horrible fears came to mind that I would become infected by unknown, sinister diseases. I was shaken to the core. I managed to hobble home and took great care to disinfect and bandage my wounds.

Later that night, lying in bed, the fears passed and I was visited by the most blissful bodyless consciousness. I floated as evanescent awareness itself, free of it all, no matter what the physical condition! Even in the most disgusting slime I am untouched! This was the true meaning of Dasarath— the awakened consciousness not caught or affected by the senses. I felt such joy, such an exhilarating knowledge of freedom. I wanted so much to share that realization with Papaji.

The next morning, I wrote Papaji a short note saying that I was leaving for the States that day and asking if I could come up front in satsang to share my experience of bodyless consciousness. I didn't mention in the note about falling in the ditch. I omitted anything that might make me look foolish. Later I realized that would have been humble, funny, human. But the desire to impress him came up so completely and took me over again. I was serious about transcending all that frail humanness. This was my chance to sit up front with the master as his equal and schmooze about being free. I thought my dream was about to come true.

He read my letter out loud to the satsang in a tone I had never heard from him before. He spoke dryly and mechanically, without his usual humor or dramatic feeling, as if he had no interest in it at all, as if he had disdain for it. I caught a brief glimmer then that something was off, but I couldn't really get it. He said I could come up and talk with him, speaking in a kind of ominous tone of "are you sure you really want to do this?" It was a challenging or warning tone, but I didn't quite grasp that either, my hopes were so strong that I would finally get my chance to rap with the master.

I had no sooner started to say something about consciousness when Papaji cut me off and yelled angrily at me. There was no way I could speak to him! he shouted. I was like a pig trying to speak to an elephant! He hotly pointed out that I started off my note matter of factly saying I was going back to the States without any reference to God or truth. He accused me of arrogance and when I tried to respond he yelled even louder at me to be quiet, that he would not allow me to speak to him, that I was just a pig and that I did not deserve to speak with him! He was ferocious. I had never experienced this from him before—such a withering blast of anger, like a flame-thrower of overwhelming power. Every once in a while he would stop, and begin speaking with someone else in his usual loving tone, then abruptly turn to me, praising their devotion in contrast to my arrogance. He would again disdainfully tell me to be quiet. It felt like he kept pounding me to make sure I was out for the count. When the satsang ended I was standing near the door Papa usually exited, so he had to walk right past me on the way out. As he did so, he came directly up to me, looked me straight in the eye and commanded forcefully, "You be quiet!" and walked out.

I was absolutely crushed, crumpled up by the wall, crying and aching with pain. I have never felt such devastation, such humiliation and shame. It was a total rejection by the master in front of everyone, for the entire world to see. There was no escape. I was destroyed, shell-shocked. It felt as if my chest had been torn open and the tender, hurting flesh exposed.

Some people consoled me, telling me what grace it was, that Papa only did this to his favorites, that it was the quickest way to burn up the most stubborn vasanas. I had heard from his older students that in the past Papaji was more of the ferocious, ruthless slayer of ego, that he would bear down intensely on his students. In my first two visits I only experienced Papaji as the loving, gentle father. Now I saw the roaring lion.

Even in the midst of my pain I recognized the grace of the gift and was deeply grateful to Papaji for attending directly to the arrogance that controlled me. My loving guru was only fulfilling my request for a mercy killing. In the first satsang he was gentle and joking about attachment. But I didn't get it and the arrogance sprang back up to assert itself again. I realized that it took such overwhelming force to obliterate that arrogance. Only the guru could do that. It took making a fool of myself in front of everyone to undermine that addiction to wanting to be seen as high and holy. There was no way I could possibly claim that now. My beloved master played it out and gave me what I wanted.

I was in a state of shock when the taxi came to the satsang hall to take me to the airport. On the flight back to the States I experienced the most contradictory mix of feelings. I felt as if a neutron bomb had exploded in my chest, sending my fragments hurtling in all directions into space. Within this vast emptiness reverberated a deafening silence. I felt as if I were outer space without any sense of definition or location. I felt the most tender, raw vulnerability, embarrassment, hurt. At the same time I knew the grace of this explosion and was filled with waves of laughter, gratitude and bliss, all of it arising within stillness. This odd constellation of experience—raw vulnerability, silence, joy, bliss—stayed with me in varying degrees of intensity for the next eight months. It felt as if the guru had performed some operation on me, without anesthesia, and all I could do was to feel and allow it.

Later I remembered that G had told me that the ritual she performed that night in Ithaca was laying powerful depth charges in me that would go off later, and that no matter what it seemed like, it was all for the good. That night G's form had transfigured into Papaji. The master was speaking to me then. All of that was the incomprehensible mystery of the guru doing whatever was required to destroy ignorance.

Back home I consulted my astrologer on what the chart said about those fateful days with Papaji in late August '93. I purposely omitted telling him any of the details of what happened, as I was curious to check the accuracy of his reading. He pointed out that the Sabian symbol for the degrees during my stay in Lucknow read: "A man walking blindfolded toward the opening of a deep pit." I was astounded to hear how specifically accurate that was. The astrology seemed to map out how it was all a divine set-up. He also pointed out that the chart said I had been "looking for an authentication of an interior experience," and that the aspects on the day Papaji blasted me described "a confrontation with ego." All completely accurate. He said this aspect comes only once every thirty years, so if I didn't think I had enough or learned my lesson, I should go back to Papa within the next two months to make sure it was complete. I was sure that I had had enough.

I could no longer bear the thought of speaking or teaching the dharma. I saw vividly that all the speaking I'd done was manipulation to prove some state. I was blessedly relieved of the compulsion to speak and the constant, underlying tension of having to know or explain anything, or affirm myself. I dropped all interest in talking about freedom, and didn't give satsang again for another four years. It seemed pointless. In fact *anything* that I could say seemed like arrogance. I was supersensitive to the flavor of "I" in everything I tried to do, in any position I took, in any thought I held. It was very clear that ego *is* mind, and that it is *all* arrogance. There was no way to escape it except to be quiet.

I had fallen deeply in love with silence. Over and over again I heard Papaji's voice within me: "Be quiet! There is nothing to say." This had been the master's only teaching to me from the beginning. The stillness was soothing, it was home, my refuge from suffering. I kept wanting to write him, yet anything I might say seemed egotistical or superficial. Why say it? The underlying silence was sufficient. I only wrote Papaji once in eight months, a brief few lines of love and gratitude for his immense grace. The master never wrote me again.

Yet the non-verbal inner communication with the guru was strengthened as I allowed my life to be guided more from within. I saw the arrogance of any doership, worrying about success or failure and trying to make life happen any particular way. I sensed the moment-to-moment newness and unknowableness of the movie. For the next year, I had minimal interest in my consulting and seminar work. It seemed meaningless and beside the point. All I wanted to do was sit quietly and disappear. Miraculously, the work continued, unfolding just as Papaji had told me it would. I simply accepted and allowed it to happen. There was an openness to what comes, even a willingness for the work to collapse. Amazingly, the work kept improving, becoming deeper and, with some momentary dips, even more financially successful, as I opened to share myself more freely with people. Papaji's blast had humbled me and left me in love with stillness.

I Am With You Wherever You Are

Regarding Grace, it doesn't make any difference whether you are physically close to the Teacher or not. But if the physical presence of the Teacher is available that should be given preference. . . . —Papaji

I visited Papaji in Lucknow three more times, in the springs of '94 and '95, and January of '97. Over that span there was a gradual relinquishing of my desire to be with the external guru and a firm recognition that the formless Satguru within is my own true Self.

On my return to India in April 1994, at the first satsang, Papa saw me in the crowd as he got out of the van, came over and greeted me with a warm smile and a special word: "When did you arrive?" That seemingly small gesture made me feel completely welcomed and back together with him. Any apprehension had completely disappeared in the wake of the master's warmth. The next day when I came over to pay my respects and was told by his household that he was busy, he sent someone to come after me and bring me back to the house, just so he could tell me personally that he was involved in an interview and would see me the next day. I saw Papaji only a few times in the two weeks I was there. He wasn't feeling well and about half the satsangs were cancelled. I didn't speak with him in satsang, and was content to sit quietly and drink in the silence. I only visited him twice at his house. Though he was sweet to me, we had very little conversation. Still, the presence was enormous and obvious, sometimes in the most surprising ways.

One night while sleeping in my room I awoke in the middle of the night with an electric shock of great energy. In the upper right hand corner of the room near the door to the bathroom, I saw Papaji's head glowing——no body, just his head very clearly delineated and glowing with light in full color. He was looking at me, as if he had been there for some time. Then he disappeared. I lay there with the comforting sense of his presence watching over me, and fell back asleep. It was a clear sign that there was no need to be with the guru physically, that he was always with me.

My next trip to India in March-April 1995 was a deep immersion in the reality of the formless Satguru within. I spent the first week at Ramanasramam in Tiruvannamalai, South India to be in the presence of Bhagavan Sri Ramana Maharshi, Papaji's deceased master and my spiritual grandfather who lived deep in my heart. The ancient temple city of Tiruvannamalai with its many holy men was a major pilgrimage on the non-dual circuit, visited by many of Papaji's students. On this holy terrain where Papaji had awakened, Bhagavan had lived his entire life after his self-realization, much of it on the mountain Arunachala which Ramana claimed was his guru. The Hindus say that Arunachala is a physical incarnation of the supreme, all-pervading consciousness they call Shiva. Shiva, so goes the myth, is so vast and powerful he required a mountain for his embodiment. A mere human figure could not contain such immensity. In this sacred place I saw how the Satguru was showing up as an entire lineage of great masters— Shiva, Arunachala, Ramana, Papaji—all of them embodiments of the same Self. Even a half-century after Ramana's physical passing the deep silence of the Maharshi's presence still hovers over the land and envelops one in its power. In my cottage at the foot of Arunachala, I studied Ramana's teachings and was immersed in the silent mysteries of the guru.

It was in Ramana's presence that Papaji fully realized the unlimited Self. Papaji told the story many times that, after his awakening in Tiruvannamalai at the time of the partition of India into Muslim and Hindu states, Ramana told Papaji to go up north and take his Hindu family out of the primarily Muslim areas where they were living (now Pakistan) because he saw political trouble coming. When Papaji demurred, saying he wanted to stay with his beloved guru, Bhagavan reassured him: "I am with you wherever you are." This made a great impact on Papaji who realized that the formless Satguru or Self is always present, and was freed from any lingering attachment to the physical form of the external guru.

My stay in Ramanasramam touched me in a similar way. As I made the pilgrimage around Arunachala, climbed the sacred mountain and visited the caves where Ramana had lived, I sensed the presence of the Satguru within me.

Annamalai Swami

Satguru is within your own Self and nowhere else. Your Satguru dwells in your Heart and in the Heart of all Beings. Since you don't understand his language, by Grace he takes a form to point you Within. The Real guru is within. —Papaji.

While at Ramanasramam I experienced the guru lineage through another one of Ramana's living disciples, Annamalai Swami, who had spent many years with the sage of Arunachala and was now himself a teacher to a new generation of students.

I had heard about Annamalai Swami from Papaji's students in Lucknow, especially from David Godman who had lived at the ashram for many years and had just written the Swami's biography, *Living by the Words of Bhagavan*. Annamalai Swami, like Papaji, an enlightened disciple of Ramana, had a small ashram next door to Ramanasraman where he met with students and presented the Maharshi's teachings. While I had no strong interest in seeing him, feeling fully satisfied with my guru Papaji and somewhat annoyed when people suggested I should visit someone else, I did have a little curiosity.

One afternoon after having my coffee and feeling very high, I headed out toward Arunachala, strolling along the back wall of Annamali Swami's ashram. As I was walking I felt a glowing in the center of my chest—the glowing face of a swami who was smiling and calling me. This was very similar to the time I saw Ramana's face glowing in my chest just before meeting Papaji. I felt the same sense of presence of the guru, and followed it by walking closer to the wall, debating whether to ignore it as just my imagination. As I got closer to the outside gate a group of Indian *sadhus* saw me and immediately beckoned me to come up to the gate. I hesitated a moment and they beckoned again, very animatedly, with reassuring looks on their faces, as if I were being ushered in. When I came up to the gate, they opened it and pointed me to the inner gate to the garden. As I stood at the inner gate and looked back at them, they gestured for me to open the inner gate and walk into the swami's private garden.

I hesitated again, and then all of a sudden saw the swami standing there in the garden, a skinny little brown man with a dhoti wrapped diaper-like around him, looking startlingly like Ramana. He saw me, smiled, and beckoned me in with his finger. I entered and followed him to the mandir, the open air, screened-in temple where he gave satsang. We sat down facing one another. After we were alone for a while, his translator came in and asked if I had something to say. I was completely empty so we just sat there in silence. He was looking at me, yet as if he was not seeing anything. Then, just to say something I said that I was a friend of David Godman. David had told me that Annamalai Swami loved him and was very happy with the book. On hearing David's name the swami became very animated and happy, laughing and clapping his hands. We both laughed together. It seemed so absurd, there was nothing to say in the midst of this silence and bliss we were sharing. We sat for a while when other devotees began to come in and the translator gestured it was time for me to leave. I left, empty of all thought and filled with happiness, as if I had been given a great blessing. I continued my walk around the mountain in deep peace, again filled with the sense of being ushered into the guru, embraced by and infused with the guru, certain that the whole movie was in the hands of the guru.

When I returned to Lucknow the next week to be with Papaji I finally read David Godman's biography of Annamalai Swami. I was especially drawn to the swami's descriptions of his relationship with Ramana and how the guru functioned.

"At a certain point of spiritual maturity, the Self manifests to you as a guru to turn you to yourSelf. The guru shows up in the maya, in the dream, to awaken you from the dream to the Self. In the dream the guru and the disciple are real. In the waking up there is no dream, no guru and no disciple, only the Self. Even though you know it is all the Self, that doesn't mean you do not respect and honor the guru and treat him as an ordinary person who is no different from other manifestations. You honor the guru anyway."

Annamali Swami used the example of the dream in which an elephant is being attacked by a lion. The roar of the lion in the dream awakens you from the dream. "Your original question was: 'is the guru-disciple relationship real?' From the standpoint of the Self, one would have to say that it is all maya [illusion or imagination], but one could add that it is the best kind of maya. One can use a thorn to remove another thorn. Similarly, one can use the maya-like guru-disciple relationship to root out maya in all its manifestations. Maya is so firmly established in us that only the illusory guru-lion in our own dream can give us a big enough shock to wake us."

The outer guru shows up in form to tell you of the reality of the Self, turns you within to focus attention on the inner guru, gives instructions and quiets the mind. The inner guru pulls you home to the Self.

"The relationship with the outer guru lasts as long as it is necessary," the Swami continued. "It lasts until the disciple knows from direct experience that the Self alone exists. In my case a time came when it was no longer phys-ically possible for me to be with the form of the guru. Bhagavan severed the physical relationship because he wanted me to be aware of him as he really is. When you pass your exams at school, you graduate to the next class. We cannot enter the same class again. I graduated from regarding Bhagavan as a form and came to regard him as the formless Self. After that I was never given the chance to have a relationship with Bhagavan's physical form again."

"When a calf is very young its mother gives it milk whenever it is hun-gry. But after it has learned to eat grass the mother gives it a kick whenever it tries to drink milk again. After I had learned to make contact with the form-less Self, Bhagavan gave me a kick when I still tried to carry on drinking the grace from his physical form. He wanted me to get all my spiritual nourish-ment from the formless Self."

Are You Going Now?

The Self is the Satguru, you will get help from Within. Here your true Guide is, here all wisdom and knowledge is. —Papaji.

I felt the same kick when I returned to Lucknow that spring of '95 to be with Papaji. The formless presence was revealed, and the outer guru was withdrawn. Like my visit the previous year, Papaji was kind and friendly but now showed no interest in me whatsoever and offered no time together. This trip he barely even looked at me. If I were in the house with him, and he had something to say to me, he would say it to someone else to pass on to me, as if I weren't there. One night sitting in Papaji's house for four hours in the silence of his presence, a total reassurance came that it is all completely done and taken care of. I had strong intimations that my work would be extraordi-narily successful and that the guru's presence would be continuously present in everything that happened in the movie.

It was the custom of Papaji's students who wanted to spend time with him at his house, to wait by the front gate to be let in. Even though I knew sub-liminally it was all over, on occasion I still came to the gate in hopes that I could get in to see him. I remember clearly, almost exactly three years after I first met the guru, I wrote in my diary: "Standing at Papa's gate today I get the feeling I don't have to do this, that it is unnecessary, beside the point. For a week or two I've been sensing that I'm in touch with the inner guru, that the guru is everywhere, the guru is the Self, and that there is no need for attach-ment to Papa's form. In fact attachment to the form, any fascination with the movie around Papa, any thought that I need to be with him, is a distraction. It pulls away from the inner consciousness and strengthens the illusion that I am not that and that I need to be with a guru to help awaken. The sense of the all-pervading Self is strong. I am that consciousness. Surrender fully into the inner guru. The inner guru is the pull home and the outer guru has done his work. He is telling me it is over. Papa shows no interest in me. Take the hint."

When I visited his house before leaving for the States, again Papaji wouldn't address me directly. Even when I was sitting just a few feet away, he gave the letters I was going to mail in the States to someone else to hand to me, ignoring me as if I weren't there. It was so odd to realize that I didn't exist for him. He was clearly done with me. Then he stood up and started to leave the room. At the door he turned around and looked directly at me, smiled a big grin, and asked: "Are you going now?" It was such a loving, playful goodbye. It was obvious to me that he was asking, "Are you done yet? Are you ready?" I laughed and replied, "I'm outta here, Papaji." What a sense of exhilaration and freedom, what a joy knowing he had had enough of me! It was clear that my work with Papaji the outer guru was over. From then on my devotion was to serve the formless guru everywhere.

An Exploding Star

My guru is not dead. I never thought that my guru is just the bones, skin, blood and marrow. I see my precious Teacher only and That Teacher is within. —Papaji.

When I left Papaji in the spring of '95 I assumed that was my last visit to India. Yet I simply could not turn off my desire to be with the master again and returned to sit at his feet one more time for the sheer joy of sharing the presence of being.

During my trip to India in January 1997, Papaji was recovering from a long illness and began holding satsangs again just as I got there. I had no individual time with him, just the traditional checking in on my arrival and departure. While he spoke very little in satsang and seemed physically weak, merely sitting with him was a profound sharing of silent awareness.

My time with Papaji was so extraordinarily powerful that on returning to the States I immediately planned to return for a full month in September-October '97, to be there for Papaji's eighty-seventh birthday on October 13. He was getting older, his health was deteriorating, and we didn't know how much longer he would be around. My yearning to be with him was so strong I planned to be there at a peak work time for me.

All year I was looking forward to my full month with Papaji in the fall. We had scheduled my daughter Lila's surgery for that summer, which left plenty of time for me to be around for her recovery before leaving for India. When the surgery was postponed until early September, a week before my planned departure, I had some concern that the surgery might be delayed again, or worse, that there might be complications which would delay my trip. I felt selfish that I viewed the possibility of delays as an obstruction of my time with Papaji. The guru resolved this dilemma in the most mysterious way.

During my consulting work at Harbin Hot Springs the last ten days of August, the blissful consciousness I usually associated with being around Papaji's physical form arose gently on its own. There was a clear sense of the master's presence, including some dreams of him in which I felt him close within me. It became obvious that he is here, that the essence—the grace—that was showing up as Papaji's form is everywhere and that there was no need to go to India or to be around Papaji. I was relieved knowing that if Lila's surgery were delayed I would give up the India trip.

On one of my last nights at Harbin, sometime in the first few days of September, I dreamt I was in the hospital looking for Lila who was having surgery there. I was roaming the halls, not knowing which room she was in, disturbed that I couldn't find her. Then I realized it was not Lila I was looking for, but Papaji. I knew that Papaji was in the hospital, that something was happening to him, and that I needed to find him. I awoke, puzzled and a bit disturbed, yet also blessed by his presence, which seemed even stronger than ever. Two days later, on returning to Ithaca, I received a call that Papaji's health had deteriorated rapidly, that he had been in the Lucknow hospital for a few days. They had put him on a respirator, but he didn't want any more life support, and they were expecting him to pass away at any time. The next day, September 6, 1997, I received another call that the master expired an hour or so earlier.

Papaji's passing filled me with a mix of powerful emotions. Intense currents of joy and sorrow, love and gratitude, tears and laughter all flowed through me. It freed me of any residual desire I had for his recognition. Or perhaps it was that in his dying he gave that acknowledgment finally and fully in such a way that I could not deny it. I sensed a transmission coming from him, as if he were passing into me all of his assurance and love. It felt like a final blessing and permission to be who I am and to share it with others. There was an exhilarating sense of release. I spoke with many others in Lucknow who also dreamt or sensed that Papaji had come to them in the last days. It was as if a great star had exploded and its awesome energy radiated out to be absorbed by those around him. His death was his last act of freedom for himself and for his students as well. The work of Papaji, the outer guru, was over.

With Lila's surgery a success, and her recovery so rapid, I was thrilled to go to India in mid-September to celebrate our master with the satsang family. I arrived in Lucknow the day everyone had returned from Hardwar where they had cast his ashes into the Ganges. As I watched the videos of Papaji's cremation, the rituals and devotional chanting, and the casting of his bones into his beloved sacred river, I again felt the full range of emotions and gratitude for the gift he had given all of us. Old students and devotees came from all over the world to the satsang house in Indra Nagar to celebrate the master's birthday in an ecstatic rejoicing of devotion, music, dancing, laughter, tears and overflowing love.

It was a month of great stillness in which the idea for this book was born and I began writing about the mystery of awakening. Satsang started to do itself. It was obvious that only the Self can give satsang. No "I" can do it. It just flowed naturally on its own. I began sharing informal satsang in Lucknow with friends, as the speaking came through without any effort or self-consciousness. The doubts and reservations were gone. On my return I began giving satsang in the States.

My corporate work also became infused with satsang, as I could no longer separate this consciousness from my retreats and coaching sessions with clients. Previously, no matter how supportive and encouraging Papaji was about my corporate work, I had always considered it to be less than "spiritual." It seemed too bogged down in serving ordinary egoic needs, and wasn't as "high" as the satsang that some of Papaji's other students were giving. On leaving India in the spring of '95, I had begun to write about how to integrate the nondual awareness in the workplace and support people to realize their true nature in their work. After the master's death I brought those writings together in my book *Wisdom at Work*, which was dedicated to Papaji. At the same time, any residual fears of becoming dysfunctional in my work were erased as I witnessed the increasing success of my business. All activity flowed effortlessly from the silence just as Papaji had said it would in our first meeting. I watched with wonder as my clients began to have tastes of peace and clarity in the midst of their corporate offices and high-tech conference rooms. The coaching and retreat work seemed to have a life of its own as this mindbody organism was moved along, informed and energized by guru's grace. Papaji's presence infused it all and touched my clients. I finally realized that *this was my work*, that my activity in the workplace was the satsang I had always wanted to share, that it was all happening full blown, here and now, in the corporate world. There was nothing down the road to wait for. This was it.

At that time I had another dream of the guru. I was running on the beach feeling free, yet somehow wanting something for "me." A group of us were all racing to build our houses on the beach. As we each ran to get started on our projects, I had some sense of being concerned with getting ahead of them or just getting my house built. Then I met the guru, a majestic, powerful man up on the high dunes overlooking the beach. He had the distinctive feel of Papaji and I knew I was in his presence. He told me to serve others' enlightenment, not to be concerned with building my own house, but to help others build theirs'. It would be a collective house for all. Serving others' freedom is my joy and devotion. Everything needed to do this work, all the insight, energy, and guidance simply flows from this internal source, which is doing it all.

Living Mystery

Eventually you have to get rid of the name and form of both your master and yourself. . .The guru has no body, visible or invisible. Do not depend on any body . . . The guru is your own Self, not ego-self, Self here and now. Reject the form of the guru and only the Supreme is left. —Papaji

Freedom is unconditional surrender to being lived by mystery, which is ultimately a recognition of *being* the mystery. It is resting as the silent unknowing, beyond the illusion of control and the controller, simply present to the unfolding of life.

By '94-95 I had become aware of deep-lying control tendencies that had operated unconsciously throughout my life. I saw more clearly than ever my need to understand what is happening and to direct the movie. The immersions in formless consciousness seemed to agitate these vasanas and brought into stark relief the addiction to the basic survival mechanisms, which both expressed and reinforced the illusory sense of a controller.

The prospect of letting that all go and dwelling in mystery brought up moments of intense fear for me periodically during my times in India, especially after '94. In the midst of clarity and peace, I would be zapped by shocks of fear, jolts of energy that flowed like currents of electricity through my body. I was plagued by fearful thoughts that things wouldn't work out, that I wasn't holding it together, that it was all slipping through my fingers. Sometimes it manifested specifically as the fear of being robbed, of getting sick, of losing my passport or tickets, of missing my plane, being stuck in India, and not being able to get back to my life. At times it seemed like actual paranoia, as if I was being taken over by moments of insanity, filled with an ominous sense of being at risk, threatened by everything, and having to shore up control, security, identity. These fears were a reflection of a frantic clinging to existence, expressed in how badly I wanted to get back to my old, familiar drama.

Papaji had pointed out that people would come all the way to India for freedom, yet they would tie a rope to their body that kept them securely bound to their old, familiar life. He cautioned us to untie that rope, to surrender to freedom here and now. It wasn't until my last visit to India in October '97, after Papaji's passing, that I realized how tightly I had tied that rope, how much I clung to my comfortable and busy life, and how I always tried to fit Papaji and my India trips into that framework. My fear was associated with not losing all that. The more I knew it was all sandcastles on the beach, the more I feared their dissolution. I finally knew that it was time to untie the rope that bound me to the movie, that I could only live untethered, trusting the Self and allowing the movie to unfold as it will. That meant accepting that my business might collapse if need be, that my life might not work out as I wished.

Looking back, I see that my original question to Papaji—if I could be free in my life as it was—was placing a condition on freedom, trying to set it up the way I wanted. Of course, Papaji said "yes," since one can know oneself anywhere under any conditions. But I was still trying to make a deal with God. I wanted it all. I didn't want to choose between freedom and my secure, comfortable life. "I" was still trying to manipulate and control "my" destiny. Papaji had said that when people say "Thy will be done," they are really wanting *their* will to be done. They want life to happen their way. He insisted that one must place freedom first above all things without laying any conditions on it. I now had no doubt that freedom was unconditional. You cut no deals with the absolute.

So living mystery meant giving up the strategic controlling tendency and wanting to know what will happen, giving up wanting to plot out my life so that everything will work out right. It sees that the Self really is doing it all, that the movie is unfolding perfectly, and that no one is touched by the play of the movie, no matter how it turns out. Whenever a question about what to do came up, I would turn to the silence within and the internal guru would say: "I'll take care of that, just be quiet. There is no need to think about or plan anything. No need to be concerned about the movie in any way." In a metaphorical sense Papaji's presence seemed to take over and provide guidance though the trackless unknown. It is such an odd paradox, having a sense of guidance and knowing that it is just an anthropomorphic way to experience the intuition by which the Self guides itself through its own projection.

To be fully guided by the Self meant to me giving up the astrological insight and advice I had been receiving on a wide range of issues for the past fifteen years. After meeting Papaji, my focus in the astrology sessions was increasingly on charting the most auspicious dates for travel to India to be with the guru. The perceptive readings were crucial to placing me fully in the master's orbit and the flow of intuition. It was so successful that by '95-96 I recognized it was time to let go of dependence on the chart, time to be total-ly guided from within.

My shift in view was not a criticism of my astrologer's expertise, nor of the validity of astrology, but rather that it seemed to chart the apparent evo-lution of the illusory individual self and its drama of individual existence. My attachment to astrology still reinforced the belief that I was a separate sub-ject concerned about how "my life" would turn out, seeking to chart "my course" and to know or influence "my destiny." I was using it as a survival tool of the "I" and my interest kept me locked into identification with a seek-er and the stressful pursuit of its strategy. There seemed to be a conflict between checking out the stars and my own intuition of being free and fol-lowing inner guidance.

I realized that I didn't want to forecast the future or to follow guidelines laid out by the chart. Simple planning is fine, but all of my previous worry and strategic forecasting pulled awareness away from itself and obscured the truth that is untouched by events and personal tendencies. It was such relief to live in the moment and discover life as it unfolds.

I later came to recognize, from a deeper appreciation of the nondual per-spective, that astrology was also an expression of the same guru-function of the Self. In mapping out the impersonal patterns of the cosmic play, it pro-vides both guidance and an elegant invitation to awaken from the dream of individual doership to the One that is showing up as everything.

Ultimate Guru

The Satguru is greater than all else, even God. The Satguru is Truth-Awareness-Bliss, and is like the sun; you no longer need a torch to see. — Papaji

The mystery of the guru is fathomless, impossible to understand. The guru showed up in the external form of Papaji to turn my awareness to the invisible Satguru within, my own Self. I first knew him as the gentle, wise master who tenderly and patiently answered questions, encouraged me, and cleared away doubts. Papaji gave me everything I asked for. He played along with my need to be acknowledged and feel special, and allowed me the lime-light I had always wanted. And when enough was enough, he became the rag-ing lion who ferociously devoured arrogance and tore away illusions. In the end he was simply the empty mirror whose indifference to my personal drama reflected only my formless nature. However he manifested, it was always love, the uncompromising love of the Self for the Self.

Papaji's ultimate teaching, as he declared many times, is that there is no teaching, no teacher or student, no awakening, no realization, no transmission. For him it was all a big joke. "Everything in this world is a big joke, including my teachings," the master confided, tongue in cheek. "I tell people, 'If you do this you will win enlightenment'. Or I say, 'You are already enlightened. Why are you so miserable?' Or I may say, 'Don't do anything. Don't listen to anybody, just be quiet and see what happens. . . . I say all these things every day but in my Heart I know it is all a big joke, I know there is no world; I know that there is no one striving for enlightenment and I know that no one has ever attained it. This is my unshakeable experience. If I say anything else you can take it as a joke. "

Here is Papaji's final legacy after a lifetime of spiritual investigation and experience:

"I will tell you the bare truth," he told David Godman at the end of his three-volume biography, which the master entitled: *Nothing Ever Happened*. "There is no birth, there is no death, there is no creator, there is no creation. This is now my conviction, my experience." Like the great advaita sages Gaudapada, Shankara, and Ramana before him, Papaji was fascinated by the enigma of how the manifestation could be happening and yet not be happening at the same time, how something could seem to exist and yet be nothing at all. When we wake up, we wake up from the *seeming*—call it a dream, mind, imagination, illusion—in the same way that when we wake from a dream we see that it was only a dream played out by dreamed characters. It only *seemed* to happen—nothing actually happened to anyone. This was Papaji's precious gift—the knowledge that this "I," the very narrator of this story, is but the play of consciousness. There is no one who becomes free or remains in bondage, there is only That which can never be understood or described.

I loved Papaji most of all precisely because he continually pulled the rug out from under any position, any identity, any concept. There was nothing at all to stand on or hold on to around him. He warned us not to attach to his teachings, joking that he didn't understand what he was saying or why. That to me was the ultimate guru, revealing nothing and leaving nothing, and yet, in that very process illuminating the mystery, the essence that you, I, all beings, are beyond ignorance and enlightenment.

Still, within the sweet dream of the guru-disciple, my thankfulness pours out to him, as if his name and form were magnets that give love a target. Love of the guru is a way the Self enjoys the experience of thankfulness for being itself. While it is clear that he is my own being, it still has the special flavor of Papaji. I feel him as a presence in my heart, bubbling up as intuitions of inner guidance, a silent partner in the playful banter of truth with itself.

In the years since Papaji's death the guru has kept coming occasionally in dreams as vivid experiences of blessing and guidance. He said a number of times that when you dream of the guru, it's not a dream—the guru is really with you.

In one dream that took place in Papaji's house in India, I was a member of his household, and was surprised and happy to be so close to him. I was a bit apprehensive, sitting in his room when I saw him come in, his huge figure looming toward me, silhouetted by the doorway. He sat down beside me and began talking in the familiar, reassuring tone of a close friend, discussing his schedule, what we were going to do that day, treating me as an equal. I felt completely embraced and affirmed. Here was the relationship I had always wanted with him—close friends just sharing life and truth together. How sweet that the Self would fulfill that desire in the dream.

The following summer I dreamt Papaji and I were Krishna devotees. We were sharing the devotional heart together in a way we had never done when he was alive. We were lying down together, our faces so close, looking into one another's eyes just inches apart. It was such an intimate scene, sharing a silent understanding. I whispered to him with a sense of wonder: "All this life is just possibility; all this form, all this manifestation is just a possibility arising within the sea of potentiality. None of it is reality. It is all just imagination dancing in empty consciousness." I was telling him and asking him at the same time, looking into his eyes, which were smiling with joy. He nodded and affirmed: "Yes, yes," he said laughing, "none of it is really happening."

Such a mysterious, liberating knowing. All of the drama, the yearning for freedom, the years of spiritual practice, the travels to India and the awakening with Papaji, the struggle with doubt and arrogance—yes, it all happened and yet . . . none of it has any lasting reality. Through Papaji's grace I came to see that thoughts, doubts, emotions and all manner of experience arise and disappear, yet nothing sticks. It all comes and goes, and silent presence is here, behind and within it all. It includes being someone and being nobody. There are times of identification, of emptiness and fullness, of contraction and expansion. In this sense the awakening is reborn and refreshed each day as quiet releases, small epiphanies, gratitude and wonder. And each time it is the same awakening, the realization of being the ground of spacious awareness, wholeness and peace underlying the surface fluctuations. All forms, all experiences—including identification and the appearance of separation—arise in this space that allows it all to be as it is, perfect expressions of freedom's dream.

Biography

Dasarath, born David Davidson in 1941, has been a student of the nondual traditions for over thirty years. He has studied and practiced with masters in Zen, Vipassana, Yoga, and western transformational approaches. In 1992 he met Advaita Master Sri H.W.L.Poonja (Papaji) in India, in whose presence his true nature was revealed and his teaching turned fully to sharing awakening.

Dasarath received his Ph.D. from Yale University and taught History at Cornell University for five years. He has been a counselor and seminar leader on personal growth and relationships, a corporate consultant and trainer, and has led meditation retreats and satsangs. He currently coaches leaders at Corning Incorporated and offers retreats on being awake and effective at work. He has also written *Wisdom at Work: The Awakening of Consciousness in the Workplace,* Larson Publications, 1998, published under the name Let Davidson.

Dasarath can be reached by e-mail at dasarath@baka.com or dasarath@aol.com, and through his website:

http://www.letwisdomwork.com.

ALSO FROM THE BOOK TREE

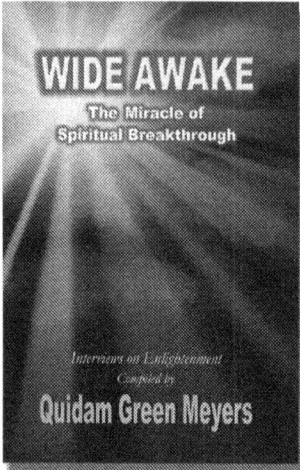

Wide Awake: The Miracle of Spiritual Breakthrough
by
Quidam Green Meyers

What is the reality of Enlightenment? How is spiritual freedom being lived in the 21st Century? In this revealing text, Quidam Green Meyers speaks to some of the West's top spiritual teachers and writers on the topic of Contemporary Awakening. Each was asked the same set of questions for the sake of comparison, yet their answers differ greatly. What is revealed is a stunning glimpse into the simple-yet-powerful life transformation that can take place when our Awakened Self is recognized and lived. Wide Awake reveals that there is no set path for Enlightenment. The men and women speaking in this book offer an impassioned plea for us to give up the search, since Truth is to be found eternally alive and present in every human Heart. Those interviewed include Matthew Fox, Alan Cohen, Rev. Michael Beckwith, Catherine Ingram, Lama Surya Das, Saniel Bonder, Isaac Shapiro, Arjuna Nick Ardagh, Satyam Nadeen, Dasarath, Neelam, Akash, Wayne Liquorman, Howard Raphael Cushner and Antonio Duncan.

BT-37X · ISBN 1-885395-37-X · trade paper · 200 pages · $18.95

CALL FOR A FREE CATALOG 1 800 700-TREE (8733)
www.thebooktree.com

www.ingramcontent.com/pod-product-compliance
Lightning Source LLC
Chambersburg PA
CBHW032059080426
42733CB00006B/337